ATTACK ON GOVERNMENT

also by David P. Levine

Normative Political Economy: Subjective Freedom, the Market,
 and the State
Subjectivity in Political Economy: Essays on Wanting and Choosing
Self-Seeking and the Pursuit of Justice
Wealth and Freedom: An Introduction to Political Economy

ATTACK ON GOVERNMENT
Fear, Distrust, and Hatred in Public Life

David P. Levine

PITCHSTONE PUBLISHING
Charlottesville, Virginia 22901

PITCHSTONE PUBLISHING
Charlottesville, Virginia 22901

Copyright © 2004 by David P. Levine
Printed in the United States of America
First edition, 2004

Library of Congress Cataloging-in-Publication Data

Levine, David P., 1948-
  Attack on government : fear, distrust, and hatred in public life / David
P. Levine.-- 1st ed.
      p. cm.
  Includes bibliographical references and index.
  ISBN 0-9728875-4-7 (hardcover : alk. paper)
1. United States--Politics and government--1989----Philosophy. 2.
Political culture--United States. 3. Political corruption--United States.
4. Capitalism--United States. 5. Democracy--United States. 6.
Citizenship--United States. I. Title.

  JK275.L48 2004
  306.2'0973--dc22
                                              2004009465

CONTENTS

INTRODUCTION

Who Governs?

When the citizens of Minnesota elected Jesse Ventura governor, they created an apt symbol for government as many Americans think they know it. What many Americans think they know about government is that it is corrupt and incompetent. For them, government at its best offers a sadly comic spectacle, at its worst an opportunity for the abuse of power. The closer we come to government, the more likely we will be corrupted by it. The ideal of governing is that government would be taken over by those who have had as little to do with government as possible.

If this is what we need, Jesse Ventura fit the bill. Neither a lawyer nor a professional politician, Ventura's resume (high school graduate, member of a California motorcycle club, bouncer, professional wrestler, sports commentator) carried only one blemish: he was the mayor of a Minneapolis suburb. Jesse Ventura was not elected because of any demonstrated aptitude for, knowledge of, or experience in government. On the contrary, he was elected because he fell so far short in each of these categories. His stint as a mayor was his only relevant qualification, and probably the least important for his election.

He claimed that facing death as a Navy SEAL had prepared him for anything, adding that [his opponents in the race for governor] would "wet their pants" in SEAL training. "They would be crying for their mommies after the first day," he said, as if inexperience on the ropes course would be a liability when it came to governing.[1]

The choreography of professional wrestling, in which nothing is what it seems and everyone knows it, was for many just the preparation for a leadership role in government. In professional wrestling, the audience can watch as much brutality as it can stand, knowing that when the match is

7

over no real harm has been done. Perhaps in electing Jesse Ventura, the citizens of Minnesota were hoping they could now say the same thing about government: that it might be brutal without anyone getting hurt. Beyond power and brutality, then, Jesse Ventura represents a caricature of power and brutality. We elect him governor to make government a mockery of itself.

That Jesse Ventura would be a clown in high office made him, for some, more real than most elected officials, since in Jesse's case there would be no façade of serious purpose and calling. With Jesse in office, the government would become, like professional wrestling, a spoof of itself. While no doubt this is all good for a laugh, there is, of course, a darker side. When wrestlers put on a show, we judge it by its entertainment value; but the government has a job to do. And, when we insist that it become a self-denigrating show put on for our amusement, that job is unlikely to get done well. Then, it cannot be said that a brutal government hurts no one, as, for example, victims of welfare reform can attest.

The spoof of government tells us much about it, not only because of the spoof's sharply critical intent, to express feelings of disappointment and anger recast as humor, but also because of its specific content. Jesse Ventura's image tells us much about our attitude toward what we perceive as the power of government. By mocking it, we seek to belittle the power we fear government has over us. Those who most fear government power, and would do most to weaken government, have least to fear from Jesse Ventura in office. Thus, Ventura can simultaneously symbolize the power we fear in government, and the contempt we have for it.

One might imagine, given the frequent and often substantial failures of government, that the caricature is real enough. In other words, we might imagine that the attitude toward government embodied in the Minnesota election was no more than one might expect given the sort of government we have, which is, after all, a government that invites contempt. Yet, this sort of interpretation is, in the end, much too easy. By appealing to it, we evade our culpability for the government we have, which may be, as the saying goes, the government we deserve.[2] It ignores the ways in which we need our government to be the way it is. It refuses to consider how difficult it would be for us to cope with a government that did its job well.

Why do we want and need our government to fail? Why do we want and need it to be too powerful, and to be corrupt in its power? Why do we need to have a government deserving of our contempt? And, finally, why do we need our government to be a suitable target for our fear and hatred?

These questions cannot be answered if we take it for granted that the prevailing attitude toward government is simply a reality-based response to what government has become. To answer these questions, we need to consider a reality distinct from, if related to, the one with which we are most familiar and take for granted.

Psychodynamics of Public Life

In her study of institutions as ways of defending against anxiety, Isabel Menzies Lyth notes that the ostensible purposes for which institutions are organized, and the associated tasks we assume they are designed to accomplish, are, at best, "limiting factors." Within the limits they set, the organization, mode of functioning, and goals of the institution "are determined by the psychological needs of the members," especially the need to deal with anxiety by externalizing it.

What holds true for social institutions holds true, albeit in a somewhat different way, for public life more generally. Public life includes not only institutions, but also the ideas and symbols that represent collective, or potentially collective, experience in groups large and small. Public life is, then, more complex, and possibly more diffuse, than the institutions in which it is sometimes embodied. Yet, public life shares with institutions the quality that Lyth and others have attributed to them. It carries on a dual existence: one on a level of conscious awareness, seemingly rational discourse linked to reality, well known and agreed upon goals; one at a level on which the ends are quite different and often in conflict with those of which we are consciously aware.

The tone of the debate over the appropriate activities and limits of government exemplifies this difference. One stream of the debate is about the everyday lives of citizens: inflation, unemployment, environmental degradation, social welfare, and social security. Another stream is about moral character and responsibility. We can observe the convergence of these two streams in the crusade for a balanced budget, which often becomes less a matter of the likely consequences of deficits for economic variables and every day life, more a matter of the struggle between good and evil:

> On Capitol Hill an impressive number of Republican congressmen were holding stolidly to the belief that by their sustained and earnest repetition of the words "balanced budget" they could

restore the American economy to a state of fiscal grace. Although not yet swinging incense pots or walking around in circles, they disdained to listen to people who pointed out that the arithmetic makes no sense, that a government forced to balance current revenues and expenditures would cease operations in a matter of weeks. Nor were they to be troubled with the nuisance of real numbers. What they apparently had in mind was the salvation of souls, and having defined debt as sin, they had gone forth to the conviction that the federal budget resembles the monthly checkbook kept by the upright father of an exemplary American family (two sons, two daughters, six bibles) back home in nineteenth-century Indiana.[3]

The two levels of public experience are not easily disentangled, since they may not be separated in time and space, and those discussing the issues rarely see them as separable accounts of the problem. Put another way, public life has a psychic meaning distinct from, yet as or more powerful than, the one we normally attribute to it. It is my purpose in this volume to make clear how ignoring its psychic meaning assures that public experience will be poorly understood, and that the outcome of public debate will not be to solve the problems it is ostensibly meant to address, but to assure that those problems persist.

As I suggest above, the best single indicator that public discussion has shifted to the level of psychic meaning is the transformation of issues into matters of good and evil. Good and evil are the building blocks of the moral orientation toward the world, so we can also say that to know the psychic meaning of public experience is to know the moral significance of government. We will not understand government if we restrict ourselves to thinking about it as a locus or instrument of power, as a method for collective decision-making, or as a way of mediating struggles over resources. Rather, to understand government, we need to consider it a repository of moral and psychic meaning.

Beyond considering government a repository in this sense, I consider the processes by which government takes on the meaning that it does. These are the processes by which psychic content is moved across the boundaries between persons, and between persons and institutions. These psychodynamic processes tie the individual to the group, and to the institutions that organize group life. Psychodynamic processes move feelings and self-experiences from the inner world to the world outside (projection), and from the world outside to the inner world (internalization). The more intense the emotional connection (whether negative or positive) to the external world, the more reason to expect that such movements are involved. We experience our government as irresponsible, self-interested, corrupt, powerful, and so on because we project onto it our irresponsible, corrupt, power-seeking selves. This projection is an effort to rid ourselves of unacceptable qualities that, if acknowledged, would provoke powerful negative feelings and harsh self-criticism.

It is not enough, however, to imagine the government as a repository for disavowed aspects of the inner lives of its citizens. If the story stopped here, we would have an essentially good government that is nonetheless perceived to be bad, and thus hated for what it is not. This situation is inherently unstable, since the reality of the government, if it is indeed a good government, must conflict with the fantasy we need to maintain about it, which would make maintaining the fantasy that much more difficult and unsatisfying.

Collectively, we can solve this problem by provoking government to act in ways consistent with the fantasy, thus reassuring ourselves that it is not a good government, and is thus worthy of our scorn. This provocation constitutes an instance of what Melanie Klein refers to as "projective identification." Arthur Hyatt-Williams defines projective identification as the "splitting off and projection of parts of the self and the forcing of them upon another person who may then be attacked for seeming to be responsible for those parts...."[4] According to this definition, individuals use projective identification to rid their inner worlds of aggressive, especially hateful and destructive, feelings. As Vamik Volkan points out, however, the same process can be used to deal with positively valued (or good) aspects of self-experience. This becomes necessary when the inner world is a dangerous place for the good self, and it therefore becomes necessary to place that self outside "for safekeeping."[5]

A good example of projective identification of positively valued parts of the self is the relationship between the believer and his or her god. In the Christian religion, Jesus Christ contains the good selves of the members of the Christian community. Their connection to Christ represents their way of being good, which they cannot be in themselves, but only by connecting to something outside that has been invested with their goodness. They cannot be good in themselves because they are sinners, and a sinner is clearly not a safe container for the good self. We can see in this the link between the psychodynamic process and moral thinking already emphasized.

Here, I consider this same process as a way of binding public institutions to the community's psychic life. Volkan emphasizes how, at a certain point in individual development, the external containers for projected aspects of self-experience (which he terms "suitable targets for externalization") come to be shared among group members. Groups select for their members which containers are good and which are bad, so that connection to what is good (now outside the individual psyche though still within collective psychic life) means connection to the group through its chosen symbols, memories, customs, institutions, and so on. Similarly, disconnection from what is bad means rejection of that which is outside the group (its enemy).

The group, community, or nation satisfies the need to keep the good aspects of the self outside the individual, yet in a place where they remain accessible to him. The individual can thus maintain an intimate relationship with the good while still keeping it at a safe distance. This means that the group or community has a moral significance by definition. It is only well defined in a moral universe. The problem for government is that, within this moral universe, it is made to take on a role in opposition to the good. For the community, this problem is understood to arise because the government is not firmly enough connected to the community and therefore loses the moral standing derived from that connection. Within this moral structure of meaning, any disconnection of government from community (variously conceived as the nation or the people) makes the government bad.

The resulting animosity toward, distrust of, even hatred of government expresses the opposition between government and community. So far as the problem is attributed to the separation of government from community, the solution seems to be the merger of government into community. The pressure toward merger of government into community has the implication, however, of undermining the capacity of the government to get its various jobs done. The solution to the problem of government failure assures that government will fail. For some, the solution is to replace government by the market; for some, it is to reestablish the unity of government and nation; and, for some, it is to reassert the identity of government and people through enhanced democracy. The movement to redefine the relation between individual, community, and government is the subject of this study.

Collective Psychic Life

The notion of projective identification offers a solution to a problem that has blocked the development of an understanding of the psychic meaning of government, and thus the application of psychoanalytic ideas to the larger institutions of public life. The difficulty arises because of the tendency to confuse psychodynamic interpretations with the reduction of social reality to matters of individual psychology. There is always the prospect that political institutions will be seen as emanations of individual psychic life, as epiphenomena of the inner world of the individual, much as Marx imagined them epiphenomena of material life.

We reduce the social to the psychological when we treat individual psychopathology as the reason for institutional or organizational dysfunction. It can be tempting to do so. It is easy enough, after all, to find in the psychic make-up of those who occupy public positions the same inner conflicts and defensive maneuvers that affect people more generally. It is also easy enough to see in the character flaws of public office holders the root cause of their failure to protect the public trust. To proceed this way is to seek psychological explanations of social realities. This is not my purpose here. Whatever their specific psychological make up, the failure of government stems not from the unique and private character flaws of office holders, as those who attacked Bill Clinton on the character issue wished us to believe. Rather, we need to consider how office holders occupy a position in the community's psychic life. If the community chooses them because their character fits its needs, all the better. But then we must explain why they are chosen, which we cannot do on the basis of purely intrapsychic considerations.

Institutions bear a needed psychic meaning, which then shapes their conduct vis-à-vis individuals so as to reinforce and recreate the need that led to the original psychic use of the institution. When the attack on government deprives it of the resources it needs to do its job, government must fail, and in failing government confirms the basis of the original attack. Welfare reform forces those dependent on government to get along on their own. The resulting deprivation, especially of children, builds a future class of individuals damaged in their capacity to function without the direct support of government. Not without reason did the senior Senator from Massachusetts refer to welfare reform as legislative child abuse. The attack on welfare assures the perpetuation of the welfare problem. Government, by acting out a punitive social agenda, helps recreate the type of citizen most likely to provoke and justify that agenda.

It is this reciprocal relationship that concerns me here. It can be considered an instance at the societal level of the operation of resistance to change and of the urge to reenactment so prevalent at the individual level. In thinking about reenactment at the societal level, I think it will be helpful to adapt Ronald Fairbairn's distinction between closed and open systems.[6] Within a closed system, internal, or psychic, reality remains strongly defended against any external influence. In an open system, internal reality remains connected to and influenced by experience of an external reality, which is to say a reality not governed by the individual's wishing and willing (the reality Freud refers to as governed by the "pleasure principle"). As we will see, the attack on government seeks to secure its position within the community's closed system either by destroying government or by redefining its relationship to community in a way that assures the absorption of government into community. This assures that government will not force the community to acknowledge another reality, one it finds alien and threatening.

Ronald Reagan, in his second Inaugural Address, acts as spokesman for what I refer to here as a closed system.

> Four years ago, I spoke to you of a new beginning and we have accomplished that. But in another sense, our new beginning is a continuation of that beginning created two centuries ago when, for the first time in history, government, the people said, was not our master, it is our servant; its only power is that which we the people allow it to have.

Reagan goes on to refer to this relation between government and people as a "system," one that "has never failed us" although we have failed it. This system is the one created when two conditions are met: the people are united into one, and the government is subsumed into the people. It is the closed system to which I refer here.

It may be said, of course, that Reagan speaks only for a particular part of the people, and in some ways this is correct. Yet, in advocating movement toward a closed system, Reagan speaks for more than a particular interest. We can see that this is the case by considering how those of a sharply different political persuasion also support the "system" to which Reagan refers. Thus, in their book, aptly titled *Government is Us*, two professors of public administration see in the "system" the solution to the problems posed for public administration in an "anti-government era." While Reagan's solution to the problems of our time includes less government and more reliance on markets and enterprise, their solution appeals to participation and closing the distance between the government and the people.

> In American politics can people be who they are? ... If they could, people and government would be one, which is clearly not the case. Examples of ordinary people directly involved in governing are few and far between. ... Not only are there occasional outbreaks of aggressive anti-government action, but the feeling that Government isn't us is widespread.[7]

Like Reagan, these authors look for solutions to the problems perceived in the relation between government and the people in the "system" that makes the government subject to control by the people, or, in the limit, makes the people govern themselves.

The idea of a closed system expresses at a psychic level the fear of separation of the government from the people and the pressure to merge the two into a single unit. It needs to be emphasized that the pressure to move in this direction originates in anxiety. It is fear that fuels the closed system, and it might be worth asking, even at this preliminary stage of our investigation, what sort of fear this is and what sort of object it has. I will suggest in chapter 1 that the primary fear has to do with the problem of maintaining a sense of the goodness of the community, and therefore of its members. Maintaining the goodness of the community means fending off the bad, especially keeping it outside. Put another way, the system closes around, or in order to protect, the assumption that the community is a (or the) repository of goodness, that it is good.

Energy must be devoted not only to protecting this assumption against those outside, but also against internal threats. Protecting the assumption, and thus securing the relation of government to people as a closed system, demands the mobilization of substantial amounts of aggression. Closed systems then are held together by aggression, and the more extreme their closure, the more intense the aggression needed to protect them. In the limit, this aggression takes the form of hatred and destruction, as it does for those bound up in the more extreme movements against government. We will see in chapter 4 how the attack on government is meant to serve the end of establishing a closed system that has come apart, a unity that has fallen into division. Whether we consider the more or the less extreme expressions of the closed system mentality, we need always to bear in mind the prominent place aggression plays in the emotional life of such systems.

To summarize, the importance of the psychic meaning of political ideals, institutions, and process can be understood in the following way. One method individuals use to cope with inner conflicts involves externalizing, which is to say attributing a problematic internal psychic experience (a feeling, wish, impulse, self-representation, etc.) to something outside: another person, an institution, or a group. This attribution of an unacceptable internal experience works best when the external reality actually exhibits the qualities attributed to (or projected onto) it. Thus, the more the objective reality can be made to exhibit the needed qualities, the more the individual can avoid taking responsibility for them, which is the psychic purpose of projection, and becomes the psychic meaning of the objective, or external, reality. To take this idea one step further, so far as individuals can act in ways that promote or stimulate an external response consistent with their projections, the process of projection is doubly hidden from its original subject. Then, the subjective, or psychic, reality disappears into the objective, which becomes an overpowering external fact. The individual's loss of his or her subjective experience becomes the psychic meaning of objective reality.

We can also say that central to the processes just summarized is control. To assure that the institution plays the part scripted for it, that institution must be subject to control. Indeed, control is an implication of the process of projective identification. When successful, that process assures that no dissonant note will be heard that might impede the institution from playing its part in a collective psychic drama. In the worst case, there simply exists no external reality that needs to be acknowledged, since the community produces the "reality" it needs. Then, the government is shaped by the wish that all reality could be constructed so as to satisfy psychic need. As a result, we have a closed circle connecting institutions and individuals. In this closed circle, neither individual nor institution is the causal moment. Each provokes in the other the response needed to maintain its psychic meaning.

Emotional Connection

Psychic meaning refers to the place of an experience or object (in our case government) in a configuration of forces organized around a central psychic reality. This is the reality of emotional meaning. Emotional meaning is the connection an object or experience has to the personality's driving force. Our emotions are important because they mark connection. In the words of Jonathan Lear, our emotions provide "a framework through which the world is viewed."[8] To say things matter is to say we are invested in them, which is to say that we are emotionally connected to them. Psychic meaning can be shared, can be invested in groups and institutions; it can be both inside the individual's mind and a larger social reality for the individual.

If emotional meaning is the central reality of psychic experience, we may also wonder what has, or might have, such meaning. I think that the most powerful answer to this question is that particular things (including groups and institutions) have meaning because of their involvement with what is for us the most salient of all objects, our distinctively human character. We speak of our humanness in various ways, but always in a way that hopes to identify a center of activity "distinct from other centers of different kinds of activity—be they stars or nebula, atoms, plants or animals."[9] It is this center of activity that has for us the greatest meaning; or, put differently, their having a connection to this center gives things their significance for us. This center of activity is what Heinz Kohut refers to as the "self," and what Donald Winnicott refers to as the "true self."

In identifying the reference point for the self, Hans Loewald emphasizes the meaning we invest in the mind taken as a whole. "Self, mind, personality, identity, are terms referring to a totality seen from different perspectives."[10] When the whole of our person becomes the object of our emotional interest and connection, we can be said to have found our selves. This means that to have a (cohesive or integrated) self, one must have the capacity to make an emotional investment in the personality as a whole, not only in certain parts, or at certain moments, or in specific circumstances. To have a self in this sense means, then, to find meaning in an integrated life experience. This is not always easy to do. To fail means that we must seek something other than the experience of having a self around which to organize our lives.

I will suggest that movement toward a closed system is driven by a specific psychic experience. In this experience, the personality's center of meaning has been lost. No loss can be of greater significance, and none can provoke a more intense response. At the heart of the response to loss is the drive to shift the loss onto others, either by sharing it with them, or by giving it over to them altogether. All of this is done, of course, in the name of retrieving what has been lost.

When loss is the binding force of community, the community must form itself into a closed system. The system closes in around loss, organizing itself through connections between members consistent with preserving loss as its prime reality. The community replaces what is lost (the individual's center of meaning and the personal identity in which that meaning is invested) with group identity, which is the identity of shared loss. To make loss the basis of identity means to impose loss on others.

One of the most important expressions of the closed system at the societal level is the attack on government. Here, I will interpret the attack on government as an instance of the effort to impose loss on others. If the attack on government (the effort to weaken or destroy it) is a part of the effort to impose loss, then, government must in some sense be the agency responsible for preventing loss, or for helping the individual retrieve what has been lost so far as that is possible. By administering justice and protecting rights, the government expresses the community's commitment to preventing loss. If this is correct, then to assure the imposition of loss means to frustrate government in its effort to prevent loss, and even enlist government in the effort to make loss universal. In other words, the purpose of government must be perverted, so that government comes to represent the opposite of what it could be.

Government secures the space for individual initiative and self-determination; it must, therefore, be weakened to assure that no safe space exists for the self in its world. Government represents integration; it must, therefore, be weakened to assure the predominance of division and opposition. Government takes power away from the group, and thus threatens the group's domination over the individual; it must therefore be weakened so that the group can be made strong.

Since all of this must be done in the name of preventing the loss of self-feeling, it must be made to appear as the opposite of what it is. Our desire to dominate others so we may destroy their sense of themselves as centers of initiative, and thus destroy the center of meaning in their lives, becomes, via projection, the desire of government to destroy us. Government must be weakened so that its power will not be used against us, though weakening government assures that there will be no power to protect us from those who would impose loss on us. Draining this power means replacing government with markets, where power is diffused to the point that it can no longer do harm; or it means replacing institutions of government with popular participation, which is assumed to assure the use of public power for good rather than evil.

In all of this, the moral current runs strong. Indeed, as we will see, the moral current is nothing but the movement of loss through the community. The moral dimension and the significance of loss to it are nowhere more vivid than in the rhetoric of character. Central to the phenomena of public life is the confusion of character with self-repression and self-hatred. The moral ideal makes loss (of self-love) the basis of character. If this is what we mean by character, the free market builds character by assuring that everyone exists permanently under threat of loss. To cope with this threat, the individual inures him or her self to it by scorning any dependence on others that might create vulnerability. In contrast to the market, government destroys character by fostering dependence, and therefore vulnerability. Participation in a democratic community builds character by requiring repression of the self (therefore loss of self-feeling) in the interest of community, so that serving the group replaces self-interest. Advocates of enhanced democracy insist that institutions of government separated from the people destroy character by breeding passivity and disinterest in community. These are the themes with which I will be concerned. They express the psychic meaning of government. They are also the greatest challenge our government and we as a society face in attempting to solve the problem of governance.

The Anti-Government Fantasy

The standard alternative to understanding the psychic meaning of public life is to treat the public world as an arena for the clash of interests, and government as an institution bound up in satisfying or frustrating the needs that drive those interests. Central to this understanding is the idea that individuals and groups act rationally in the pursuit of their ends. Since this assumption is the main alternative to explanation based in psychodynamic processes and psychic meaning, I will consider it more closely to see how it connects to our concerns here. To do so, let me consider a specific example.

In his book *Losing Ground* (1984), Charles Murray argues that government policy often causes the problems it is ostensibly meant to solve. Because of this, he concludes that the goals of social policy would be better served in its absence. In drawing this conclusion, Murray echoes a sentiment common in economics since Adam Smith insisted that the goal of economic growth would best be achieved if the government did the least to promote it. I will have occasion to consider this line of argument more closely in chapter 6. Here, I would like to raise a question not only about Murray's book, but also more broadly about how we understand attitudes toward government.

Does the argument in Murray's book constitute evidence of a specific attitude toward government involving, for example, significant animosity toward, or distrust of, government? On the surface at least, this would not seem to be the case. Indeed, there is little in the book to suggest an affinity between its author and those, for example, who hate government, know they hate government, and do not hesitate to express their feelings in words and actions. Instead of the expression of an underlying attitude toward government, what we find is a conclusion argued to follow inevitably from a simple assumption about human nature: that people act rationally in the economist's sense. To act rationally in the economist's sense means, roughly speaking, to order alternatives according to their expected impact on levels of satisfaction, given available information. Rationality in this sense leads to perverse effects of government policy when government income subsidies and welfare payments make working less remunerative than not working. Then, the rational individual faced with the choice of working for less or not working will presumably choose to remain unemployed.

> It is not necessary to invoke the Zeitgeist of the 1960s, or changes in the work ethic, or racial differences, or the complexities of postindustrial society, in order to explain increasing unemployment among the young, increased dropout from the labor force, or higher rates of illegitimacy and welfare dependence. All were results that could have been predicted (indeed, in some instances were predicted) from the changes that social policy made in the rewards and penalties, carrots and sticks, that govern human behavior.[11]

In Murray's view, the welfare system offered some individuals and families an alternative superior to seeking employment and living off an individual or family wage. It follows that the result of providing non-market income support is to draw people away from the market toward dependence on government.

Given this premise, there is nothing surprising in Murray's conclusion that eliminating social welfare will eliminate the problem social welfare is meant to solve. He proposes to scrap "the entire federal welfare and income-support structure for working-aged persons," thus leaving them "with no recourse whatsoever except the job market, family members, friends, and public or private locally funded services."[12] For Murray, the problem lies not in the character of the poor, but in the incentive system surrounding them. The poor are responsible for their situation only in the sense that, given the institutional setting, they make rational decisions that lead them to unemployment and dependence rather than employment and independence.

We will not be surprised to discover that following the rationality assumption leads many to favor markets over government when considering the institutional setting that will best solve problems of income distribution and the use of resources. Neither market nor free market solutions follow inevitably from the rationality assumption. Adequate information may not be available. Factors such as economies of scale may foster market imperfections that yield sub-optimal outcomes. Nonetheless, the rationality assumption has remained a powerful one for those who favor limited government.

Thinking about government in the way just summarized leads us to what we might call the typical vision of a world without government, or with a minimal government. In this vision, each individual is on his or her own. Each enjoys a radical autonomy that denies dependence, and rejects the support structures that express dependence on others. We will have occasion to return to this construction at various points in the following pages. It is not the only vision of government, and we will consider others. But, it is currently among the most prominent, and I will pay special attention to it. What I would like to do here is consider this construction not as a theory of government and its relation to society, which is how it appears for authors such as Murray, but as a fantasy, indeed as the typical anti-government fantasy. There are some risks in treating this construction as a fantasy, since the term carries connotations that involve a contrast with reality. In using the term fantasy here, I will not emphasize the contrast with reality, assuming instead that fantasies might be real in some important respects, or they might be made real (or we might attempt to make them real) if they are not.

The issue in considering fantasy is not reality and unreality, but the wishful quality of the construction.[13] What, then, distinguishes fantasy from theory or description is that it contains and is driven by a wish. To consider psychic meaning is to consider this wishful quality often hidden in what is presented to us as hard reality, or a purely logical construction of the type Murray insists he develops in his book. A theory may well be a logical construction made up of assumptions and conclusions derived from them by the rules of inference. At the same time, it may also be the expression of a fantasy. The fact that the element of fantasy is denied, or seemingly left out altogether, makes it no less a powerful force driving the construction. We can say, then, that theories operate on two levels, one the explicit or conscious level of deduction, the other the level of fantasy, which is the level of hope and fear, of gratification and deprivation. Our problem is to identify the hidden fantasy about government in the rhetoric and theory with which we are all familiar.

Identifying the fantasy does not in itself uncover the theory's psychic meaning. This is because whatever meaning the fantasy has is expressed not directly but indirectly, as a narrative describing the wished for individual in a wished for world. To find its meaning, and thus the psychic meaning of the original idea, the fantasy must be interpreted. We can consider the entire activity of identifying first the hidden fantasy and then its psychic meaning under the heading of interpretation. Interpretation in this sense is what I propose to do here, and what I have in mind by uncovering the psychic meaning of government specifically and public life more generally.[14]

Interpreting fantasy involves identifying the hope or fear that drives it, then finding the formative psychic experience from which that hope or fear originates. The connection of fantasy to a formative psychic experience involves fantasy in the processes of repetition and reenactment, which are essential elements in interpretation of psychic meaning. Formative experience provides a mold for subsequent relatedness, and sets up dynamic forces that shape life experiences. The fantasy, then, is not an original construction. It consists, rather, of variations on a theme, or set of themes. These variations have as their purpose such goals as solving problems, gratifying wants, and shifting the burden of unacceptable feelings away from the self.

The resolutions offered in fantasy are, of course, just that, resolutions in fantasy. Thus, fantasy may simply offer a pleasurable alternative to reality, a temporary refuge from the constraints of living in the world. It may also offer a mental procedure for trying out possibilities, some of which might be made real. But, fantasy may push beyond these limits. The pressures driving the fantasy may be so great that any conflict between fantasy and reality, any obstacle between wish and its fulfillment, cannot be tolerated. Then, reality must be forced into the shape of the fantasy, and the border between fantasy and reality overcome. This erosion of the border between fantasy and reality plays an especially important part in public life precisely because of the overriding fantasy that the social world can be remade by acts of collective will.

This involves the effort to enlist others in the solutions laid out in fantasy, so that the fantasy now becomes a threat to the boundaries that separate self and other. The pressure to overcome the boundary between fantasy and reality can be seen operating not only in the anti-government movement, but also in the ideal of the good society, a variant of which I consider in chapter 7.

With these comments in mind, let me consider again what I refer to above as the typical anti-government fantasy to indicate more concretely how the method outlined here will be applied to a particularly important modality of public life. The conscious construction in this fantasy is one of radical independence. In the fantasy, we can get along by ourselves and on the basis of our own resources. Government is not needed as an external support structure since the individual is strong enough to get along well enough alone. In the fantasy, getting rid of government allows the individual to flourish, since government only saps the individual of his or her initiative, will, and therefore power. Without government social programs, the poor will find jobs, develop their autonomy and initiative, and realize their potential in ways prevented by dependence on government. The fantasy is one in which social problems disappear with the disappearance of government.

What I have said so far refers to the conscious fantasy. If we follow the suggestion made above that this aspect of the fantasy simply represents a formative experience and a possible way of resolving the emotional problems that experience posed, then we need to identify the original experience that drives the construction of the fantasy. We have now to take the characters in the fantasy (the government and its citizens) not as literally what they appear to be, but as symbols for more primitive objects in psychic experience and psychic life. What psychic object might the government represent?

Central to the anti-government fantasy are the connected issues of vulnerability, dependence, and the availability of a reliable authority capable of providing security and support. In the fantasy, authority is unnecessary, ineffective, intrusive, or harmful. As a matter of formative psychic experience, this points us in the direction of an original experience with authority and dependence of a particular kind. This is the experience of parental neglect and abuse.

Neglect can take a number of forms ranging from the actual loss of the parent to the failure of a parent who is physically present to provide for the child's basic needs including security, guidance, limit-setting, and affect regulation. The fantasy of a world without government, or with only a minimal government, can be said to express the neglected child's wish that he or she could get along perfectly well without the parent. This is a variation of the grandiose fantasy typically employed to compensate for powerful feelings of inadequacy and vulnerability. The fantasy incorporates the resolution of a problem, which is the child's desperate need for adequate parenting capable of securing an atmosphere of safety and the guidance needed so that personal development can take place. The reality of parental neglect is overcome in fantasy by the idea that the child does not need the parent.

This same construction can be transferred in the adult world onto institutions, including those of government. Here, the government plays the part of the absent or neglectful parent, so that the relationship with government replicates the formative relationship with the parent. The fantasy invoked to deal with the original dilemma is now repeated, if in revised form, with the government. The result is the anti-government fantasy and the policy measures associated with it.

The anti-government fantasy can be linked in this way to the experience of parental neglect, and to the wish that the neglectful parent is unnecessary to the child's well-being. Alternatively, we can link the anti-government fantasy to the experience of parental abuse by focusing attention not so much on the idea that citizens would thrive if left to their own devices, but on the idea that government represents a capricious and harmful power over them. Then, the reenactment is not of the experience with the absent parent, but with the abusive parent who represented a capricious and harmful power acting against the child's aspiration for a personal development as an autonomous center of initiative. We can see, then, how variations on the anti-government theme express variations on a fantasy of a world without government, which is a world in which either the government is not needed or in which its harmful force is minimized or eliminated. These fantasies express formative experiences, solutions to the problems they create, and escape from the dangers they pose.

So far, I have considered the fantasy of limited government as a kind of wish fulfillment, a way in which the real problems faced by the child, problems the child cannot solve with the resources available, could be solved, if only in the mind. There is, however, another possibility, one that has particularly significant and ominous implications in public life. This is the possibility that the fantasy resolves the problem by shifting its burden from self to others, or, at least, sharing it with them. The burden of abuse and neglect, and of the impaired self-esteem that develops in the child as their result, becomes all the more difficult to bear when the child feels singled out, when he or she imagines that others have attentive and competent parents who act in their interests. To reduce this burden, the fantasy can include the element of shared neglect and abuse. If this is the case, then the effort to limit government is less an effort to escape deprivation than an effort to visit it on others so that all can be made to live in a world where authority is unreliable or even abusive. Then, activity meant to provoke government to act in ways consistent with the fantasy seeks to make government neglectful (by dismantling social programs) or abusive (by stimulating a harsh response to an attack, as happened for example in Waco). Here the fantasy involves a significant element of sadism, which is then acted out in conduct aimed at forcing reality into the mold of the fantasy.

So far as this line of interpretation is correct, we can conclude that, whatever the overt content of the rationality postulate, it also contains a sadistic element. So far as this postulate is the conscious expression of a fantasy of the type considered here, it has a substantial psychic meaning. While the knowledge of this meaning made available through interpretation does not bear directly on the question of the postulate's validity, it does bear on how we understand the effort to make the hypothesis valid by making the world conform to it. Interpretation enables us to understand that the postulate is not simply an observation about human nature, but a fantasy about relatedness and its absence, a fantasy that, for some, must be made real, through policy (Murray) or through provocation (the militia movement).

1 THE PROBLEM OF CHARACTER

Introduction

Late in the 1996 Presidential election campaign, when, despite an effort to gain ground by offering the electorate a tax cut, the Republican challenger, Bob Dole, remained far behind, he turned from issues of the economy and the pocketbook to an issue at once more ephemeral and more profound: the problem of character. Bill Clinton could not be trusted; he did not have the strength of his convictions, even assuming he had any convictions, which the challenger doubted; he did not have the will, and therefore he did not have the character, to govern.

By attacking the character of the incumbent, the Republican challenger hoped to engage an electorate in a campaign that had, up to that point, offered voters little to inspire them. Missing in the campaign had been any emotional involvement. Neither candidate had made himself the focal point of anger or hope; the incumbent was winning by default in a context of generally favorable economic news. The character issue had the potential, it was thought, to make the incumbent the object of the electorate's anger, and to make the challenger the vehicle of the electorate's hope. The election would be transformed from a dry debate over budgets to an emotionally charged referendum on good versus evil.

In the end, the strategy failed, and the incumbent was reelected. Yet, the issue of character remained. Indeed, it was generally accepted that the President had a weakness in his character. When asked to name the best aspect of Clinton's character, the most frequent response among voters was that "he does not have one."[1] Those who voted for the President did not do so because they found him exemplary, or even above average, when it comes to matters summarized under the heading "character." They did not, however, much favor the challenger, and they feared the power of a

26

government in which the same party controlled both the executive branch and the Congress.

The issue of character has a powerful moral connotation. It is not about the kind of character the President is, or whether the President was acting in character. It is, instead, about whether the President had that mix of knowledge and will that enables us to know right conduct, and to act on that knowledge. Having character in this sense means that you would not be swayed by the corrupting influence of those who would bend your conduct from its orientation toward what is good and right to an orientation governed by desire and interest. Having character means having the capacity for moral judgment and moral conduct. The first and the most salient item in the indictment of government is that those in government fail the test of character, that they are weak, self-interested, corrupted by pressure groups and by their own desires.

Concern with character in an electoral campaign contrasts sharply with concern over "issues" and "policies." Should we elect those leaders who, because of the inherent goodness of their character will make the right decisions; or should we elect those leaders whose stated policies attract our support? Or should we assume, as some do, that having the "right" policies is the mark of good character? When, during the election campaign just considered, Dole resigned his position in the Senate and returned to his "home," Russell, Kansas, he announced that he was now running neither as a long-time public servant knowledgeable about the workings of the political system, nor as a Republican candidate with a public platform of policies and goals, but just as a "man from Kansas." To be from Kansas meant to have roots in small town rural life, and thus to embody the mythical values represented by family, community, hard work, religion, and so on. A man is good because of his origins and the values associated with the kind of world he comes from, and a man does good because he is good.

If we seek to elect someone because he or she is good, then what we hope to find in our government is not good policies, but goodness itself. Our goal, then, is not specific accomplishments but a moral standing, one we gain for ourselves by forging a connection to an institution that is good. Just as we can secure our goodness by joining a Church because the Church is the repository of what is good, we can secure our goodness by being linked to a nation that is good because its leaders are good.

The same issue arose, of course, during the crisis of the Clinton presidency associated with his affair with Monica Lewinsky. In response to the

revelation that Clinton had an affair and then lied about it, some respond-
ed that they could no longer trust the President and he should therefore
resign or be removed from office. While there were numerous issues
involved in the matter of resignation and impeachment, one was clearly a
matter of trust. If Clinton lied about the affair, would he not lie about
other matters? Doesn't the lie about the affair indicate a proclivity to lie?
A man with a proclivity for lying is not a trust-worthy man, which is to
say he is not a good man. And, again, we cannot trust a man who is not
good to do good, whatever his policies may be and whatever the political
pressures we normally assume determine action in the political arena.

We can see here a clash between two ideals of leadership. According to
one, we should have as our leaders men and women whose goodness com-
mands our confidence that their actions will also be good. According to
the other ideal, we should elect those leaders whose policies we support,
assuming that the constraints of office dictate conduct. In the first case, we
insist that the office and the man are inseparable; in the second we insist
that we are electing an office holder, whose action in office will be governed by political commitments and pressures, rather than by character.
In the second case, we distinguish office-holder from man, and character
becomes a secondary consideration.

While the distinction just drawn may seem clear enough, we need to
be alert to another possibility. This is the possibility that what makes a
man or woman good is what they do rather than what they are. Thus,
those who line up on the "right" side of an issue are good. This construction reverses the relation just considered, although it often appears to simply express that relation. If being good means adapting conduct to the
appropriate "values," then being good is derivative of doing good, and
thus our ability to count on those who are good to do good does not
amount to much. Yet, while relying on those whose goodness derives from
what they do to do good does not amount to much, it still carries a substantial emotional significance. Indeed, the difference between deriving
inner goodness from right conduct and being good points us toward a
basic distinction in moral thinking that has much to do with problems of
public life. In this chapter, I consider this difference and some of its implications for governing.

The goal of having others judge our conduct to be "good" and "right"
powerfully influences what we say and do. In universities as in government, few issues spend much time under discussion without someone
defining them as moral tests. In small ways, and sometimes in ways that

are not so small, where we stand on issues determines whether we are good or bad, right or wrong, and thus establishes whether we have character. All of the problems tangled up with matters of "political correctness" (for those who are and for those who are not) stem from the association of good and right with "correct." The result is to make moral-political concerns govern what is taught, how it is taught, and by whom.

This preoccupation with having character, with being and doing right, contrasts sharply with another attitude common among students, many of whom are convinced that what is right is a matter of opinion. Then, the intensity of the desire to do and be right is matched by the conviction that the criteria by which we judge what is right are contingent and purely subjective. This contradictory attitude is important, and, if we can understand it, will tell us something important about the preoccupation with character alluded to above. To understand the combination of beliefs, attitudes, and feelings that define the problem of character, we must understand better what about the individual makes possible, or impedes, ethical conduct. In this chapter, I consider the capacity for ethical conduct, and why it has such significance for us.

Good and Bad

We usually assume that being capable of ethical conduct means being able to distinguish right from wrong and act according to what is right rather than what is expedient or self-serving. Distinguishing right from wrong can mean knowing the rules of right conduct. Equating ethical conduct with adherence to rules, however, sidesteps the issue of how psychic organization does or does not make someone inherently ethical in his or her orientation to the world, focusing instead on questions about how we know and make ourselves do what is right. Knowing and making ourselves do what is right makes ethics an external constraint on action, and sets up an opposition between the demands of the self and those of ethical conduct.

An alternative way of thinking about ethical conduct emphasizes how psychic organization makes ethical conduct a natural expression of our character rather than the result of an inner conflict. Ethics, then, refers not to adherence to rules, but to the regard for others that becomes a part of our sense of our selves. For simplicity, I will refer to the first way of thinking about ethical conduct as morality and the second as ethics.[2] Their psychic meaning and origins are decidedly different, and a high moral tone as often as not signals a weakness of ethical character. The distinction just drawn has importance for the issue with which I began this chapter. When we speak of a "good" man who will do good because he is good, are we speaking of someone morally good, or someone possessed of ethical character? As we will see, doing good has a decidedly different meaning when linked to morality than it does when linked to the capacity for ethical conduct.[3]

Underlying moral and ethical judgment is the experience of the "good" and the "bad," which plays an important part in the psychic meaning of government and in the symbolic dimension of public experience. As I suggest in the Introduction, the intrusion of moral categories, which is to say categories organized around good and bad, is our first indication that a shift has taken place to the hidden and unconscious collective agenda. It is necessary, therefore, to explore the psychic meaning of these categories before we can consider the way they play out in the public arena. The categories good and bad have a primitive emotional significance, primitive in that they express the earliest human connections, and the most primitive of human aspirations. By understanding this link between early experience and moral thinking, we can also understand the moral language of politics, and the shape of public experience that arises out of it.

In psychoanalytic interpretations of the child's earliest encounters with others, good and bad are attributes of the child's primary object (his or her mother, mothering person, or caretaker). Here, psychoanalysts generally treat good and bad as more or less synonymous with satisfying and frustrating. Initially this equation seems clear enough. The object takes on significance for the infant because of its ability to satisfy the infant's need, archetypally to satisfy his or her hunger. When the mother satisfies her child's hunger, she is good, and when she fails, she is bad.

While we can speak of good and bad as attributes of the object, we can also consider good and bad objects internalized products of experience. That is, we can say not that the object is good or bad, but that good and bad experiences become internalized as a part of fantasy life. Thus, the early experience of severe frustration is transformed "into the fantasied image of a bad mother."[4] Formulating the process in this way has the advantage that it links experiences in the world (relations with external objects) with the construction of an inner world. This transformation of external object relation into internal psychic reality, or psychic structure, is important in understanding the phenomenon of hate, which is central to our concerns here.

In thinking about the matter of satisfying and frustrating objects, it will help to consider Ronald Fairbairn's suggestion that the object of the infant's need is not satisfaction in the more traditional sense, but the forming of a relationship.[5] As he puts it, libido is object seeking rather than pleasure seeking. This would seem to demand that we rethink what we mean by satisfying. Here, it might help to distinguish a satisfying relationship from a relationship that satisfies. The former refers to satisfaction in a relationship, the latter to a relationship that can provide satisfaction of a need not inherently involving relatedness. A satisfying relationship is an end in itself, and makes the other valued in him or her self, at least potentially.[6] A relationship that satisfies is a means to an end and makes others instruments valued for what they can provide, not for who they are. What is bad about bad objects, then, is not simply that they fail to satisfy need, but that in their failure they disrupt a relationship. We can say that bad, therefore, means withholding of love, or unloving.

In general, objects are not simply bad or simply good, but sometimes bad and sometimes good. If the caretaker's attitude toward the child is, at least to some extent, one of ambivalence—the caretaker's preoccupation with the infant is not complete—then the caretaker takes on at different moments the qualities of both the good and the bad objects. Coping with good and bad experiences becomes the central emotional problem of maturation. Since it is a problem about connection, it is, at least implicitly, a problem about the moral attitude toward the world. We need to bear in mind the significance of connection in the psychic meaning of morality. While connection is not the whole of the story of primitive human desire, it is vital to that story.

The bad object poses a dilemma for the child, who is absolutely dependent on it, not only for sustenance, but also for that relatedness without which the nascent person within the child withers. The bad object rejects the child and especially the child's love. According to Fairbairn, the child adopts the obvious strategy for dealing with its dilemma: it seeks to remove the bad object from its world in order to make the world a place within which it can live and hope to find love.

To accomplish this end, the child has only one place to put the bad object, which is inside him or her self. This means that the child becomes bad himself (or herself) in order to protect the object, and therefore the world, from being bad. The bad child becomes a vessel for the badness of the world. Now the child is bad and the world is good. But, this only reproduces the child's dilemma in altered form. When the object was bad and the child good, the object rejected the child and therefore obstructed the needed relationship. Now that the child is bad and the object good, the child obstructs that relationship. Being bad now means being unworthy of love, so the child has made the object loving by making him or her self unworthy of the object's love. To be bad in the sense of unworthy of love is to be bad in a moral sense.

To have an internal bad object is to have a life-forming idea that you are bad along with the associated bad feeling about yourself. Speaking of internal objects means that our primary feelings of love and hate have taken on a concrete meaning that is not simply or primarily conceptual, but experiential, and that the meaning of love and hate are internalized, which implies that they shape our sense of self.

The language of internal good and bad objects can be a puzzling one. While the elusive quality of the language cannot be altogether avoided, it might be worthwhile to make the point in another way. Fairbairn depicts the dilemma faced by hatred for the object that must be loved in a religious language when he notes that it is better to be a sinner in a world ruled by God than to live in a world ruled by the devil. For the sinner there is always hope for redemption, which is to say for love in a world suitable to love. Thus, the child becomes the sinner so that those who rule his or her world can remain good. Not only does the child take on the idea that he or she is a sinner, but the child also acts in ways a sinner would act because doing so assures that the badness lies within the child and not in his or her world. Now, for example, whatever the mother does, she remains the good mother since any seemingly hostile or sadistic behavior on her part is prompted by the child, and is just punishment for the child's bad behavior. When the child provokes sadistic behavior he or she secures the needed relationship. The bad behavior makes this relationship real, or more so. The result of this maneuver is that the child is bad, or has a bad self. When the child is prompted into this role, he is, in psychoanalytic language, identified with his bad internal object, or his identity as a sinner.

As infants and children (perhaps even as adults), we can do nothing to change the world outside except to take its badness into ourselves; we cannot really make the world good. So, to cope with a badness that has become our own, we must do something with it inside ourselves. This something is the repression (into the unconscious) of the (internal) bad object. Internalization and repression of the bad object and of our relationship with it seals both object and relationship from the influence of changing circumstances in the world outside. Fairbairn sees repression of the bad object as the next step in the drama of the child's effort to cope with his or her dilemma. This repression is a continuation of the strategy of removal of the bad object, except now the removal is wholly internal, into the unconscious. Repression is our way of not knowing our own badness. But, not knowing our inner world prevents us from changing it. There is much in the phenomena of hate that involves not knowing a vital part of who we are.

Consider in this connection a group of college students who organized an effort to cope with what are sometimes referred to as "hate crimes" around the slogan "Erase the Hate."[7] This slogan expresses with special force the denial of hate as a way of coping with hate. Indeed, this denial of hate is already implied in the category of hate crime, which insists that hate is itself a crime and should be punished over and above the punishment associated with the same crime were it not motivated by hate. The special treatment of hate crimes also insists that the great majority of even violent crimes are not motivated by hate. Only those crimes explicitly, which is to say consciously, motivated by a desire to destroy a group are acknowledged as "hate crimes," so that the very category of hate crime already erases the hate underlying most if not all crimes of violence, and many crimes not involving violence. Erasing the hate in this case does not, of course, remove hate, but only our awareness of it. Similarly, the effort to identify a very small group of crimes as hate crimes seeks to cordon off society's hate. Here, we can see the repression of the bad object on a societal level. This repression also involves projection, which is the next step in coping with the dilemma posed by the rejecting object.

The Bad Object and the World Outside

When the child responds to the badness of the neglecting or abusing object by taking its badness inside, the child becomes bad so that the object can be made good. This means that the original deprivation experienced in relation to the primary caregiver now becomes self-deprivation, which becomes more tolerable to the degree that it can be visited on others. Then, the deprived become the depriving. When this happens, the meaning of good and bad becomes complex. Originally, bad means depriving, good means satisfying. As a result of internalization and repression, however, bad comes to mean self-satisfying (it is bad to be self-indulgent), and good comes to mean self-denying (it is good to be industrious and frugal). This reversal makes sense once we recall that the child understands being good (in relation to the narcissistic parent) to mean satisfying the parent's needs and not his or her own. Being good in relation to the bad parent requires self-denial.

One important implication of this dynamic is that to make the parent (world) good, the child creates an ideal parent by taking on responsibility for the bad relation with the (now good) parent. So long as this bad remains within the child (the child is bad), the psychic experience of the child will be dominated by feelings of inadequacy and self-hatred. The more intense such feelings become, the less they can be tolerated, the greater the pressure to find a way to relieve them. Relief from the pain of self-hatred and the feeling of worthlessness that goes along with it comes in the form of externalizing via projection. When feelings of self-hatred are intense enough, the badness (bad internal object or bad self) can no longer be contained inside. It must be put outside, which is to say it must be attributed to an external object, which is bad. This process secures the desired identification with the good self (the child is his or her good self) at the expense of making a part of the world bad. Because the child is frustrated and deprived by the now externalized bad object, the child can be said to hate that object, and wish to remove it from the world.

The whole process has created a divided external world made up on one side of an object made altogether good by internalization of the bad object relation (the creation of the self as the sinner in a world ruled by God) and on the other of an object experienced as altogether bad because it is the container for the projected bad self. This experience of a divided world is an essential element in the phenomena of hate. Hate movements aim to attack, control, and destroy this externalized bad object so that the good object can once again rule in the world. Removal of the externalized bad object becomes a project involving the world outside; it is no longer an internal psychic maneuver, but an action taken in the world, from which the object must be removed.

The project of removing the bad object from the world has substantial significance for the psychic meaning of public experience. The attack on government is bound up with the idea of purifying the public realm (an idea also involved in the various forms of ethnic and racial cleansing that periodically emerge in the international arena). Purification assures that what is is good, and that those who are good do good. The necessity of protecting the ideal from the real suggests the importance of notions such as contamination and corruption. As it turns out, the notion of corruption also plays a central role in the attack on government. Indeed, the failures of government are frequently summed up in the notion that government is corrupt. Then, we can only assure the goodness of the nation by reclaiming it from the government.[8]

The Moral Defense

Internalizing the bad object makes the child bad. If all the child has with which to identify is an internalized bad object, he or she can be nothing but bad. Externalizing the bad object may relieve the pain associated with the feeling that the self is bad, but it also voids the inner world of a sense of self and the associated capacity to direct action in the world. To deal with this problem, the child can internalize a good object to counter the bad. Then, so far as the child identifies with his or her internal good object, he or she can be good, but only conditionally so. That is, to be good is to reject the internalized bad object and the part of the self identified with it. Thus, being good means being good against the self.

This element of self-denial (the attack on the self) is essential in distinguishing the moral stance from ethical character. The former is built around the idea that we are originally bad (as expressed in the notion of original sin), and thus around the internal divisions implied in that idea. The moral stance is also organized around the idea of repression of the self, which is bad. In the psychic drama of government, self-hatred plays a primary role.

We should note that the good object (or good self-construct) internalized to cope with the bad has some peculiar qualities that make its goodness suspect. The most notable of these qualities is its purity. The internalized good object is simply (and therefore perfectly) good. The internalized good object is, then, a kind of caricature of the good. And, the part of the self patterned after it is a kind of caricature of a self: the good self. We can see here again how the internalized good and bad objects are not good and bad selves, but parts of a self that can never quite put itself together. The good (part) self strives to be always and only good. Yet, this means that the internalized good object is alien to and rejecting of the self (or the child's aspirations to constitute a self) since a self is not always good. This implicit rejection of selfhood suggests why morality displays such a penchant for sadism. Indeed, because it is an attack on the self, the moral defense forges a link between morality and sadism. This link to sadism becomes especially important when we consider the psychic meaning and psychic roots of the attack on the welfare state. We can begin to understand the punitive attitude some adopt toward those dependent on welfare if we understand first the punitive attitude they have toward themselves.

The attack on the self means that in acting we cannot trust our selves, which have lost their moral authority. Rather than trust in our selves, we seek to identify with an external authority (the external good object) capable of directing our conduct in the world. That is, we can act according to rules of right conduct given to us. If we then equate being good with following the right rules, or doing good, we have an answer to the question, Who should govern?, rooted in the moral orientation. This answer is that those who govern should be those who are good, and those who are good are those who follow the approved rules of right thinking and right conduct. Put in the language with which I began, those who are good in this sense are those who engage in moral conduct even though they do not have ethical character. When they do so, of course, they act against the self, which tends to make the morality of rule-bound behavior one of denial and restraint, first of the self, then of others. Being good against the self fosters the natural transition from morality to moralizing.

The effort to foster the good self as an antidote to the bad is well expressed in the rhetoric around issues of tolerance, where the emphasis is sometimes placed on teaching and learning tolerance. This emphasis denies the emotional roots of intolerance, and especially the psychic meaning and roots of hatred. Instead, hatred is to be understood as learned behavior, or an attitude taken up because of peer pressure or parental example. While it might seem plausible to suggest that we unlearn intolerance, it seems hardly plausible that we could unlearn hate if only because hate is not something we learn, but a complex emotional response to a frightening early experience. Then, so far as intolerance is linked to hate, we can no more unlearn intolerance than we can unlearn hate.

We can see in the struggle over the self (between good and bad selves) the root of another quality important in understanding public experience, the rigidity of thought typical in public debate. Intolerance of those who disagree is fueled by the conviction that what is at stake in the debate is not alternative policies, but who will be made to carry the burden of being bad. Thus, public debate becomes a contest between good and evil. Once framed (psychically) in this way, there can be no room for tolerance or compromise. This construction of debate as a moral contest, while most evident for those who explicitly frame the issues in a religious language, is not restricted to those wishing to mix religion with politics. The moral defense has an affinity for the religious construction of the world, but it also has its secular expressions. These expressions are common in public life when matters of the nation, national identity, and national pride are involved. The idea of the goodness of the people or the nation also expresses the moral stance, and especially the presence of what we have referred to here as the moral defense.

The stronger the moral current the stronger the attack on the self and the greater the difficulty the individual has with genuinely ethical conduct. The stronger the attack on the self, the more powerful the sadistic trends in the personality and the less suited it is to fostering a genuinely ethical attitude toward others. As I will argue below, the power of the bad internal object and the preoccupation of the ego with its repression subvert the formation of ethical character.

Guilt

Melanie Klein uses the notion of the depressive position to depict the situation in which the child discovers that the mother he or she hates for being the bad object is the same mother he or she loves for being the good object. At this point, the child develops a relation to a whole person, whole in the primitive sense of both good and bad. To accept the goodness of the bad object and the badness of the good (that they are the same object) enables the child to accept that he or she is also both good and bad. Thus, accepting the wholeness of the object is the other side of achieving wholeness of the self. This achievement establishes the basis for guilt as a response to harm done to the (good) object. We feel bad about harm we have done to others when we recognize those others as good. Guilt is important because it expresses recognition of the self-in-other and the capacity to take responsibility for harm done. The connection of guilt to recognition of other and responsibility for self links guilt to ethical character.

True guilt arises because the child recognizes the identity of the hated and loved objects.[9] The child recognizes that love and hate are directed at the same, or more accurately at one, person. More importantly, however, guilt arises because the child realizes that he or she is both good and bad, and therefore cannot escape his or her own badness. True guilt, then, expresses our love for the hated person. But, it also expresses our love for ourselves since it expresses acceptance of the fact that we are not unconditionally or inevitably good. This acceptance involves the modulation of feelings toward self and object that marks ethical character. Combining love and hate produces a more moderate attitude, which is the essence of genuine tolerance and thus a genuinely ethical attitude.

The connection between morality and sadism already emphasized separates morality from true guilt and links it instead to hatred. Hate circumvents guilt by treating the object as all bad. When the object is not good, harm done to it does not mean harm done to the good object, and guilt does not arise. Those who commit the violent acts we associate with "hate crimes" are not subject to normal guilt that expresses regard for the other person (for the self-in-other). This does not mean that such individuals have no guilt-like experience. On the contrary, they may experience the most savage internal attack on the self, involving intense self-hatred and feelings of worthlessness. Following Melanie Klein, Arthur Hyatt-Williams points out that these individuals "have a persecutory superego that is savagely punitive." These intense and distorted forms of what we normally think of as conscience have the most profound consequences, especially involving the externalization "into dramatic enactments."[10] These enactments provoke a harsh response, which when internalized, reinforces the development or persecutory internal objects. An individual under intense and sadistic attack internally seeks relief by turning the attack on the self into an attack on others, who become identified as the bad self. Then, what begins as a distorted form of conscience becomes sadism and cruelty.

The provocation of authority figures referred to by Hyatt-Williams appears in public life in the relationship with government, the ultimate authority figure for society as a whole. The violence of government in response to those who attack the civil community enables them to exercise the option of experiencing the attack on the self as coming from outside (from government) rather inside. This relieves the inner conflict and pain. It also suggests how inadequate is the plan of those who would raise the stakes for crime by intensifying punishment, since they ignore how preferable punishment can be, no matter how cruel, to psychic pain.

The Self-Ideal

Once the primitive separation of good and bad objects fails in the face of recognition of the wholeness of self and other, the terrain of the struggle between separation and integration shifts. The struggle now takes place over our internalized ideal self. The formation of the ideal self establishes purpose in our lives on the abstract plane of goals and ideals. Being good now means being our ideal self, and being bad means failing to do so. Yet, whether we can be good also depends on how we deal with being bad, and, in particular, how much badness we accept as part of ourselves. Put another way, psychic integration depends both on the attainability of our ideal and on our ability to tolerate failure. Attainability depends on how absolutely good that ideal is, therefore on how much room it allows us to fall short of perfection and still consider ourselves worthy of love. Tolerance of failure depends on how severe the consequences of failure are expected or imagined to be.

Splitting good from bad prevents the knowledge that we might be bad from infecting our ego ideal, which is patterned not on a whole object that is both good and bad, but on an idealized object that is always and only good. The purity of the idealized object reflects itself in the perfection of the ideal. Forming an absolute and formal ideal leaves little room for tolerance of self and other. Perfection of the ideal makes it unattainable and places us in the position that we can never satisfy our own internal self-expectation, a situation that reproduces as an internal matter our original interpersonal dilemma.

Andrew Morrison considers how the experience of shame expresses the disparity between the actual and ideal selves. Shame, he suggests, reflects feelings about a defect in the self, with the attendant lowering of self-esteem, and the inevitable falling short of the values of the ego ideal.[11] Our shame invokes a threat of abandonment or rejection, which would affirm our unworthiness for love. The experience of shame involves the depletion of the self, and is "overcome through attainment of a cohesive, plentiful self which allows for self-acceptance" and therefore also acceptance of the self-in-other.[12]

To avoid the experience of shame, the depleted self seeks fusion of ideal and actual selves. In the words of Otto Kernberg, "there is a fusion of ideal self, ideal object, and actual self-images as a defense against an intolerable reality in the interpersonal realm" with the result that the individual identifies him or her self with his or her self-ideal.[13] This assures that the individual can avoid the experience of shame. In other words, protection against feeling ashamed of the self is provided by "the building up of an inflated self concept" sometimes referred to as a "grandiose self." Ideals unattainable in reality are attained within the grandiose fantasy that takes the place of a connection to interpersonal reality.

The fantasized fusion of actual and ideal constitutes a manic defense closely associated with an attack on the externalized parts of the self, especially in the form of cruelty toward others. Hyatt-Williams describes how manic defenses protect against psychic pain by acting "against feelings of tenderness, unrequited need such as the need for love, feelings of compassion and concern both for the kind and tender parts of the self and for the well-being of others." By acting against these feelings, the manic defenses "also act against feelings of inadequacy, smallness, lack of intelligence or skill, inability to compete with others, lack of beauty or of social graces."[14]

The fantasized fusion of real with ideal, because it is predicated on the externalization of the devalued parts of the self, constitutes a grandiose self on one side, and, on the other, an external world made to contain those parts of the self that involve inadequacy, dependence, and so on. The attitude toward that world combines fear and contempt. We fear the world because in it we find the projected parts of ourselves, parts that we expect, in their externalized form, to attack us out of envy for what we imagine ourselves to be. We hold the world in contempt because in it we find our projected dependent and therefore inadequate selves. The fear and contempt for what is real (external) stimulates an impulse to control objects in the world, since only control of objects can protect the grandiose self from them and assure that they behave in ways consistent with their use as containers for disavowed parts of the self. Thus, the fusion of real and ideal is maintained through relationships with others marked by a significant element of cruelty.

The fusion of self and self-ideal has two important consequences for understanding certain attitudes toward government. First, it carries an implication about dependence, a concept vital in the ideal of small government or no government. Second, it carries an implication about the perception of others, who are made via projection to contain unacceptable self-images, which is to say those images that undermine the fusion of self with its grandiose ideal. Kernberg notes how the fantasy of fusion denies "normal dependency on external objects."[15] It is, after all, the failure of these objects that the grandiose self must make right. Where objects fail, the self must step in, and in so doing establish its independence of objects, which it can only do by denying its limitations as one in a world of others.

Denial of dependence is a vital theme of the psychic experience of government. This theme involves both denial of dependence on government, and cruelty toward those who become dependent on it. Here we can see both implications of the fusion of actual and ideal selves in action. The grandiose self has no need for objects, is self-sufficient, and therefore has no need for government. Similarly, the grandiose self treats with sadism and contempt those who are in need of government since they are the repositories of the projected shameful self. It will not be surprising, then, if we find the experience of shame playing a central role in the attack on government, especially in its more violent forms.[16]

The Feeling of Security

The good parent satisfies because he or she secures a sense of relatedness for the child. Thus far, I have placed exclusive emphasis on relatedness or connection without considering more specifically the content or object of that relatedness. Vital to understanding the quality of connection is the way connection implicates the nascent self of the child. Arnold Rothstein describes two alternative meanings connection can have.[17] The first he refers to as "object-related love" by which he has in mind a maternal orientation "in which joy is derived primarily from nurturing the child for its own sake." In object-related love, the separateness of the child is respected, and his or her needs become the parent's primary concern. By contrast, in narcissistic love, the child is treated as a "narcissistically invested extension of the maternal self-representation." Here, the child is "of value only insofar as he aggrandizes the parents' self-representation."

The path to ethical character made available by object-related love rests on the feeling of security the child develops in relation to the parent. Nothing threatens the building of ethical character more than insecurity. Indeed, a key quality of the moral orientation is feeling insecure in an unsafe world. Insecurity is a vital element of the attack government, which, if successful, removes from the world a primary source of security for the individual.

When narcissistic love dominates over object-related love, the parent creates an uncertain environment for the child by making connection contingent. Being good means doing whatever sustains connection, which is to say being for other rather than being for self. This syndrome sets up in the child a primitive idea of the good, and provides a foundation for what Donald Winnicott refers to as the "false self," a concept with clear and compelling relevance to understanding how the moral defense obstructs the development of ethical character.[18] As the child matures into adulthood, the idea of the good becomes more complex, and its roots in the striving to secure the relation with the parent become obscure, although no less powerful. The adult formed in this way continues to believe (if unconsciously) that being good in the sense of conforming to an ideal originating outside (a moral ideal) will assure merger with his or her idealized object; it will assure that he or she is only and altogether good.

To achieve such an ideal places us in an ethical dilemma. The ideal has the subjective meaning of merger with the parent and rejection of everything bad, which excludes others (especially if they have accepted that they are sometimes bad) and even obliterates the distinctiveness of the self. Since realizing the moral ideal means merger and merger denies difference, realizing that ideal is part of a striving to deny boundaries and thus the integrity of others. Realizing such an ideal therefore stands opposed to ethical character. Yet, the moral ideal contains the sum of our notion of right conduct in the world. It embodies our sense of what we wish to be, including the sense of what we ought to be. It builds on moral strictures (however idiosyncratic)—of right and wrong—presented to us by our parents early in life as the money accepted in payment for connection with them. Thus, identification with our moral ideal links us to canons of right conduct, but it does so in a way that denies the integrity of others since its aim is merger rather than difference. The link between morality, the ego ideal, and merger fantasies has important implications for understanding groups and certain kinds of community.[19] This connection will be important when we turn to the question of democratic community and to the question of the tension between citizenship and group identity.

Narcissistic love, because of its connection to merger fantasies, can be thought of as an all too intense connection between parent and child. In its way, however, it is no connection at all, but the denial of the otherness of the child, which is to say denial of the child's true self. The resulting repression of the true self will later have substantial consequences for the ability of the adult to accept difference where difference expresses the individual's creative potential. We can say in a sense, then, that however intense the relation with the parent may seem when it is organized around narcissistic love, it constitutes deprivation by refusing to satisfy the child's need to have his or her separate self recognized and nurtured. After all, narcissistic love informs the child that he or she (his or her self) is not worthy of love, except insofar as his or her self is adapted to the alien self of the other (the parent). The neglect associated with narcissistic love shapes the child's inner world in a specific direction.

Trust

At the beginning of this chapter, I noted the connection between the problem of character and the problem of trust. Because the President lied about his affair with Monica Lewinsky, he cannot be trusted. He lied, and therefore cannot be trusted because of a weakness in character. This weakness in character means that he falls short of a standard many believe we ought to apply to those in public office, especially the paramount public office of President.

If we ask the question, Why is trust of such paramount importance in governance?, a number of answers emerge. Some would link honesty to democracy. They insist that democracy means that the people are the ultimate governors. But, if the people are the ultimate governors, they must have the autonomy to decide on issues, which they cannot have if they are manipulated by the control over information. Dishonesty on the part of public officials, then, corrupts democracy. I will explore the matter of democracy at length further on. For the present, I would like to focus attention on another dimension of the problem of trust, one closely connected to the salience of character in public life.

A second answer to the question, Why does it matter that the President lied?, evokes more directly the psychic meaning of trust. Here, trust takes on importance in itself, not because it is important to other ends, such as democratic self-governance. Now, the issue of character takes center stage. This happens when the President's character is made to represent the character of the nation, and thus the president's character flaws become flaws in the national character, which means flaws in our character as citizens of the nation. The idea that the President is a model, especially for young people, expresses this idea more concretely. A flawed President creates a flawed nation. His dishonesty serves to validate dishonesty as a social matter, for all. In other words, the President's character failure corrupts the character of the nation, of its people, and especially of the young.

Given what I have already said about character, the idea that the President's conduct could corrupt character will seem implausible. The formation of character takes place in a setting where distant figures such as the President can hardly be expected to exert significant influence. Yet, we should not too quickly dismiss the claim that the President's flaws corrupt the national character, since, however true or false as a practical matter, it may yet have a powerful psychic validity. This psychic validity has two aspects. First, it involves the idea that character is learned behavior and, second, it expresses a profound psychic preoccupation with the experience of being lied to.

Treating character as learned behavior fits well with the idea of morality, and indeed is a part of that idea. The moral standpoint concerns itself with rules and strictures that govern conduct from outside. Patterning behavior after others, especially those in positions of authority, means that the quality of our behavior is determined by the pattern that we are given or that we choose. This standpoint sidesteps the whole matter of psychic experience and psychic structure, thus leaving aside what is arguably the essential driving force in practical judgment. It also insists on subordinating conduct to external expectations, thus sacrificing internal initiative and judgment to compliance (in Winnicott's language subordinating the true to the false self).

Equally important, however, is the salience of lying. When it became apparent that the President had indeed lied, the fact was clearly of greater salience to some than to others. Indeed, some found it virtually intolerable, while others viewed it as possibly of consequence to his family and close associates, but not to the nation as a whole. How might we account for what I refer to here as the salience of lying for those who found the prospect of dishonesty in the President intolerable?

We can find one answer to this question in the idea of narcissistic love considered in the previous section. For those whose experience of connection with the parent is one of narcissistic love, their experience of the most significant relationship in their lives embodies a lie. At the center of this lie is the matter of gratification, and especially of who gets gratified. Narcissistic love insists that gratifying the parent is what gratifies the child. It, therefore, offers deprivation in the name of gratification. This relationship, then, provides a template for judging other relationships, and the emotional issues built into the original relationship become the issues that give meaning to subsequent relationships.

The significance of narcissistic love becomes clear when we acknowledge that narcissistic love is not love at all, but its opposite. In other words, narcissistic love is itself a lie. It is a lie in that it offers hate in the name of love. If love sustains and affirms the other's self, while hate seeks to destroy that self, narcissistic love is really a form of hate. Narcissistic love is the hate offered by those who should love us. It is, because it carries the name of its opposite, the ultimate lie. For those who have been the victims of hate in the name of love, to be lied to has tremendous psychic meaning regardless of its practical consequences.

So far as this is correct, we can say that telling lies is the mark of the bad object, and that we must expect the bad object to lie to us. Then, of course, those in whose psychic world Bill Clinton already occupied the position of the bad object will naturally assume that he cannot be trusted, and are gratified to find objective proof to support their assumption. As it turns out, the Special Prosecutor's relentless search for proof, if it did not force Clinton to lie, certainly placed him in a position where lying became more and more likely. We can say, then, that the Special Prosecutor acted as the agent of those who required that external, or objective, reality be made to conform with psychic reality.

That Clinton was, for them, already a bad object follows from what originally defines bad objects, which is their refusal to gratify. Indeed, the bad object stands as the main obstacle to gratification. Thus, were it not for a Democratic President, nothing would stand in the way of Republican control of government. The Democratic President, then, becomes the main obstacle to their control over the source of gratification. Proving him unworthy of the public trust validated their judgment, their hope in advancing such proof being that the people would rise up against him and deliver the government to those worthy of having it.

This observation can tell us something important about hatred of government. Hatred of government results from the involvement of government in psychic drama. In this drama, the government can take the part of the bad object; and when it does, it becomes the object of our hatred. Hatred of government is closely linked to the perception that government is corrupt, which is to say that those who govern act in their own interest rather than the people's interest, just as the narcissistic parent acts in his or her own interest rather than that of the child. So far as the narcissistic parent is capable of love, it is love for self, not love for other. The hatred provoked by narcissistic love is, then, a deep pool from which to draw upon for hatred of others, and of institutions such as government.

We need only add to this the observation that the organization of our public life, especially the process by which we elect and otherwise connect with our leaders, insists that they manipulate us for their own gain. In other words, we insist upon their narcissism, as we insist that they lie to us so far as the truth might be damaging to their prospects of success in office or reelection. Corruption in high office affirms our deepest convictions about government, and assures that in government we have a suitable container for the disavowed aspects of ourselves we then criticize unmercifully in public servants.

Our need for narcissism in office has its most vivid expression in the grandiose fantasy we require our leaders to endorse for us, however implausible it might be. In America, no one who offers a realistic assessment of the nation can hope to get elected. Rather than realism, we crave and demand a fantasy of power and goodness. We must be told that we occupy a "blessed land," that "our nation is poised for greatness," that we are "a nation still mighty in its youth."[20] We must be told that "America's best is the best in the world," and that "America must lead."[21] We must be told that we "have what it takes … to make our values … the strongest force on earth."[22]

If we demand narcissism in office, we should expect to get it. That we are then enraged that the narcissistic office holder behaves narcissistically only suggests that we have gotten the government we deserve, and that one of its functions is to provide a suitable outlet for our rage. That narcissism in office means corruption and dishonesty comes as no surprise, and should be understood not as a personal failing of elected officials, but as their success in playing the part in the collective psychic drama for which they were recruited.

The Sense of Otherness

The sense of otherness achieved by uniting the good and bad objects creates a primitive interpersonal relationship with the primary caretaker, interpersonal because the relationship connects two different persons for the first time, primitive because the relationship encompasses no more than two persons, one of whom is only incipiently or potentially a person. The absence of a third makes the interpersonal relationship susceptible to regression into a single unit; the pressure toward merger remains strong since the prospect of merger remains vivid. And, after all, if the whole interpersonal world consists of two, who remain so much alike, difference has little room to flourish. Ethical character demands not only the recognition of a relation to another, but something more.

The significance of the Oedipal situation stems from the part it plays in the development of difference. In the classical Freudian theory, the son's defeat in the Oedipal struggle means renunciation of the desire for the opposite sex parent and, eventually, seeking to replace him or her with someone from outside. Thus, the Oedipal struggle has significance in the development of difference. Oedipal defeat also means recognition on the part of the child that he cannot always get what he wants. This involves a connection to reality, or renunciation of life within a fantasy world. Thus, the Oedipal struggle eventuates in a movement from omnipotence (the expectation that all needs will be satisfied in the mother-infant dyad) to reality (renunciation of the desire for the mother), and from a dyad, within which difference is always vulnerable, to relations with many others. Both achievements have ethical significance. The whole person, who has integrated good and bad, must now become a separate person, who can relate to others without denying his or her difference from them. Just as splitting gives way to integration, merger gives way to relating.

Failure to traverse the Oedipal phase means failure to accept the separateness of persons. Those who fail treat the demands of difference and relating to others as narcissistic blows directed at their fantasies of domination.[23] Others may want differently than we do, and they may be different from us, valuing different things or leading a different sort of life. The desire to submerge others into ourselves cannot accommodate such differences. Pursuit of merger can also take the form of an ideological commitment that binds group members in an effort to create the sense of oneness that dispels difference. A group built on this foundation cannot tolerate the non-member, and seeks to absorb or destroy those outside.

Intolerance of difference mirrors intolerance of self. The rejecting, punitive, sadistic self equates ethics with self-renunciation. The individual who carries this burden of self-denial may seek to impose it on others by insisting they pay the same price—renunciation of self—to attain moral standing. If the child equates regard for others with renunciation of self, this means that regard for others cannot be a natural extension of the self.

Progression from the moral standpoint to ethical character brings with it a transformation of the nature and perception of right conduct. The progression sets out, as Lawrence Kohlberg observes, from formal rules, which can only be obeyed or defied. Knowing these rules means knowing how to follow them. Such rules are abstract in that we know them prior to and outside of any rich context of thought and experience. We know them without thinking much about them. In another sense, however, these rules are concrete. To know them is to be able to follow them without much thought, by associating experiences in which they have proven appropriate. To this extent, the meaning of the rules remains experiential. This suggests that the rules are concrete rather than abstract since the experiential quality of rules severs their connection to reason. Rules cease to be rules when they are known to make up a part of a larger and comprehensible whole, when they follow reason(s) rather than orders. The larger whole is what Hegel refers to as ethical life. Considered internally, this larger whole is what we mean by ethical character.

The idea that moral conduct means conduct in accord with conventional (and in this sense arbitrary) rules links morality to group experience, since it is the group that defines the rules, and the psychic purpose achieved in following the rules is group connection. Since the moral orientation puts group connection at stake, establishing that in our conduct we are "right," meaning in conformity with group norms, has the greatest significance for us. At the same time, since what makes conduct right is conformity with group norms, the criteria of right are essentially conventional, even subjective. Thus, the link between morality and belonging in groups helps explain the apparently conflicting attitudes alluded to at the beginning of this chapter. Establishing that our conduct is right is vital to us, while we believe (as my students insist) that the norms of right conduct are purely conventional, even a matter of opinion.

Ethical Character

Good enough parenting should enable the child to develop a secure enough inner world with adequate integration of good and bad selves. This means formation of a whole person. Wholeness requires integration as an internal matter, but it also requires boundedness as a matter of placement of the person in a larger world.[24] This presupposes the sense of security within the self that mirrors an experience of a safe environment in the world outside. Janine Chasseguet-Smirgel speaks of this as maturation of the ego ideal. It is also the formation of ethical character, whose secure self-boundaries form the basis for recognition of the boundaries of others, and whose self-regard forms the basis for regard for others. For the moral actor, the content of right and wrong is determined by arbitrary rules of conduct. For ethical character, the content of right and wrong is determined by respect for the integrity of others. The difference expresses the different subjective meanings of their self-ideals.

The idea of ethical character, rooted as it is in a singular conception of what it means to be a whole and well-bounded person, leaves less room for idiosyncratic judgment, possibly linked to group identity, in determining what is right. Moral thinking, with its emphasis on internalization of rules, makes the content of the rules less central than their subjective function in relation to certain infantile aspirations carried over into adult life. Put another way, moral thinking tends to separate content from subjective function. The content of the rules does not much matter. What matters is adherence to them. By adhering to the rules, we attach ourselves to a group (which represents subjectively the primitive dyad or the family unit). By contrast, for ethical character the content of the good is inseparable from its subjective function. The subjective function is to instantiate regard for self and others in the interaction of persons, and this regard for self and others is also the content of ethical order. This idea, rooted in psychoanalytic theorizing, fits well with an ethics centering on reciprocal recognition of personhood, or mutual regard.[25]

The separation of content from subjective function is one of the more important conclusions we can draw from our discussion of the moral defense. Moral conduct means (subjectively) whatever conduct provides security in an uncertain world. In other words, moral conduct means complying with rules given from outside, sanctioned by rewards and punishments. Moral, then, means compliant, regardless of the specific modes of conduct that happen to be complied with. In this world, what is wrong ethically might be right morally since the community, or other authority that defines the good, need not have ethical character, that is, does not encourage ways of life incorporating mutual regard. A community has ethical character when it enables its members to do so. If it does not, it is more than likely that good conduct means conduct acceptable to an external authority that is itself bad (i.e., lacking ethical character).

If the distinction between the moral attitude and ethical conduct involves the matter of compliance with authority, then it leads to the question of agency and responsibility. Here we encounter a telling reversal. Morality suggests right action rooted in the volition of a subject who bears responsibility, a theme that dominates in public life and in ways centrally linked to the use of government to affirm a fantasy about independence. Yet, what distinguishes the moral attitude is division of and struggle against the self. Since the moral self is inherently divided and acts morally only when in compliance with authority, the moral actor can never be fully the subject of his or her actions, and thus is never really responsible.

The complexity of psychic structure, the significance of the unconscious, and the possibility of divisions within the personality, pose significant problems for the usual attributions of responsibility and agency to the apparent subject of action, the person in the everyday sense of the term. Agency and subjectivity become complex.[26] This complexity becomes apparent when we seek to equate agency with free will. This equation plays a large role in the attitude toward government organized around the danger dependence on government poses for the citizen. In chapter 5, I explore the idea that character is a matter of will, and develops in the struggle of wills. This idea, deeply embedded in the public consciousness, shapes an ideal of government, and promotes punitive social policies predicated on the premise that, in the words of R.H. Tawney, will is all, circumstance nothing.

2 A FANTASY ABOUT GOVERNMENT

The Dark Tunnel

If fantasy is the portal to psychic meaning, who better to guide us through it than Jimmy Stewart and Frank Capra? After a decade of depression, and on the eve of World War II, Capra and Stewart made a movie about the people and their government.[1] As the movie opens, the political machine in an unidentified western state faces a crisis brought on by the death of one of that state's Senators. The Senator's death occurs just as a bill to fund a dam, and thereby line the pockets of the local political machine, will be reaching the Senate floor. The remaining Senator (Joe Paine) wonders why they don't just drop the dam project, and is answered by the head of the machine (Jim Taylor), who reminds the Senator that they've "been quietly buying up all the land around that dam and holding it in dummy names." To drop the project now would prompt an investigation that would "show that we're going to sell it to the state...under phony names."

Rather than drop the dam project, they consider how to fill the vacant Senate seat with someone they can rely on to support funding. After considering several possibilities, the Governor's sons (Peter and Jimmie) offer a suggestion: Jefferson Smith.

> Governor: Well, forgive my abysmal ignorance, but I don't know
>   Jefferson Smith from a hole in the ground.
> Peter: Gosh Dad, head of the Boy Rangers!
> Governor: Oh, a boy!
> Jimmie: No, no, Dad, Jeff's a man! Jeff Smith! Biggest expert we got
>   on wild game and animals and rocks.
> Peter: Yeah, and right now he's the greatest hero we ever had. It's in

all the headlines.

Jimmie: Didn't you see about the terrific forest fire all around
　　　Sweetwater?

Governor: I did. What about it?

Peter: Well, Jeff put that out himself.

Not only does Jefferson Smith know the animals and protect the forest, he "can tell you what George Washington said, by heart." Jefferson Smith also edits a newspaper called "Boy Stuff" read by "all the boys in the state," whose content the Governor assumes must be "childish prattle." Despite his initial inclination to dismiss the suggestion, the Governor quickly decides that Jefferson Smith is exactly what they need to replace the deceased Senator and save the dam: "...the simpleton of all times, a big-eyed patriot. ... A perfect man. Never in politics in his life. Wouldn't know what it was all about in two years, let alone two months." As the secretary of the deceased Senator puts it, "You scratch this thing and you'll find they need a dope here for a couple of months."

Enter Jefferson Smith played by Jimmy Stewart in his patented aw shucks, gee whiz style. He hardly considers himself suited for the work of government, which he imagines to be a task worthy of George Washington and Abraham Lincoln. In his boundless naiveté, he believes that those in government must meet a standard set by the Founding Fathers. Jefferson Smith is a simple, honest, naive man, driven by fundamental values and common sense, rooted in small town country life. As his name suggests, he is a combination of Thomas Jefferson and Everyman.

The simplicity of the character is clearly expressed when, on arrival in Washington, he is asked if he has any ideas that would be good for the country. "I have got one idea," he answers, a National Boys' Camp. "You see, if we could just get the poor kids off the streets, out of the cities for a few months in the summer and...let them learn something about Nature and the American ideal." Mr. Smith has not only an idea, but a plan. He knows where he wants to locate the camp and how to fund it. What will it cost the government? "Nothing, nothing at all. You see, my idea is that the government just lends us the money for the camp and the boys pay it back by sending pennies, nickels...nothing more than a dime." As Mr. Smith sees it, the government's "got enough on its hands already."

Taking boys out of the city has a special significance that Jeff Smith learned from his father, who was a newspaperman, a dreamer, and a "champion of lost causes." After referring to the wonders of nature that fill "every rock, every ant-hill, every star," his father used to say: "Have you ever noticed how grateful you are to see daylight again after going through a dark tunnel?" His advice was always "to see life around you as if you'd just come out of a tunnel." When Mr. Smith arrives in Washington, it is clear that he experiences the world as if he has, indeed, just emerged from a tunnel. As he tours the city, he exudes a childlike wonder at everything he sees. This ability to experience the world through a child's eyes defines Mr. Smith's character in the film. The main struggle will be over whether Mr. Smith can retain this quality against the overwhelming pressure of those in Washington who live in a dark tunnel.

Jeff Smith soon discovers that lawmaking is no simple matter. The Bills presented before congress, Senator Paine informs Jeff, "are put together by legal minds, after long study." He suggests that Jeff not concern himself with lawmaking (which is, after all, the job Jeff has been appointed to do), concluding that "[w]hen the time comes, I'll advise you how to vote." Mr. Smith sets off, nonetheless, to draft a bill. In this task, he is helped by a somewhat cynical female assistant named Saunders. Saunders is "a pure city dweller" brought up in Baltimore. As she puts it, "I guess I've always lived in a tunnel."

Mr. Smith also discovers that the location he has selected for his Boys' Camp is the same as that planned for the dam. The story follows the conflict that ensues between the ideal of a summer camp to help city dwellers find their way out of the tunnel, and the plan already in motion to despoil the countryside for profit by building a dam. Pushing his summer camp is honest but not very smart; supporting the dam is smart, but means abandoning the boys to a life in the tunnel.

This conflict over what it means to be smart, and whether it is smart to be honest plays a central role in the drama. At one point, the senior Senator insists that Smith is honest not stupid, countering the tendency in Washington to equate the two. And, indeed, we are a bit confused, since Smith is simple if he is not dumb, and sometimes his naiveté comes across as the mark of diminished intelligence. Nonetheless, Saunders wonders to one of her associates "if maybe this Don Quixote hasn't got the jump on all of us. I wonder if it isn't a curse to go through life wised up like you and me." Later, Taylor will tell Smith to get smart or get out. The theme of the smart and the dumb, the simple and the complex, dominates the characters, as it does all fantasies that government is the work of the people, that it takes no special expertise, that, indeed, expertise is the enemy of good government.[2]

The Saunders character plays on the theme of childhood innocence and the risks it encounters in the world when she explains how she feels about Smith. "I felt just like a mother, sending her kid off to school for the first time, watchin' the little feller toddling off in his best bib and tucker hoping he can stand up to the other kids."[3] Shortly after making this comment, she tells Smith, "You're halfway decent. You don't belong here. Now go home." Get smart and stay, or remain innocent and go home.

Mr. Smith is a child in an adult's world, and for a moment we begin to see that his childlike innocence (or simplicity) might stand in the way of wise decision-making. In response to Smith's objections to flooding the land he has in mind for his Boys' Camp, Senator Paine points out that he's "trying to understand a project that took two years to set up, the reasons, the benefits." When Senator Paine explains the dam project to Smith, we begin to wonder if perhaps the new Senator has something to learn:

> Now, thirty years ago, I had your ideals. I was you. I had to make the same decision you were asked to make today. And I made it. I compromised, yes! You've got to face facts, Jeff. I've served our state well, haven't I? We have the lowest unemployment and the highest federal grants. But, well, I've had to compromise.

For a moment, we wonder if the world is indeed complex, if public issues are not clear-cut matters of applying simple rules of right and wrong. Perhaps right and wrong are linked in ways that defy our effort to have what is only and always right. We wonder about this, but only for a moment.

The moment passes quickly, and with it our anxiety that we will be left with ambiguity rather than the assurance that doing and being good are simple matters. That is, we discover that Paine and Taylor do not represent the adult capacity to tolerate ambiguity, but corruption. We find this out when, to defend their dam project and protect their political power, they attempt to destroy Mr. Smith's reputation as a good man. To do this, they fabricate evidence that Mr. Smith owns the land he plans to sell to the government, to be paid for by those nickels and dimes contributed by boys hoping to find their way out of the dark tunnel. Mr. Smith, then, is made to appear to be the threat to good government, while Taylor and his gang appear as the defenders of virtue.

In doing this, Paine and Taylor seek to take from Smith not only his reputation, but his innocence, including his belief in the goodness of government as represented in the ideals of the Founding Fathers. And, for a moment they succeed, as they drive Jeff Smith to despair: "A lot of junk about American ideals. Yeah, it's certainly a lot of junk all right. ... Yeah, a lot of fancy words around this town." Mr. Smith has lost his faith in those he thought he could trust, those he looked up to, as the son might lose his faith in his father. When this happens, what can he fall back on except disillusionment, which can easily turn into the very cynicism we find in those who have taken over in Washington? If this happens, then Taylor has indeed succeeded in destroying innocence.

But, at this point, Saunders falls under the influence of Mr. Smith's goodness. She shifts her allegiance from the Taylor gang, and reminds Smith that he is indeed the fighter for lost causes. All good men must call upon their faith to fight against evil. Saunders offers Smith an alternative to Paine and Taylor. It was not, she tells Jeff, the Taylors of the world in whom you placed your faith, "you had faith in something bigger than that. You had plain, decent, everyday common rightness, and this country could use some of that." Rather than faith in men, Mr. Smith had faith in ideals.

There is, Smith believes, an audience for "plain, decent, everyday common rightness," and it is the "people." At the last moment, when Smith is about to be dishonored and removed from office, he stands before the President of the Senate and demands to speak not to Paine and Taylor, but to the people. "I want a chance to talk to the people who will believe me. And when they hear my story they'll rise up and they'll kick Mr. Taylor's machine to kingdom come."

The thought that Mr. Smith might speak to the people strikes fear into the hearts of Taylor and his gang. If Mr. Smith can raise public opinion, he can destroy the power of the politicians. To prevent that, the Taylor machine mobilizes the news media, which it owns and controls, to reinforce the story that it is Smith who is corrupt. As Smith holds the Senate floor explaining himself and reading first the Declaration of Independence, then the Constitution, Taylor organizes a media campaign against him that prevents the people from hearing the words of the Founding Fathers.

Smith's message to the people is the message of the movie. "It's a funny thing about men, ya' know. They all start life being boys. I wouldn't be surprised if some of these Senators were boys once." That's why the Boys' Camp is a good idea, because we need to build boys into the right kind of men. There, they would learn not "fancy rules" but "plain, ordinary every-day kindness and a little looking out for the other fellow, too." As Mr. Smith tells us, there can be "no compromise with the truth. ... Great principles don't get lost once they come to light. They are right here. You just have to see them again." So speaks what the CBS radio announcer describes as "one lone and simple American."

When all seems lost, Senator Paine, who had his doubts all along, and who was an admirer of Smith's father, turns out to be one of those Senators who was once a boy, and still has some of that innocence in him. When he can no longer tolerate or participate in the destruction of a good man, he takes the badness on himself:

> I'm not fit to be a Senator. I'm not fit to live. ... Willet Dam is a fraud. It's a crime against the people who sent me here. And I committed it.

We see in this ending the distinction between those who are intrinsically corrupt (Jim Taylor) and those who have been corrupted (Joe Paine). Throughout the movie, Joe Paine expresses sympathy for Jeff Smith, even an attachment to him linked to his original friendship with Jeff's father. The Senator's ability to connect with himself before his life in Washington leads him to feel guilt for what he has done, and, in the end, to take responsibility for the violence he has done to his own best self.

The Dark Father

Frank Capra's fantasy about government is a fantasy about fathers and sons. In the fantasy, the protagonist, Mr. Smith, has good fathers and bad fathers, the former being ideal figures, the latter actual persons in his world. His good fathers are, of course, the Founding Fathers, especially Washington and Lincoln. They are the ideal image he expects to see realized in Congress when he arrives in Washington. What he actually finds are not good fathers but bad fathers, fathers dominated by self-interest and corrupted by the lure of power and wealth.

Capra provides us with little direct information about a possible connection of Smith's two Washington fathers to an original experience with his father back home. Early in the movie, however, we do learn something interesting. What we learn is made even more interesting by its source: Joe Paine. While Senator Paine did not know who Jefferson Smith was, he did know his father.

> Jeff, you're just like your father. ... Even with the hat. Same old
> dreamer. You know one look at you and I can see him. Back in his
> own rolltop desk, hat and all, getting out his paper. Always kept his
> hat on his head, [as] if he's ready to do battle. Clayton Smith; edi-
> tor and publisher and champion of lost causes. ... Now we were a
> team. The two of us. Struggling editor and a struggling lawyer. "The
> twin champions of lost causes," they used to call us.

Clayton Smith gave his life fighting for lost causes. "He and his little four
page paper. Against that mining syndicate. And all to defend the right of
one small miner who stuck to his claim." They tried to bribe and intimidate him; and, when that failed, they killed him.

We know that Clayton Smith was a courageous journalist, but we do
not know what sort of father he was, at least not directly. The intensity of
his son's idealization tells us something, or at least makes us wonder about
the other side of Clayton Smith. Was the "dreamer" disconnected from the
reality of his son's life, unable to be there for his son when it counted
most? Was he too preoccupied with his crusades to help his son grow into
a man? Was his son relegated to the role of observer as his father disap-
peared into his campaigns for lost causes? Did he die when Jefferson was
still a boy, and thus, however unintentionally, abandon him when he was
most needed?

The possibility that Clayton Smith was neglectful gains some support
from aspects of the fantasy presented in the film. We know that Jefferson
Smith identified strongly with an idealized image of his father, which he
had internalized. Jefferson Smith was Clayton Smith, or at least he tried to
be. We also know that Jeff felt deeply inadequate for the job, in part
because of the intensity of his idealization. How can we not feel inadequate when we take as our ideal the nation's Founding Fathers, or a real
father who gave his life for a noble, if lost, cause?

A curious aspect of the film to which Leland Pogue draws our attention also suggests that the hero Clayton Smith might have exhibited a dark
side to his son.[4] Part of Jeff's innocence finds expression in an ignorance
that is difficult to take at face value. How can a student of the Founding
Fathers know as little about our government as Jeff apparently does? How
can Jeff not know what anyone even distantly informed about the world
knows about lawmaking: that it involves compromise and a measure of

outright corruption? In other words, how can an adult old enough to be appointed a Senator be so convinced that those in power live up to abstract and unrealistic ideals? The interpretation that Pogue offers is that we consider the possibility that this is knowledge Mr. Smith has but cannot gain access to, knowledge that has been lost to him by repression (as expressed in the metaphor of forgetting). Since what has been lost here is knowledge of the bad object, we can conclude that Jeff's ignorance of reality expresses his effort to deny to himself any knowledge of the neglectful and abusive aspects of his relationship with his father.

Massive repression of any knowledge of the bad father is also expressed in a conscious and expressed fear that he will forget the good father. Thus, Jeff is not merely familiar with the writings of the Founding Fathers, he knows them "by heart." Additional evidence is provided in Jeff's vision of the Boys' Camp, whose purpose includes assuring that the boys will not forget their country's ideals. Ignorance of the bad father combined with fear of loss of the good father offer strong support for the hypothesis that Clayton Smith had a considerable dark side. This also means that Jeff's identification with his father has a dark side (is also an identification with a bad object), as we will see below. Jeff's identification with the bad object gets expressed in the intensity of his desire for a Boys' Camp to assure that he will not lose (forget) the good object.

The combination of repression of the bad object with worry over the prospect of losing the good object strongly supports the hypothesis of parental ambivalence. This ambivalence made it difficult for Jeff to achieve the integration emphasized in the last chapter as the basis for self-determination, which is to say living a life as an adult in an adult world.

It is possible that Jefferson Smith's experience with a neglectful or absent, and in some important ways inadequate, father provoked in him considerable fear and anger.[5] After all, his father's inadequacy left him having to cope on his own with a confusing and sometimes frightening world, at an age when he lacked the resources to do so. How was Jeff to cope with his fear and anger? How could he overcome his fear, and toward what object could he direct his anger? We can link this problem to the central metaphor of the film: the dark tunnel. If we interpret being in the dark tunnel as being dominated by dark emotions, and the bright light as the solution to the problem of what to do with those powerful destructive and painful feelings, then we should find in that metaphor the answer to our questions.

If frustration only intensifies need, Jeff's dilemma at the failure of his father to gratify his needs is the dilemma of an overwhelming need that threatens to destroy those on whom we depend. We can cope with this need by repression, but at a price. This price has much to do with the formulation of the problem of living in an adult world as a dilemma, a choice between desire interpreted as greed, and goodness interpreted as self-denial.

Joe Paine and Jim Taylor represent self-interest and greed, just as Jeff Smith represents selflessness and generosity. It is not unreasonable, then, to consider the dark fathers the projection into the world of Jeff's own greed and the self-interest attached to it. These were, after all, feelings he had to suppress in his relationship with his real father. We can surmise, then, that Jeff's needs were intensified by neglect and frustration, then repressed and projected onto appropriate external objects.

The idea that the characters of Paine and Taylor are shaped by projection implies that they are to some degree formed by Jeff's psychic need. Is there any evidence for this in the film? The initiation of the conflict over the dam project suggests a possible answer to this question. This initiation of conflict includes a significant element of provocation on Jeff's part. After all, it is never clear why his Boys' Camp must be built on the site planned for the dam. Why must Mr. Smith force the issue rather than simply seeking an alternative site for his camp, thereby allowing each party to get what it wants? The film encourages us to experience the conflict as resulting from the rapaciousness of the political machine, thereby insisting on Mr. Smith's innocence, though we can as easily see the conflict as provoked by Mr. Smith. While we learn early on that the dam project is little more than political graft, all Mr. Smith knows is that its location conflicts with his plan for a Boys' Camp.

Once we consider that Mr. Smith has provoked the conflict, we can ask what psychic purpose is served by his doing so. One possible answer would be that it uncovers the presence of the bad object hidden in the persona of the good man (here the public servant), and in so doing assures that there is a dark father in the world.

Provocation aimed at creating the bad object, or forcing it from its hiding place, plays an important part in the relationship between citizens and government, which includes a need to control government in ways that assure it will play its proper part in a psychic drama. As we saw in the last chapter, in the political drama over the Monica Lewinsky affair, the Special Prosecutor provokes the President into lying under oath, thus revealing what he knew all along, that the President was corrupt. In this, the Special Prosecutor plays the role of Mr. Smith, who also reveals a hidden truth, which was also one we knew all along. This is the same truth that Mr. Smith knows but does not know (has repressed), which is the truth about his father.

Clearly, Mr. Smith is tangled up in a struggle with bad objects linked to his father. But, we also know something else about Jeff Smith: that he has a strong identification with and attachment to a maternal object. This is well expressed in his identification with the land, and his battle to protect the land from politicians who would exploit and despoil it for personal gain. It is also well expressed in his strong assertion of feminine values. Jeff doesn't give two cents for "all your fancy rules" if they do not rest on a foundation of "plain, ordinary, everyday kindness and a little looking out for the other fellow." Identification with the mother reinforces our suspicion of paternal failure, and can be seen as an expression of the father's absence and neglect.

There is a further hint of an important gender issue in Jeff's total selflessness and devotion to others. In sharp contrast to the other Senators, who act wholly on self-interest, Jeff acts entirely for others. Thus, the film equates corruption with acting for self. The lure of self-interest is personified in the character of Jim Taylor. First he corrupted Joe Paine, and now he is attempting to corrupt Jeff Smith. When Paine tells Taylor that he wants no part "of crucifying the boy," Taylor reminds him that his "methods have been all right for the past twenty years," since he picked Paine out of a "fly-specked hole in the wall and blew [him] up to look like a Senator."

Shortly after reminding Joe that he has sold his soul to the dark side, Taylor offers the same deal to Jefferson Smith.

> Now, what do you like? Business? If you like business, you can pick any job in the state and go right to the top. Or politics, huh? If you like being a Senator there's no reason why you can't come back to that Senate and stay there as long as you want to…if you're smart. Now you take the boys here, or Joe Paine. They're doing all right. They don't have to worry about being re-elected or anything else. They're smart. They take my advice.

Here, being a man gets linked to a self-interest that treats others instrumentally, as having no significance in themselves, but only as they contribute to or impede the pursuit of power and wealth.

It is not surprising, then, that Jeff exhibits considerable ambivalence about himself as a man in a "man's world."⁶ When the Governor's son first proposes Jeff as a candidate for the vacant Senate seat, the Governor makes what seems to be the mistake of assuming that Jefferson Smith is a boy. And, indeed, as Senator Paine points out, Jeff has been "living in a boy's world" (literally as scout master and editor of a boy's newspaper). Later, Jeff insists that being a boy is what makes a man good. I think there is in this, and in his general awkwardness (vividly expressed in his bumbling retreat from Senator Paine's seductive daughter), evidence that Jeff is not comfortable being a man. The fantasy developed in the movie compensates to some extent for this discomfort by shifting responsibility for it onto men, thus making it more virtuous to be a boy.

Jeff's intense dependence on others offers additional support for the idea that he remains in important respects a boy. He is never an autonomous agent. Even at the film's climax, when he speaks before the senate, he must constantly look to Saunders for signals to guide him. He is never inner directed, but always searching for external sources, whether those be in the form of others (first Paine and then Saunders) or in the form of the ideas of the Founding Fathers he has committed to memory.

The intense dependence he develops on Saunders also suggests an important gender dimension in Jeff's dilemma. If we interpret nature as a female symbol, Jeff's ambivalence about being a man becomes that much more evident. Jeff's insistence that virtue is grounded literally in the land expresses his ambivalence about masculinity, as does his distrust of the city expressed through the metaphor of the dark tunnel. If we put this ambivalence together with Clayton Smith's inadequacy as a father, we might conclude that, due to paternal failure, Jeff has gotten stuck along the way in the transition from boy to man. Then, the core of the entire fantasy is the problem of failed development. How could Jeff develop if all he has to work with are an unattainable ideal and a dark father who would destroy his innocence and virtue as the price of admission to the world of men? How can Jeff grow into a man without giving up his ability to see the world with a boy's wonder? Growing up thus means living in a dark tunnel, and the only way to stay out of the tunnel is to refuse to become a man.

The crux of the fantasy expressed in the movie is the solution to the problem of the absent father and the failed development it implies. This solution has two aspects:

(1) Retreat from the world of men into a fantasized eternal childhood in a feminine setting (nature). The confrontation with Taylor initially drives Mr. Smith in the direction of this solution: "I'm getting out of this town so fast...away from all the words, and the monuments, and the whole rotten show." To justify retreat, the fantasy depicts the goal as unworthy. Then retreat and failure can be reinterpreted as the triumph of virtue. In the end, however, it remains a retreat and a failure, as the lead female character points out in an effort to get Jeff to stay the course. Retreat is not the act of a man, nor the solution to the dilemma of failed development.

(2) The fantasy that the father is unnecessary. Here, this fantasy takes the form of replacing the absent (real) father with the idealized image of the father constituted by a set of simple dogmas: the sayings of the Founders (the Declaration of Independence, the Constitution). In the language of the last chapter, this is a retreat from ethics to morality. We do not need to think about problems since we already know the solutions. Indeed, thinking will only reveal the problem's inherent complexity and the hopelessness of our wish for unambiguous solutions. Thinking, then, is part of the problem. It leads us into the dark tunnel. Thinking must give way to belief in the idealized father as embodied in simple dogmas ("family values"). Complexity is destroyed, and with it the need for the father and what he represents.

When we emerge from the dark tunnel, we see things clearly; we leave behind our confusion, our fear, and our anger. We are afraid that we are ill formed for adult life, and we are angry at those who have failed us (the real father). Our fear and anger, combined with our sense of our own inadequacy, make us vacillate in the face of the adult world and the sometimes difficult choices we must make there. To protect ourselves, we adopt a set of simple rules for living, rules that connect us to an idealized object so that we can share its goodness. Vacillation gives way to certainty that our simple values are all we need to guide us to right conduct.

In the dark tunnel, we hear a cacophony of sounds, all the words that Mr. Smith hopes to escape. The city offers a metaphor for this state in which we are assaulted by words we cannot understand. The city also represents a metaphor for difference; it is the place where people from different backgrounds live together. But it is not the place where people from different backgrounds find common ground and come together. That place is the country, the "Boys' Camp," a place where all those from different backgrounds can learn to live together according to the American ideal.

In the movie, the problem to be solved by the Boys' Camp is depicted as one in the external world, the city understood as a locus of conflict and compromise. We can also, however, interpret the cacophony as a state of internal or psychic conflict. Then, the dark tunnel is the inner world dominated by a struggle with internalized bad objects; and solving the problem of parental failure means escaping that world, which is to say destroying psychic experience and the meaning connected to it.

Interpreted in this way, the metaphor of the dark tunnel represents the inability to tolerate psychic experience, and the need to suppress it, destroy it, and thus escape from it. We must banish all but the idealized internal object, the object that is altogether and always good, altogether and always selfless. To remain innocent is to hold onto our identification with the good object. This object shines a bright light for us, the light at the end of the tunnel. To destroy complexity in the world outside, we must first destroy it within. All we must do to get out of the tunnel is embrace the simple dogmas that express the virtue of the idealized good object.

This destruction of inner experience is reenacted in the external world as the drama of Mr. Smith and his trip to Washington. It is also the drama of the people and the government we experience as an important part of contemporary political life. At the core of that drama is the hope that virtue will triumph over the bad external object, as Mr. Smith in the end triumphs over Jim Taylor. First, Jeff's innate goodness wins over the cynical Saunders, who falls in love with him as an expression of her repudiation of evil. Then, at the last minute, Jeff's goodness wins back Joe Paine, who acknowledges his corruption, and takes responsibility for his evil deeds.

The drama of Mr. Smith in Washington recounts a battle over the soul of the nation, a battle in which a naïve young man, armed only with his honesty, innocence, and ideals, triumphs over older and more powerful figures. This is, of course, a triumph in fantasy. The fantasy becomes a power in the world when the wish contained in it becomes a primary element in the relationship between people and government in the real world. Then, the wish that drives the fantasy has a power to shape public life.

The wish contained in the fantasy is the wish to destroy the bad object and identify with, even become, the good object. In contrast to the integration considered in the last chapter, which is the integration of the good and bad objects, the wish depicted here is for merger with the good object. It is accomplished by destruction of the bad object, here represented in the triumph over the dark father, who declares at the end of the film that he is "not fit to live."[7] The wish for merger as an alternative to integration represents a retreat from the task of development, which centers on the integration of good and bad objects. Thus the wish that drives the fantasy in the drama here considered is a wish to avoid development and replace it with an immediate identification with an idealized object.

Wilfred Bion refers to the lure of this wished for solution as the "hatred of a process of development." According to Bion, the alternative to development is the wish to arrive "fully equipped as an adult fitted by instinct to know without training or development exactly how to live."[8] In the film, this wish is expressed in the fantasy that a scoutmaster is, contrary to his own expectations, better prepared to govern the nation than are its elected officials. The distinction between the struggle for integration and the wish for merger plays itself out in public life. This, then, is the psychic meaning of the fantasy depicted in the film. And, so far as the film represents not merely the fantasy of those who made it, but also of those who view it, the wish that drives it also plays its part in shaping public experience and the relationship between the people and the government.

Stranger in a Strange Land

Thus far, I have taken paternal failure as the central interpersonal experience shaping Frank Capra's fantasy in "Mr. Smith Goes to Washington." This interpretation gains some support from comments Capra offers about himself in his autobiography, especially a comment he makes concerning his feelings about his family. There, he refers to the "traumatic shock" he experienced on learning at the age of five "that not one of my peasant clan could read." Even as a child, he knew "that peasants were poor and had to work like beasts because they were ignorant," a thought, he reports, that "must have burned itself into my child's mind; I never forgot it, never lost my resentment against it."[9] Contempt and disappointment were not the only emotions he felt for his family, and one must assume for his father, but they were powerful enough to be the first emotions that appear in his own telling of his life story.

After immigrating to America when Frank was six, the family pursued material success with a vengeance, working hard, saving money, eventually purchasing a sixteen-acre lemon grove. On the brink of success by the immigrant's standards, Capra's father is killed in an accident on his farm, with the result that the family loses all it has gained from years of hard work.

> Papa's dream of moving his family out of the ghetto and onto his beloved farm was shattered. Stunned Mama and frail Ann forfeited the ranch and returned to Little Sicily, as destitute as the day they had arrived in America fourteen years before.[10]

By this time, Capra had begun a personal escape from his ignorant peasant self by seeking an education. While the other family members are conscripted into the world of work, Frank remains in, and excels in, school. In this, his father had supported him, at times against significant pressure from other family members for Frank to drop out and go to work. Thus, while Frank's father was an ignorant peasant who had to work like a slave, he was also Frank's main support in his aspiration to stay in school and get an education. Like Clayton Smith, Capra's father was both a failure and a hero. He was a peasant to look upon with contempt, and he was an ideal to admire and emulate.

If we consider Capra as a young child of a peasant family immigrating to America, we can begin to see his movie as a variant on the immigrant's fantasy. The immigrant travels to the Promised Land in pursuit of freedom from oppression and freedom from want. Whether he finds these freedoms or not, he must inevitably find himself far from home. He is now a stranger in a strange land. The immigrant knows neither the language nor the customs of this land, and, in traveling there, risks humiliation in the eyes of its native population. If we treat this not primarily as the actual experience of the immigrant, but as a fantasy, then we can ask: Who is the stranger, and what is the strange land in which he finds himself?

The interpretation offered above of the fantasy in the film suggests one possible answer to this question. This answer is that the immigrant is a metaphor for the child in the adult world. The immigrant's fear is that he will be discovered for the child he is, which is to say unprepared for life in the world because of poverty and ignorance.

The immigrant, then, is a metaphor for the individual who has arrived at adulthood without passing through an adequate process of personal development that would endow him or her with the capabilities needed to cope as an independent person in a world of independent persons. The failure of development results from the inadequacy and even hostility of those responsible for facilitating it. This failure of those responsible ultimately results from their own failed development. The parent's failed development makes him or her a poor bet to secure the needed experience for the child. The parent's inadequacy may then be exacerbated by envy and the resulting desire to assure that the child does no better than the parent who has gone before him. If the immigrant's fear is that he or she, even though an adult, is nonetheless ill suited for adult life, the immigrant's wish is the one to which Bion draws our attention: the wish to be ready-made for adult life without undergoing a process of development.

The end to be attained by development into an adult is here a somewhat complicated matter, since it may or may not be implied in physical maturation. Equally important as physical maturation is an emotional development that establishes our standing in the world as autonomous persons. True adulthood, then, is synonymous with self-determination, or, in the language of political life, self-governance. To achieve this goal is to have a self and be a center of initiative. This is consistent with the immigrant's fantasy considered here, since, in this fantasy, the question of freedom plays a large role.

Freedom

If America is a land of immigrants, then it is the land of the immigrant's fantasy. And, if America is the land of the immigrant's fantasy, it is the land of the immigrant's wish. If we are to follow Capra's lead, the wish is a wish for freedom and for unity. Its primary symbol is Abraham Lincoln who freed the slaves and saved the union. It is to Lincoln that Capra and his character Jeff Smith both turn at moments of self-doubt.[11] Since neither Capra nor the typical immigrant to America was a slave, we need to consider the fantasy of freedom from enslavement not literally, but in terms of its psychic meaning. We need, that is, an answer to the question: What is psychic freedom?

For Capra, the starting point is self-contempt, the image of his family as ignorant peasants, and therefore of himself as an ignorant peasant. Self-contempt implies psychic division, we hold ourselves in contempt and therefore stand against our selves; and it implies psychic impoverishment, we judge our selves to be of no value. Self-hatred was clearly a problem for

Capra so far as he could not quite get beyond viewing himself as an ignorant peasant. It was also a problem for Jefferson Smith, who equated good with selfless and bad with self-seeking, and for whom any hope of achieving identification with the good object rested on his capacity for self-sacrifice.

When our selves can only be made good in the act of sacrificing them to others, we cannot have and enjoy being our selves. We are, then, strangers to ourselves. This sense of estrangement from the self can be transformed into a sense of estrangement from others, which is to say their estrangement from us, which is the immigrant's experience of being a stranger in a strange land. Then, Mr. Smith also represents the estrangement of our selves, and the immigrant's search represents a search for an estranged self.

Self-hatred signals the presence of a bad object, an object that attacks the self rather than providing it with the gratification it craves. Here, however, rather than being deprived by others, by bad objects in the outside world, we deprive ourselves. We have, that is, an internalized bad object, which is to say we are a bad object to ourselves. Then, if self-hatred expresses unfreedom, freedom means freedom from the tyranny of the bad object. This object may be in the external world, a hateful and depriving object on which we depend, or it may be in the internal world, a part of our selves devoted to self-deprivation. In either case, freedom means escape from this object as the only possible route to gratification of the self.

Since psychic freedom means feeling worthy of gratification, it can get confused with the acquisition of things. Then, the immigrant's fantasy is the fantasy of acquiring wealth. Not only does wealth represent the means for gratification, it also marks its owner as worthy of gratification, indeed, worthy in proportion to the amount of wealth he or she owns. For the immigrant, self-love depends on acquisition of material goods whose value establishes that the self is of value, and therefore worthy of love. Psychically, then, slavery and poverty are equated, so that the American dream of escape from slavery becomes the dream of escape from material poverty. Psychic deprivation is reinterpreted as material deprivation, and escape from psychic poverty as escape from material poverty. Since poverty also means psychic division (we are divided against our selves by the contempt we have for our selves), escape from poverty is linked to the second aspect of the wish: the wish for unification.

Acquisition of wealth is not, however, the only form the wish for freedom can take. Since freedom means escape from the tyranny of the bad object, it can also involve conduct aimed at overcoming that tyranny. We can overcome the tyranny of the bad object either by destroying it or by identifying with it. Further, destruction of and identification with the bad object can take place either internally or in the external world depending on where we find that object.

If the bad object is in the world, freedom takes on its usual meaning of destruction of, or at least escape from the relationship of dependency on, the oppressor. Jefferson Smith enacts this aspect of liberation when he attacks the members of congress and the head of his state's political machine. But, we know that, for Mr. Smith, however bad the objects in the world, they essentially represent projections of bad internal objects. Escape from the tyranny of the internal bad object also involves an act of destruction. This is the destruction of complexity, which makes possible identification with the good object as represented by simple and abstract ideals, and the mythical figures to which those ideals are connected. Thus, freedom here means destruction of the inner world.

Since, however, identification with the good object accomplished by this act of destruction requires a life of self-sacrifice and renunciation of any hope for a real emotional development, we can conclude that the bad object has not so much been destroyed as rediscovered as a good object. That is, since the nature of the bad object is to deprive the self of gratification, when identification with the good object means self-sacrifice, the good object contains the bad. This conclusion suggests an alternative interpretation of psychic freedom, which is identification with the bad object. We free ourselves from the tyranny of the bad object by becoming that object, which makes us the oppressor rather than the oppressed, even if the main object we oppress is our self.

So long as we exclude the possibility of integration of good and bad, and allow only for identification with one or the other, freedom can only mean destruction of, or identification with, the bad object. In either case, the state of freedom is deeply problematic, since we do not succeed in escaping the tyranny of the bad object. To be always and altogether good means to be self-depriving and thus to live under the tyranny of a bad object, however we have reinterpreted it as the good object. To be bad means to exercise tyranny over others and thus to place both self and other under the tyranny of which we have spoken here. Thus, so far as we cannot overcome the state of self-estrangement implied in splitting, we can never achieve real psychic freedom, and we cannot escape the tyranny of the bad object.

We can only escape from this tyranny by integrating bad with good rather than attempting the destruction of the bad. The hope for integration plays a large part in the fantasy as Capra presents it. The final scene in the screenplay for the movie, which was not included in the filmed version released by the studio, includes a reconciliation scene. A parade is held in Jeff's hometown. He and Saunders are riding in the back of an open car with confetti falling on them. At this point, Jeff leaps out of the car and runs to the curb where Joe Paine is watching.

> Jefferson: Please sir!—come with me!
> Paine: No, Jeff—please!
> Jefferson: I say it's your parade, sir! You've got to come.

He then pulls Paine with him to join Saunders in the car.[12]

The hope for integration is also expressed in Mr. Smith's main goal in Washington: to pass a bill establishing a National Boys' Camp. At this camp, city boys from different backgrounds will come together through a connection to the land, and through exposure to the nation's ideals. There is in this an implied bringing together of a family that has come apart: the ideal father, as represented by the nation's ideals, with the real father; the mother, as represented by the land, with the sons; and the sons with the fathers who had lost their way in the dark tunnel. Psychically, the unification of the family also represents the unification of the self.

The act of bringing about this unification involves an important reversal of roles in which, rather than the parent leading the child, the child leads the parent, as Jeff Smith leads Joe Paine. This leading of the parent to the Promised Land is represented in the movie by the moral leadership exerted by Mr. Smith over at least some of those he finds in Washington. In this fantasy, the child leads the father out of a world of grave dangers into a place where a bright light shines: from danger to safety, from poverty and humiliation to freedom. In doing so, the child finds guidance in the ideals of the Founding Fathers, ideals that take the place of knowledge, and thus make ignorance, specifically the ignorance of a peasant and immigrant, a virtue. The child tells his story, and hearing it makes a difference.[13] A stranger finds a home. This is the immigrant's fantasy, and it is also a primary fantasy of the people and their government in America.

The Anti-Government Fantasy

It is worth considering the relationship between the immigrant's fantasy just considered, and what I refer to in the Introduction as the typical anti-government fantasy, as both the similarities and differences are significant. In both fantasies, the dilemma that needs to be dealt with has to do with the loss of a secure and unified family structure to facilitate the child's development into an adult. The result is a sense of being alone or isolated in a dangerous world. In both fantasies, what must be done to solve the problem is formulated in the language of freedom. Thus, we have, in the anti-government fantasy, the idea of freedom as liberty, a state in which the individual flourishes by him or her self, and without dependence on authority. In the immigrant's fantasy, freedom means abundance in the Promised Land.

There is also, however, a vital element in the immigrant's fantasy missing in the typical anti-government fantasy: the prospect of merger with the good object in the world. The sadistic element in the anti-government fantasy implies identification with an abusive or neglectful caretaker, which means identification not with the good, but with the bad, object. Thus, those who would impose the policy measures associated with minimizing or eliminating government would make themselves into the image of the bad parent, who is motivated by self-interest, and whose goal includes imposing deprivation on others. This result is then made to adopt the opposite meaning, which is to save the worst off from the danger posed by dependence on government.

I note above how merger with the good object in the immigrant's fantasy, while intended to express the successful destruction of the bad object, does not destroy the bad object so much as internalize it and turn it against the self, a result expressed in the ethic of self-sacrifice. In this respect, the two paths of escape from the tyranny of the bad object considered above (destruction and identification) will not appear so different. And, indeed, it can be difficult to distinguish them since both involve the essential element of the attack on the self. Does this mean that we can draw no meaningful distinction between the anti-government fantasy and the immigrant's fantasy?

On one level, the two are closely aligned, since both involve an attack on the self. They differ, however, in where they locate the self they attack. For the immigrant, the attack on the self is primarily an internal matter of self-sacrifice and self-negation. Because of this, the sadistic element in the attack on the self is muted. In the anti-government fantasy, the attack on the self is primarily an attack on other's selves, and thus the sadistic element becomes primary.

The two fantasies also differ in the emphasis placed on unity. The wish for unity plays a part in the immigrant's fantasy that it does not in the typical anti-government fantasy. Not only is this wish expressed in the problematic form of a wish for merger with the good object; it is also expressed in the form of a wish to reunite with the bad object, albeit once that object is made tolerable by confession and guilt.

The two fantasies would shape the relationship of government to people in importantly different ways. The anti-government fantasy is to weaken or destroy government so it will do no harm. The immigrant's fantasy is not to destroy government, but to retrieve it from "selfish men,"[14] and thus renew it as a vehicle for doing good, which means primarily reestablishing a lost unity. The two fantasies are not always clearly distinguished. They both contain harsh criticisms of government, centering especially on the charge of corruption. They both find much to distrust in government as it is. For this reason, they sometimes work together in the effort to destroy government as it is, though one would replace it with a better government, the other would replace government, so far as possible, with private contracts and voluntary associations.

3 THE PEOPLE AND THEIR GOVERNMENT

Splitting

The government depicted in Frank Capra's film is not one to command the trust and respect of its citizens. On the contrary, this is a government that provokes feelings of distrust and animosity. Recent surveys of public opinion suggest that most Americans adopt a view of government consistent in this respect with the fantasy depicted in the film. That is to say, they view government as a bad object. It needs to be emphasized that, as in the film, the distrust of, and animosity toward, government expressed by Americans is not directed at the basic institutions of government, but at those who occupy positions in those institutions, and who have thereby taken control of, or taken over, government. As two students of public attitudes toward government put it, "the public has considerable confidence in the *institutions* of government, but not much confidence in the *individuals* charged with operating those institutions."[1] To be more specific: "In 1997, fewer than 10% of the public had 'a great deal of confidence' in Congress, and roughly one quarter had 'a great deal of confidence' in the presidency or the Supreme Court."[2] This does not mean that Americans want to abolish the Presidency or the Congress and replace them with other institutions. Americans are satisfied with the institutions, but not with the people who occupy offices in them. Thus, the institutions remain connected to the ideal, while office holders must bear the burden of the limitations we attribute to the real.

We have, then, a split attitude toward government. We do not hold the institutions responsible for the corruption of those who occupy them; we hold the corruption of those who occupy institutions responsible for institutional failure. This allows us to protect institutions we see as the embodiment of basic values (freedom, democracy, representation, and so on) from the harsh judgment we direct at the way those institutions fail to live up to the values they embody.

Distrust of government should be linked to qualities the electorate attributes to those in office. These qualities can be summed up in one word: corruption. Thus, one Harris pole found that nearly two-thirds of voters thought government was corrupt, and three-quarters thought that special interests had too much control over government.[3] Surveys done by the Pew Research Center found that only 34 percent of Americans "basically trust the government." They also located the cause of distrust in the perceived moral failing of elected officials. In particular, they concluded, "discontent with the honesty of elected officials is a leading cause of distrust of government."[4] While this survey found some softening of the negative attitude in light of recent economic trends, they also found that despite the favorable economic climate "distrust of government remains substantial. No matter how the question is posed, it is a decided minority that has a positive opinion of government."

Of special importance for our concerns is the negative moral judgment of government officials. The Pew Survey found that at no time between 1973 and 1997 did as many as a third of Americans judge the ethical and moral practices of government officials excellent or good. The perceived moral failing of government officials was matched by a perception of poor job performance. Only 25 percent of Americans judge the job the government does running its programs excellent or good.

Not only is there evidence that, for the majority of Americans, the government is a (morally) bad object, there is also evidence that Americans seek to isolate the bad object (government) by splitting. Perhaps the best-known example of this phenomenon is the way the electorate simultaneously holds a low opinion of Congress and a high opinion of their own representatives.[5] But there are other results that point in the same direction. Thus, in contrast to negative ratings of government, specific government agencies, aside from the IRS, received generally favorable ratings.[6]

Especially interesting evidence of splitting is to be found in the attitude about responsibility of government for managing and solving problems. Majorities of those surveyed considered the government responsible for managing the economy (68 percent in 1997), conserving natural resources (52 percent), ensuring that food and medicine are safe (73 percent), trying "to do away with poverty" (74 percent), and seeing that no one is without food and shelter (72 percent). Yet, at the same time, 64 percent believe that the government "controls too much of our daily lives" and 57 percent believe that "regulation does more harm than good."[7]

We can see the same partitioning of thought in public attitudes toward taxation and spending. According the Gallup Organization, "Americans think they pay too much in taxes, and like the idea of tax cuts in general."[8] They found that, in 1998, 66 percent of those polled judged federal income taxes too high. There is also evidence, however, that Americans do not support tax cuts when those cuts are seen to affect specific spending programs. Thus, the National Opinion Research Center at the University of Chicago found strong support for spending in the areas such as education, fighting crime, health care, and environmental protection.[9] Indeed, the only specific areas that failed to receive at least 50 percent support for spending were foreign aid (25 percent) and welfare (38 percent).

Perhaps the most important evidence of splitting, however, has to do with the sharp difference between attitudes toward government and attitudes toward the nation, a split that parallels the one between attitudes toward institutions and attitudes toward those who hold office in them. The animosity and distrust Americans feel for their government is not mirrored in any comparable negative sentiments about their country. On the contrary, of those polled in one survey, "96 percent say that they are proud to be American; 89 percent say they are very patriotic; 80 percent characterize their love of America as "very" or "extremely strong"; and 71 percent say their feelings about the flag are "very" or "extremely good."[10]

Maintaining this complex attitude requires that the distinction between government and country be sharpened into an opposition. This opposition allows us to direct our feelings of disappointment and hostility toward those in government, without thereby losing affection for our country, thus protecting our country from the hostility we feel toward its government.

The opposition between country and government expresses, at the level of public experience, the failure to fully integrate the good and bad objects, a failure that is expressed in the need to keep the two apart, or to split the one from the other. This splitting of good and bad is then part of establishing government as a bad object. Splitting and establishing government as a bad object are, of course, central in the drama of Mr. Smith's experience in Washington.

Setting country in opposition to government poses a problem for us. Where—in what set of institutions and relations—does our country exist in the absence of an effective government? Problems arise because the government is the institutional existence of the country, which, in the absence of effective government, exists only as an ideal.[11] This existence of the country as an ideal brings to mind the nation or the people, the idealized objects of patriotic sentiment. However corrupt our government, we can place our trust in the (goodness of the) nation and its people.[12] Making the people the repository of goodness grounds not only nationalistic arguments, but also arguments for strong democracy. A more democratic society places decisions into the hands of the people, thereby assuring the goodness of outcomes. In Chapter 7, I consider those who see in democratic community the positive alternative to government.

While "nation" and "people" seem to refer to actual groups of persons, we have good reason to doubt that the terms connect us to reality in this way. On the contrary, the terms invoke not so much an empirical reality as an idealized (mythical or fantasized) entity. This entity is constructed by setting aside a decisive part of what makes for actual persons. When we oppose country, nation, or people to government, then, we oppose ideal to real. In understanding the psychic meaning of government, it will help to understand what the nation and the people are ideals of, and why hostility is reserved and directed toward the realization of the ideal in the occupants of institutions.

To do this, let me begin with the way the ideal of the people appears in communications between office holders or candidates for office and their constituencies. First, consider the rhetoric in a campaign speech delivered by Harry Truman on October 11, 1948 in Willard Ohio, a railroad town of 4,000 people. The town of Willard, we are told, was named after Dan Willard, President of the Baltimore and Ohio Railroad, a man who, according to Truman, "liked and respected the people who worked for him."

> Now, Dan Willard did not sneer at the "whistlestops" of our country. He trusted people, and people trusted him. I think this is a good principle. It is a good way to run a railroad, and it is a good way to run a country. ... The Republican candidate and the Republican Congress do not trust the people. They just work along at their old problem of trying to fool the people into voting for the interests of the few.

Here, Truman collapses two seemingly different propositions into one: that the people are worthy of trust and that their elected officials are not. Elected officials of the other party have tried and will continue to try "to fool the people" so those officials can serve the interests of the few. But,

Truman trusts the people not to be fooled. We can say then, if we follow Truman, that not only are the people worthy of our trust, but they are too good to be fooled.

Now consider another President, Ronald Reagan, speaking on the issue of the role of government and its relation to the people:

> From time to time we've been tempted to believe that society has become too complex to be managed by self-rule, that government by an elite is superior to government for, by, and of the people. Well if no one among us is capable of governing himself, then who among us has the capacity to govern someone else? All of us together, in and out of government, must bear the burden. ... We hear much of special interest groups. Well, our concern must be for a special interest group that has been too long neglected ... It is made up of men and women who raise our food, patrol our streets, man our mines and factories, teach our children, keep our homes, and heal us when we're sick—professionals, industrialists, shop-keepers, clerks, cabbies, and truck-drivers. They are, in short, "We the people," this breed called Americans.[13]

Reagan goes on to refer to this "breed called Americans" as heroes. There are heroes, he tells us, "going in and out of factory gates." You meet them across counters. Their taxes support government; their contributions support church and charity. "Their patriotism is quiet, but deep. Their values sustain our national life."

As with Truman, Reagan links faith in the goodness (heroism) of the people to the integrity of the office-holder. Those in office who trust the people will not serve special interests. The people have no special interests. They, like Jefferson Smith, have values and ideals, especially faith in God and love of country. They are, Reagan tells us, "the special interest group that has been too long neglected."

The problem is that government, rather than serving this special interest group (the people), serves other interests, those driven by motives other than patriotism and national values. Thus, "government is not the solution to our problem; government is the problem." For Reagan, the people stand in conflict with the government, and the best way to serve the interests of the people is to reduce the power of government. It is his intent, then, "to curb the size and influence of the federal establishment...."

Limiting government is one solution to the problem that government falls out of the hands of the people and into the hands of those whose special interests are not rooted in values and patriotism. But, it is not the only solution. Truman proposes not so much to curb government as to retrieve it (from the Republicans and the special interests they represent). In either case, the vital element is the development of an opposition between government and people. When this opposition develops, the goodness of the people stands against the evils of a government separated from them. The result is an idealization of the people (as heroes too good to be fooled) and an attack on government as it is.

It will help, in this connection, to recall the close link between idealization and fantasies of omnipotence and perfection. Such fantasies act as defenses against feelings of profound worthlessness. Indeed, we can say that the need to idealize is inversely related to the underlying devaluation of the self. The more intense the (internal) attack on the self, the stronger the impulse to protect it by retreating from reality into a fantasized fusion of actual and ideal selves. For this fusion to hold, those aspects of the self not consistent with the fantasy must be projected outside, onto others, or onto institutions. Thus, we can treat the degree of idealization, for example of the world to be won by the battle against the government, as a measure of the low esteem in which the self is held, however unconsciously.

This process appears vividly in public life when doubt develops about the goodness of the nation. One such time was 1964 when Lyndon Johnson delivered his "Great Society" speech. Less than a year after the assassination of John Kennedy, as the Vietnam war escalated, and in the face of an emerging civil rights movement, Johnson asked the nation to take hold of the "opportunity to move not only toward the rich society and the powerful society, but upward to the Great Society."[14] The Great Society rests on "abundance and liberty for all." But, while we think of the Great Society as a set of social welfare programs, for Johnson it was much more than that:

> The Great Society is a place where every child can find knowledge to enrich his mind and to enlarge his talents. It is a place where leisure is a welcome chance to build and reflect, not a feared cause of boredom and restlessness. It is a place where the city of man serves not only the needs of the body and the demands of commerce but the desire for beauty and the hunger for community.
>
> It is a place where man can renew contact with nature. It is a

place which honors creation for its own sake and for what it adds to the understanding of the race. It is a place where men are more concerned with the quality of their goals than the quantity of their goods.

But most of all, the Great Society is not a safe harbor, a resting place, a final objective, a finished work. It is challenge constantly renewed, beckoning us toward a destiny where the meaning of our lives matches the marvelous products of our labor.

Johnson goes on to consider how far we are from the Great Society, noting that it is "harder and harder to live the good life in American Cities today," that the "catalogue of ills is long...." But this only heightens our mission. The link between the ills of society and the grandiose fantasy of the Great Society is nowhere more clearly articulated than at the end of the speech when Johnson enlists his audience in his mission to build a Great Society:

For better or for worse, your generation has been appointed by history to deal with those problems and to lead America toward a new age. You have the chance never before afforded any people in any age. You can build a society where the demands of morality, and the needs of the spirit, can be realized in the life of the Nation.

Idealization of "the people," doubts about those in government, grandiose expectations of the future often linked to the ideals of the past, insistence on the possibility that the people can govern themselves, all mark the rhetoric those in office use to communicate with the electorate. In dong so, they suggest the presence of a collective fantasy, held in common by presidents with otherwise diverse political agendas. To be sure, this fantasy appears in different versions, and is adapted to the needs of time, place, and party. Yet, it also exhibits some remarkable continuities.

The primary elements of the fantasy are those we found in the drama of Mr. Smith's experience in Washington. On a psychic level, this fantasy expresses splitting, idealization of the good object, dissatisfaction with reality, and the hope to establish in the future a merger of reality with a lost ideal. All of these elements also indicate that government has gotten caught up in a moral drama.

The Moral Standing of Government

Idealization is closely linked to moral thinking. Idealization, when applied to the problem of government, treats government as a moral institution, and concerns itself with government's moral standing. What does it mean to say that government has a moral significance? First, it means that as part of a nation-state, we acknowledge and consciously express our connection with others. We often invoke the term "community" for our sense of connection and belonging to a greater whole. The ethical or moral significance of both government (negative) and country (positive) derives from their involvement in establishing the connection we associate with community. Psychically, there is nothing surprising in this. After all, the primitive notion of the good is the notion of a (positive) connection: between child and parent. At the level of political and public life, the elements of the nation-state have ethical significance because they involve a particular type of connection with others.

The ethical significance of this connection has two meanings closely linked to the distinction between ethics and morality developed in the last chapter. Connecting self to other can mean recognizing that selfhood exists in the varied concrete forms of different selves: individuals with different qualities, interests, and ways of life. Alternatively, connecting self to other can mean treating others as persons (possessed of selves) only so far as they share our qualities, interests, and ways of life. The ideal, then, can involve recognizing others as selves though they remain different from us; or, it can involve recognizing others as selves only so far as they are the same as we are. This is the distinction between recognition of self in other and identification of self with other.[15]

We have already encountered this distinction in another form, as the opposition between two ideals of integration, one involving the integration of good and bad objects, the other merger into the idealized good object. The first represents what I refer to here as recognition, the second as identification (with the idealized object).

This distinction has considerable psychic significance. It involves levels of psychic development, an earlier one marked by relating as identification, and a later one marked by relating as recognizing self-boundaries. Indeed, Freud describes identification as "the earliest expression of an emotional tie with another person.[16] Recognition raises identification to a higher level. When we recognize (different) self in other, we also identify with the other, but no longer with his or her concrete particular qualities, interests, and way of life. Rather, recognition means identification with a more abstract other: the self in general rather than in its particular forms.

Those for whom identification, which seeks sameness, tends to displace recognition of difference claim that loss of self into the community marks an ethical life.[17] What makes a connection ethical, then, is either that it recognizes self-boundaries and the integrity of others (involves recognition), or that it does not (is rooted in identification). It is important to bear in mind how the term ethical can refer to connections of two decidedly different kinds, indeed, how it can have opposed and inconsistent connotations. I suggest in chapter 1 that we speak of this opposition between two ethics as a distinction between ethics and morality. This opposition plays a central part in the development of the split in attitude between government and nation.

The element of difference that enters into ethical thinking centered on recognition disappears when ethical thinking centers on identification. Central to the perceived failing of government is the connection between government and differences of a particular kind: the differences that separate private interests. Those critical of government, whether they favor free market or democratic solutions, point out how government has been captured by private interest, and thus is no better, indeed no different, than a particular or partial interest. Some have turned this observation into a theory of government, insisting that its subordination to private interest is inevitable, even desirable.[18] Being captured by private interest places government into the psychic space of the bad object, whose primary characteristic is that concern for the needs of the child is displaced by concern with the parent's needs (self-interest). When this happens, government falls short of the ethical ideal, whether interpreted along the lines of recognition or identification. It matters, however, whether we perceive this failure in the language of identification or of recognition.

The link between government and private interest may mean failure because the government has been captured by the wrong interests, that is the interests of others. Here, government's involvement with difference makes it fail in the eyes of those whose notion of connection is shaped by the need for identification (sameness). Lamenting the loss of "allegiance to a common culture," including a shared way of life, suggests a commitment to connection as identification. Thus, Speaker of the House Newt Gingrich insists that America is a set of "habits;" and he worries that we are no longer teaching ourselves "how to be American."[19] The same sentiment is expressed by Patrick Buchanan in a speech announcing his candidacy for the Presidency:[20]

> "One nation, indivisible," is what the Pledge of Allegiance declares, and the millions of immigrants who have come here in recent decades to become part of the American family shall be welcomed as our adopted sons, daughters, brothers, and sisters. But, as they have learn, we have a duty to assimilate them into the American family—to teach them our heritage, our traditions, our customs, our history, our culture, and our language. ... All students must be introduced to American history, and our unique culture to which all who have come here have contributed.

Love for country gets wrapped up with the drive for identification and the imposition of sameness, that, in this case, will define who is and who is not an American according to their habits and ways of life.

For those at the extreme of hatred for government, the government has been taken over by alien forces: "alien people have taken control over our people."[21] Hatred for government means, in this case, hatred for a government that has been taken from its true people and from its true values. It is not the government of the real America, but the "Zionist Occupied Government". It is a government taken over by alien races, thus the rallying cry of Louis Beam, quoted by Morris Dees: "Never let any race but the white race rule this country.[22] For those operating at the level of identification, taking sides with partial groups is not the problem. Government is not illegitimate because it fails to be universal. Government loses its legitimacy because it has sided with groups who are not really American. In this understanding of the illegitimacy of government, moral judgment based on identification dominates.[23]

Alternatively, the government's involvement with particular interests may mean failure not because it has been captured by the wrong interests, but because it can no longer rise above partial interest. Then, it fails to represent a meeting point for the common aspirations of all individuals, who embody selfhood regardless of their differences, including different habits and ways of life. To the extent that the state serves the interest of a particular group, it loses its connection to selfhood in general. This is a failure to support connection through recognition of self in other. Loss of government's commitment to the universal calls into question its ethical standing. Such a government warrants feelings of disappointment and even hostility. Psychically, a government acting this way repeats the parent's inability to consider the child's different self. Then, the missing universal has the meaning of a missing respect for the freedom of the child to develop in his or her own way and direction.

I have suggested that the distinction between the attitudes organized around identification and recognition centers on difference. The first cannot tolerate difference, and sees the good as the negation of difference. The second sees the good existing in many different forms each capable of realizing the ideal of what it means to be a person. Linking the good to identification makes difference a threat to it. The threat difference poses is the threat of opposition and limitation, the opposition to and limitation on the self associated with the existence of others in the world, and with the existence of a world outside the subject (a world not governed by the subject's wanting and willing). This difference is a flaw in the world that must be fixed.

The real is marked by differences, and, because it is, the ethics of identification (morality) makes it necessary to protect what is good from what is real. When this happens, the ideal loses its capacity to be part of our lives in the world. The good is placed outside the world, where, if attainable at all, it is either in the future (for example, after death) or in renouncing the satisfactions of worldly pursuits.[24] Placing the good outside the world protects it from the bad, but, at the same time, assures that what is, in the world, becomes as bad as the ideal is good.

Gender

The opposition between country or nation and government sometimes appears in the language of gender, the nation being associated with the female, the government with the male. The patriotic ideal, then, connects with the idealization of women, and the corruption of government with the fall of man. "Family values," which are closely linked with hostility toward government, refer to the organization of family and social life in a way that will preserve the goodness of women and protect them from the corrupting influence of the world outside, which includes the world of public life. Here, to protect women we must contain them within the family; so protect means circumscribe and control.

Two recent phenomena exemplify this trend: Louis Farrakhan's "Million Man March" and Bill McCartney's "Promise Keepers." Each demands that husbands and fathers take up their "responsibilities," meaning to provide security and protection for, and thus to assure control over, women and children. As we will see, in the attack on government in the United States, the matter of responsibility looms large: "To be an American ... is to be responsible."[25] This idea is a central tenet of the Promise Keepers, who insist "wives should be treated with love and respect and included in decision-making, but the man is 'the head of the household and women are responders.'"[26]

Renewal of the traditional family structure with its traditional gender roles offers a solution to the perceived "breakdown of family and society." This solution will not be found in good government, but in the family. Thus, according to Steve Farrar, a Promise Keeper's speaker, "when you take the major pressing issues that are facing us—violence, teen pregnancy, broken families—and reduce them to their lowest common denominator, you're going to find a lack of male leadership at the root."[27] The gender role envisioned for men emphasizes taking responsibility for moral decay, indeed "moral chaos," which is understood to result from the way men have abdicated their leadership role in the family.[28] Thus, in a similar vein, Louis Farrakhan describes the Million Man March as a "day of atonement," a time for black men who have failed in their obligations to apologize to "their women."[29]

The theme of leadership and authority is bound up with a theme of sacrifice. Leadership in the family does not mean the subordination of the family to the husband's power. Rather than power, the head of household must offer "total submission." Specifically, Promise Keepers urges members "to form 'accountability' groups ... within which they are expected to submit all aspects of their lives to review and rebuke."[30]

Repression of the self is the theme both of Promise Keepers and of the Million Man March. It is not surprising that framing social problems in the language of morality expresses self-hatred and fosters repression, since the main organizing theme of the moral stance is the attack on the self. Moral chaos naturally gets identified with the idea of self-indulgence rather than self-sacrifice. To bring order to the world means to feel guilt for, and to atone for, the sin of self-indulgence, which means submission to a strict regime of self-denial through loss of self into a group.

We can cure moral chaos by turning hate away from others and onto the self. This solution therefore expresses parental (including maternal) failure. This failure gets transformed into idealization, especially of women. Insistence on the goodness of women would itself suggest a powerful element of ambivalence. Since it is here combined with the desire to control women as an expression of hate, we need not hesitate to see idealization as an expression of its opposite.

The protection of (the goodness of) women central to the movements just considered is also of special significance in understanding the attack on government. The impulse to protect women originates in the need to protect the good mother without whom the child has no hope of a life-affirming connection to the world. When, later in life, the split between the good and bad mother gets internalized and projected back into the world, it naturally resolves itself into a gender difference between the good mother and the bad father. This, then, helps account for the goodness of the nation (female) and the badness of the government (male), which suggests how lost those who attack government would be if they could not be assured of a bad government.

The woman's sphere (the family) is the locus of the good, and the world outside (the world ruled by government) the locus of the bad. Government cannot do good since it stands outside the family. Like the government, the father must be bad if the mother is to be good. This bad-ness gets internalized and repressed as self-hatred and guilt, and is some-times acted out as abandonment of the family. Abandonment is a signifi-cant theme in the attack on government, which, in a weakened state resulting from this attack, cannot but abandon its citizens.

We can take all of this, especially the wish to reinstate what are under-stood to be traditional gender roles, as an expression of a larger ambiva-lence toward the self. So long as society understands the self and its inter-ests as a danger to social cohesion and group identity, repression of the self must be a central goal for its institutions. At the same time, the notion of individual responsibility has no meaning in the absence of an ideal of the individual possessed of a self, acting as a "center of initiative" in the world. Since we cannot get along with or without the self, we must find a way both to include and to exclude it. Polarized gender roles is a part of the solution to this problem.

Polarization of gender roles places the active moment of having a self into one part of society: men. This part pursues self-interest in those spheres where it is appropriate to do so (especially in the world outside the family). Polarization places the passive moment (selflessness) into anoth-er part of society, women. This part cannot participate in life outside the family not only because doing so requires an active self-interest, but also because doing so can only corrupt the virtue of those who sacrifice self for others. Men have the power that stems from self-determination, but must bear the burden of society's distrust of the self. Women have the virtue of being without selves of their own, but must suffer subordination to men. Women are good because they are not for themselves. This naturally makes men responsible for the moral chaos understood to result from the lack of constraints on the self.

To have a self is to be the bearer of pride and shame. To have no self of your own, but only that of the other, means to have the other (the man) bear your pride and shame. If we assume, as James Gilligan suggests we should, that shame breeds violence, we will not be surprised to find a correlation between gender and violence. This correlation, as Gilligan points out, is built into the polarization of gender roles.[31] But, more basically, violence is built into society's ambivalence toward the self, which fosters and finds expression in the polarization of gender roles.

How does government participate in the moral and psychic drama of ambivalence toward the self and gender polarization? I suggest above that the split between government and country has its expression in the language of gender polarization, which suggests that both splits have a common root and psychic meaning. The government is the active moment (or realization in action) of the nation, its presence in the form of those who can use institutions for the purpose of governing. The country, people, or nation represents the passive moment, since, outside an institutional setting (government), they cannot act, or even achieve the consciousness of self needed for self-directed action. The two moments need not stand opposed, but polarization sets them against each other, with the resulting ambivalence, if not hatred, toward government that makes governing difficult or impossible. We can see in this how the gender issues so prominent in Frank Capra's drama well express the fundamental dilemmas posed by splitting of good and bad, and the ambivalence toward the self that results from that it.

Making the World Good

As a result of the processes just summarized, patriotism combines with a sometimes extreme animosity toward the incarnation of patriotism's object: the government as the only form in which the nation can exist in the world. The more extreme the division, the more what is real cannot be allowed to contain anything that is good, the more this failure to contain what is good becomes a matter of contamination by what is bad. So far, we have explored this split as the psychic meaning of the combination: love of country, distrust of government. This combination poses a problem, however. The problem is that the object we love does not exist in the world. So far as the good remains an unattainable ideal, the world as it exists must remain bad, or essentially so.

This dilemma can be resolved in two ways. The first attempts to recreate the world in the image of the ideal by purging it of the bad; we destroy the world so that it may be reborn. The destruction of government, which is the extreme outcome of splitting, is meant to contribute to the purification of the world: "Am I advocating the overthrow of the government?" No, "I'm advocating the cleansing" of government.[32] The second resolution is to withdraw from the public world. The two resolutions are not so different as they seem, since the latter, though it does not require destruction of government, does require that government be made weak enough that it cannot do us any harm (or any good, of course).

The bombing of the Federal Building in Oklahoma City exemplifies the first solution. For those whose objects are so bad that they can find little or nothing good in the world, destruction is the logical solution to the problem. Yet, while destroying the world is meant (consciously) to destroy the bad, it does not reinstate the good, which cannot exist in the world. For the anti-government extremist, a good government is not a government at all. Rather, we "need a government of men and women ... whose attitude towards its mission is essentially *religious*: a government more like a holy order than like any existing secular government today."[33] No actual government, acting as a government, can bring about merger with the good object. The government cannot be good, but it can be devoted to the mission of carrying on a war against evil.

The government conceived in this way, since it does not instantiate the ideal (nation) into a set of enduring laws and institutions, is no government at all, but an anti-government. Yet, without a real (institutionalized) government, there can be no ethical order, no security for the self, no connection based on recognition of self in other. If destroying government destroys the country, what is the real end of the attack on government? The answer is that the end is not bringing the good into the world, but acknowledging the triumph of the bad. We can surmise, then, that the real purpose in destroying government is not to clear the way for the triumph of the good, as is claimed and consciously believed, but to create hell on earth. Doing so assures that the individual's subjective experience of a world ruled by the bad object becomes objective reality, that the individual's original deprivation gets visited on others.

The violent attack on government provokes two responses, both with significant psychic meaning. If successful, the attack on government removes the only authority capable of providing security for the individual, protecting rights, and promoting a sense of group life. The successful attack on government, then, creates a reality of deprivation on the largest scale possible. An unsuccessful attack on government still alters the world in psychically relevant directions. Failure provokes a response: the limiting of freedom, the repression of dissent in the name of security, the strengthening of internal police apparatus, and so on. The failed attack prompts a strengthening of the authority attacked, especially of its capacity for violence against citizens, and a weakening of citizens' rights and autonomy. The attack on government assures that it will be bad, which it must be if it is to play its part in the psychic drama of those who hate government.

Thus, the attack on government either removes government and destroys freedom (which can only exist when sustained by government), or it empowers government to override citizens' rights and freedom. On one plane, the two responses are the same: the erosion of rights and security. On another plane, they are polar opposites, since one turns government into an overpowering and hostile presence, while the other removes government, leaving us all on our own.

In its less extreme form, the attack on government means withdrawal from the world that is bad into a world that is, or at least can be, good. This means withdrawal from public into private, which is also the theme of the family values movement as exemplified by the Promise Keepers. In the words of Newt Gingrich, "what we really want to do is devolve power all the way out of government and back to working American families."[34] As we have seen, the family is the locus of women and children, therefore of innocence and virtue, of what is good. The psychic meaning of the insistence that we shrink government is not that we destroy it, but that we make it too weak to corrupt the good. The good can exist, but only as a private matter. If the private world contains the good, the public the bad, then the smaller the latter and the larger the former, the better. The connection between private and good, public and bad begins to make sense when we recall the gender distinction between the two spheres. Traditionally, public and private spheres relate as the domain of the masculine and feminine respectively. The attack on government in the name of the private sphere, then, protects the goodness of the feminine principle by allocating badness to the public world, which, of course, means keeping women out of the public realm.

Hatred of Women

To this point, I have linked government with the masculine, nation with the feminine, interpreting recourse to the private world as seeking refuge in the idealized feminine. This construction sits uncomfortably, however, with an important element of the movement against government, the element that targets the welfare state. For those who attack the welfare state, the issue is dependence on government, and thus implicitly a too close association between government and the feminine principle. And, indeed, the welfare system, which, according to its critics, is the part of government responsible for undermining autonomy is, in America, associated not with the masculine, but with the feminine.

To take this into account, we need to move beyond the simpler equation of nation with feminine, government with masculine. Not only does the state divide into nation/country and government, the government also divides into legislature/executive/law enforcement (masculine) on one side, and welfare system (feminine) on the other. Then, what begins as a division between good (idealized feminine) and bad (masculine) becomes a division between good (idealized feminine) and bad (masculine and feminine). The construction just outlined also carries the potential for paternal betrayal, since it is the masculine part that relegates those who fail to the feminine world.

To understand this construction, we need to consider the association of the feminine with the destruction of will. In doing so, I think Mervin Glasser's notion of a "Core Complex" proves helpful. Glasser introduces this concept to describe the psychic impact of certain extreme experiences originating in severely narcissistic mothering. He describes a victim of this experience as being "infused with his mother's attitudes, standards and goals" to such an extent that he "came to consider her as having established an existence inside him, as if she had *colonized* him: she had somehow psychically implanted herself permanently by some process akin to projective identification."[35]

The result of this experience is the formation of a Core Complex consisting of the following elements. The first is the fantasy of fusion with an idealized mother as means to achieve security and satisfaction (Glasser terms it the "ultimate narcissistic fulfilment"). However, the mother is simultaneously regarded as avaricious and indifferent; she thus constitutes a split object. As a result of these qualities, the mother is experienced as a threat, specifically the threat of annihilation, to which the individual responds by withdrawal and/or aggression.

The victim of this complex experiences intense aggressive feelings either toward the mother, or toward the self in an effort to protect the mother. This aggressiveness connects to the prospect of the loss of self in the merged relation with a narcissistic mother. While Glasser develops this concept in the context of severe pathology, he also suggests that in milder forms it can exist more pervasively. Fear of dependency, as I suggest above, is fear of loss of self, more specifically of will, which constitutes the self as a separate and integrated entity (one that has a will of its own).

Introducing the Core Complex allows us to link animosity toward government with hostility toward women, a link already implicit in the connection between hostility toward government and the demand that men take on their traditional responsibilities, which is also an attack on men.[36] The other side of hostility toward women is the absence, or weakness, of the father, who cannot protect the child from the mother, and may even deliver the child to her. Delivering the child to the mother is what the government does to those who become its dependents. The prospect of dependence gives us all the more reason to fear government, though in this case fear of government is combined with a good measure of contempt for its weakness.

Paternal betrayal gets built into the fabric of society when women are relegated to the home, men to the world of work. This makes paternal abandonment a daily occurrence. It also secures the identification of public with masculine, private with feminine. The psychic phenomenon just summarized, then, mirrors, and is mirrored by, the division of labor between the sexes in society. Government failure, understood as a form of abandonment of citizens, reenacts the experience with an absent or ineffective father who abandons the child to the (narcissistic) mother. This begins to make clear how the fear of too strong government has its roots in government's weakness.[37] Understanding how its weakness spawns the fear of powerful government helps us see more clearly the policy dilemma posed by the attack on government, which produces and reproduces the problem it hopes to solve.

It will not be surprising to discover that splitting results in oscillation between inconsistent ideas that nonetheless imply each other, one involving the idealization of women, the other hatred of women. In one, we escape into the family; in the other we must escape from the family. This construction begins to define the psychic space the free market, which is a refuge both from government and from the family, is meant to occupy.

4 THE PLACE OF HATRED IN PUBLIC LIFE

Introduction

Whether we hate government or only distrust it, we concur in the judgment that government is corrupt. That is, we treat our government as a bad object. Our relationship with our government will, then, be shaped by the way we relate to bad objects, which depends on our formative experiences, and in particular on the extent to which those experiences facilitated the integration of good and bad. Hatred is a particular modality of the relationship with government, the incidence of which we might be tempted to assume is relatively small. This temptation is reinforced by the data we have on attitudes toward government normally associated with hatred. Thus, for example, if we consider anger toward government an indicator of hatred, then, since only 12 percent of Americans report being angry at the government, we might conclude that the incidence of hatred of government is no more, and presumably less, than 12 percent.[1]

This approach to the problem can, however, be misleading, as becomes clear when we take into account certain important features of hatred. To see this, let me first offer a preliminary definition of hatred as unmodulated destructive feelings directed at an object experienced as essentially or altogether bad. Bad here means frustrating or depriving, so hatred is a feeling directed at objects from which we seek gratification, but do not receive it. As I have suggested, this description fits government, which is an object from which we expect gratification, but often fail to receive it. Indeed, the Pew Research Center Survey found a high incidence of reported frustration with government (56 percent), which reinforces the judgment that government constitutes a bad object for many citizens.

Hatred defined in this way might be an overt, or conscious, feeling or self-state: intense anger, or rage. If we limit hatred to this overt self-state, then we would have to conclude that only a small percentage of Americans hate their government. The problem with this conclusion is that it ignores the difficulties posed for the individual were he or she to experience rage as a permanent state, and not a temporary experience. Indeed, rage as the overt experience of hate cannot normally be tolerated for any length of time since doing so would be highly destructive not so much to the hated object as to the individual who is in this way consumed by hate. Rage is difficult to sustain for a number of reasons, not the least of which is the very intensity of the feeling and the energy consumed in having it. Beyond this limitation, rage at a frustrating object may be experienced as only fuelling the sadistic gratification that object gains from inflicting frustration, and thus will seem to serve the object more than the person who hates it. Finally, the very destructiveness of rage makes it difficult to reconcile with daily life.

Something must be done with hatred in its overt form if it is not to destroy the one who hates rather than the hated object. For dealing with hate, we have several possibilities. We can repress our destructive feelings rather than having them, with the result that we do not experience our hate, even though in a basic sense we still hate. As a part of this strategy, we may turn our hate against ourselves. Alternatively, we can externalize our hate by experiencing it in others, and in the limit provoking them to hate us. Bearing these considerations in mind, we cannot treat reports of overt feeling states we might associate with hatred as convincing evidence of whether it is present or not.

The trial of Timothy McVeigh for the Oklahoma City bombing exemplifies the processes used to deal with hate. During the sometimes-impassioned testimony of the victims' families in the penalty phase of the trial, "McVeigh, as usual, showed no emotion."[2] How can someone who seems wholly lacking in emotional involvement be responsible for an act of such emotional significance? The absence of any apparent feeling on McVeigh's part intensifies the anger directed toward him, and fuels a sense of bewilderment. The puzzle can be solved once we see the destruction of the Murrah building and the people in it as a successful effort to shift an intense and intolerable feeling from perpetrator to victim. Now, the victims' friends and families express the feelings (hate) absent in the accused perpetrator of the crime. McVeigh seems emotionless because, in a sense, he is, having succeeded in turning his subjective experience into something outside himself. McVeigh attacked the hated object, thereby expressing his hate, while simultaneously shifting that hate onto others, thereby relieving himself of responsibility for it.

Timothy McVeigh expressed nothing that could be interpreted as an emotion linked to hate except the absence of emotion. As I suggest above, his original destructive act combined with his lack of emotion provoked hate in the victims' families. Thus, if we limit our concept of hate to the expression in violent emotion of our destructive feelings toward an object, we would have to conclude that McVeigh did not hate. Following this line of interpretation, we might find relatively little hate in our world. Certainly we will find less than might be discovered were we to alter our criteria to take into account the necessity that hatred be in some way disavowed.

Indeed, the source and location of hate are always problematic, since we always consider hate something provoked in us by the bad object. Even when we hate, we are not, then, the source of hate; the object is. The attribution of our hate to the object we hate is therefore built into the phenomenon from the outset, as is our sense that hate is something put into us from outside. This is consistent with the drive hate fosters in us to move it on to someone else. We must, then, find an outlet for our hate that confirms the judgment that we are not hateful, but have been provoked to hate by the hateful conduct of a depriving object. Then, our rage can be experienced not as hate, but as outrage.[3] Denial of hate goes together with a need to find acceptable outlets for individual and collective hate, including its overt expression in rage.

If no suitable objects can be found, an object must be manufactured for the purpose. Thus, members of the Cuban community in Miami turned the Attorney General into a suitable target for their outrage when their own recalcitrance drove her to use the threat of force against them in the Elian Gonzalez affair. By provoking action from the state, they provided themselves with an opportunity to express their hatred in the form of righteous indignation (a typical form of hatred). They could then hate without being hateful.

Hate that is repressed or exported onto others is no less hate. Yet, by its nature, hate offers only indirect evidence of its presence; so, we must see evidence for hate in self-states and emotions not normally thought of as expressions of hate. Indeed, even hate's opposite, love, can offer such evidence, as it does in the idea of "tough love." To find hate, we must look not for rage and overt acts of destruction, but for feelings that look very different from hate. We have seen an example of this in the absence of feeling exhibited by Timothy McVeigh. Hate, then, appears not as a specific, overt, and acknowledged emotion, but as a complex structure or organization of emotional life aimed at dealing with intense feelings and with the experiences that provoke them. Here, I would like to explore this structure, and the way of life linked to it.

Hatred

In my discussion of moral thinking, I emphasized the problem of integration. Failure to integrate the good and bad object means failure to modulate the feelings invested in those objects. Essential to the prospects for integration is the way the individual experiences and deals with his or her aggressive impulses. As Winnicott emphasizes, the aggressive impulse plays a vital part in establishing separation from the object, and thus the capacity for relating to it.[4] Aggression marks and protects the self-boundary and thus the capacity for mobilizing aggression is essential to being a self. Aggression is, therefore, bound up with difference.[5] The danger is that the feeling that grounds separation will destroy the object, because that feeling is too intense and/or the object too weak. If aggressive feelings are too intense, separation becomes problematic. This requires that the destructive feelings be kept apart from, rather than integrated into, the personality. This isolation of aggression impairs the individual's ability to establish self-boundaries and self-integration.[6]

Understanding the vicissitudes of the aggressive feelings is obviously of considerable importance in any attempt to understand hatred of government. Failure to integrate those feelings means that aggression cannot be experienced as a feeling the person *has*, but becomes, instead, what the person *is* (he or she is "consumed" by anger). To be a person who experiences anger presumes a prior integration, or subsuming, of anger into the personality. The person who is angry is also something more than and different from his or her anger. In other words, there is a whole, the whole person, who experiences anger as his or her own, but not as the sum total of his or her being. Splitting impedes the development of this attitude, locking individuals, and the groups dominated by such individuals, into more primitive forms of aggression. These more primitive forms of aggression shape the experience we know as hate.

When, in a burst of feeling, we say that we hate, this may be a momentary experience, rather than the organized campaign against an enemy we associate with hate movements in the public arena. Since these more organized movements are our main concern, we need to distinguish from the outset between the two meanings, or between rage and hate. Otto Kernberg suggests we consider hatred "a complex structured derivative of the affect rage." This complex structure, in contrast to rage, is chronic and stable, rooted in character structure, even the organizing element in character. It continues the goal of rage, which is to destroy the bad object, make it suffer, or control it. Kernberg goes on to note how hatred is inevitably linked to revenge against the object, and therefore must be understood as a response to a real or imagined attack by it. "Paranoid fears of retaliation also are usually unavoidable accompaniments of intense hatred, so that paranoid features, a wish for revenge, and sadism go hand in hand."[7]

While the phenomenon of hatred should be distinguished from the simple desire to destroy the (bad) object, it remains a transformation of that simple desire (rage). We must, then, understand hatred first in relation to the impulse to destroy what is perceived to stand in the way of gratification. We must also bear in mind the element of revenge associated with hatred and destruction, since this element will become central when we take up the problem of justice, and of the relationship between hatred and the demand for justice.

Hatred is rage organized around an external object conceived in thought, and thus the target of a complex mental relationship. This object cannot be destroyed by an impulsive act, but only by a well-organized campaign. This is because the object is potentially overpowering in its capacity and intent to do harm. Psychically, the object is the concentration of the subject's own rage organized into hatred and projected into the world. The attribution of power is vital to the relationship with the object.[8] We need to bear in mind that the power of the object is the power of the subject's own (organized and projected) rage. The more intense and destructive the individual's feelings, the more powerful and dangerous the fantasized adversary in the world.

We can see in this the individual's intense need for a persecuting object in the world. It is not enough to have the fantasy that the government is intent on harm, the government must be made to act in ways that validate that fantasy. At stake, then, is control over the government. This is not, however, control by the normal process of representation. Rather, it is control via the provocation of a psychodynamic link. Using provocation as a means of control shifts the connection with the object from thinking and reason to feeling, from thoughtful and deliberative conduct to impulse-driven action. Control of the object (government) facilitates the projection of intolerable feelings onto it, assuring that those feelings need not be dealt with internally.

Were it possible to deal with the feelings internally, the control of the object (government in this case) would not be necessary. What makes control necessary is the same thing that makes externalization necessary: the intensity of psychic pain. When psychic pain becomes too intense to tolerate, it must be gotten out, often by a violent act aimed at transferring it from self to others.[9] This is precisely what Timothy McVeigh succeeded so well in accomplishing. He was able to remain calm and seemingly without emotion, because, at least for a moment, he had transferred his intense pain onto others. Indeed the magnitude of the horror experienced by his victims is a good measure of the intensity of his own pain. This evacuation into the world is what we mean by paranoid hatred of objects, in this case government.

Those who act out of hate organize their personalities around hate. In the absence of hate, which is to say in the absence of the hated object, their personalities would lose their centers of meaning. We can say, then, that hate serves an integrating function, but only in a limited sense. It does not so much make rage a part of a whole personality as it makes the whole personality an expression of rage. The result is not the integration of love and hate, but the destruction of love so a pseudo-unity can develop organized around only the one pole, which is dedicated to destruction. To understand destruction, we need to delineate more explicitly the constructive and destructive aspects of aggression. Aggression aimed at destroying persecutory objects projected into the world has a different psychic meaning and goal than aggression made to serve the end of living in the world.

If we take aggression to consist "of the use of force to express feelings and to achieve aims," then aggression is not in itself creative or destructive, but sometimes one, sometimes the other, depending on its aim and context. Aggression can be used "to intimidate, to impress, to manipulate, and sometimes to subjugate other people and the environment and the various things contained in it." But, it can also be used "for purposes of self-preservation" or "to save, rescue, and defend."[10] Aggression, including the anger sometimes associated with it, protects the integrity of the self, and can be used to defend the integrity of others.

When aggression is used to intimidate, manipulate, and otherwise subjugate, this indicates that the individual's integrity is not well enough developed and self-boundaries are too problematic for aggression to be put in their service. Rather than defending against violations of self-boundaries, aggression defends against the original rejection experienced in relation with the bad object. Put another way, rather than defending the (separate) self, aggression attacks difference from the self in order to secure connection through identification. The use of aggression tells us something important about the individual's success or failure in accomplishing the transition from identification to recognition.

In cases of failure to make this transition, what must be defended is not the self's boundedness, but its vulnerability. On one level, the threat is to the needed connection based on identification. Yet, aggression used to protect connection based on sameness also fends off any connection based on the recognition of (different) selfhood. Thus, rage and hatred block real connection, which must involve another (separate) person. Since connection is what the individual wants, aggression acts here to block satisfaction of the individual's most deeply felt need (for connection with another). In part, this attack on connection may be thought of as a form of identification, in this case with the bad object (the object that frustrates the child's need for connection). Identification with the aggressor has much to do with the attack on government, which, if successful, assures that there will be no framework in which the individual can secure connectedness with others.[11]

Underlying identification with the aggressor is the need to protect against the experience of frustration and rejection associated with the bad object. Becoming the aggressor means shifting that experience from self to other.[12] Hatred, then, becomes a means to avoid the intensely painful feeling of rejection and the loss of love. Not only does hatred attack connection (rather than defending the self), it attacks the connection-seeking part of the self now experienced in others rather than in the self. Aggression gets directed against those for whom the hope for connection remains alive.

The Attack on Innocence

Aggression shaped in relation with the bad object does not, then, simply mean rage directed against the bad object and whoever in the present life experience represents that object. It also means aggression directed against any present-day representative of hope. The representatives of hope are the innocent victims, most tragically the children in the day-care center in the Federal Building in Oklahoma City.[13] Note how, for those involved in the militia movement, innocent victims of terrorist acts represent prior victims of the government: "For it was, after all, the taking of lives by the government at Ruby Ridge and Waco that provided the innocent blood that gave birth to the militia and the associated anti-government feeling currently sweeping the nation."[14] A press release issued by the Militia of Montana "reminded followers that 'the innocent at Mount Carmel'—the site of the Branch Davidian compound outside Waco—cried out for justice as much as the 'hearts of the innocent in Oklahoma City.'"[15] Since the members of the militia identify with these past victims, we can assume that the victims of their own violent acts represent the innocent selves they lost in the psychic (and sometimes physical) violence inflicted by their caretakers. The act repeats the destruction of their selves, but now as their own act and with others as stand-ins for themselves as victims. This destruction of others, which represents and reproduces their own experience of victimization, is then either denied by being treated as an accidental, if inevitable, by-product of aggression, rather than its real objective, or it is justified on the grounds of justice.

The attitude of the militia toward the innocent victims of their violent acts has a parallel in the attitude of those who demand welfare reform toward those dependent on the welfare system. Welfare reform also has two sets of victims: welfare mothers and their children. The former are the explicit (conscious) victims of policies intended to punish and deprive. The latter are the innocent victims punished as a by-product of the attack on their parents.

The destruction of innocence, and the link between current and past destruction, constitutes a vital theme in the hatred of government. Destruction of innocence destroys hope for love, and with it the prospect of any revival of the pain experienced in the loss of love. It would be a mistake, therefore, to treat innocent victims as an unfortunate, if unavoidable, by-product of the war against government tyranny, which is how the militia leaders consciously understand them.[16] They should be treated, instead, as a necessary part of the drama.

Innocent victims represent innocence as the victim of violence. Though destroying innocence may be placed outside of awareness, it remains the ultimate goal. Destroying innocence destroys the good, and in this is part of the work of envy. Hyatt-Williams notes that envy is the deadliest of sins "because it attacks all the virtues and attacks all goodness. The envious person attacks the good object because that object is good and has something to give."[17] Envy is the impulse to take from others what we desire but do not have, and do not imagine ourselves acquiring. We reduce the pain of our lack by seeking to make it universal. So far as all lack what we lack, we are not diminished by it, at least we are not diminished relative to what we might be. Envy is the first root of the attack on innocence, and therefore a fundamental root of the attack on government.

There is also a second root for the attack on innocence, which is not in envy but in protest. This is the protest against the appearance of innocence and goodness where neither are real. The attack on the appearance of innocence is closely linked to the demand for justice and acts of violence done in the name of justice. In the words of James Gilligan, "all violence is an attempt to achieve justice," where justice means relieving the innocent of the burden of guilt.[18] Those who feel they unjustly bear the burden of guilt denounce the false innocence of those who have transferred that burden onto them. When this means imposing the burden of guilt on those who do not currently bear it but ought to, then justice attacks the appearance of innocence.

The attack on Columbine High School in Colorado exemplifies the attack on the sham of innocence. The two young men responsible for the attack knew the false innocence we attach to adolescents in affluent suburban communities. In particular, they knew the cruelty and sadism of life in an affluent suburban school.

> The skewed community values created by administrators, teachers, parents, and the media exacerbate the natural volatility of high-school social groups. Just as rape and other felonies committed by star athletes at the NCAA powerhouses are tolerated with wearying predictability, today's high-school administrator will allow the barely controllable gangs from the gridiron free rein to commit verbal and physical aggro upon the castes below.[19]

If innocence means the absence of hate, cruelty, and sadism, Harris and Klebold knew only too well that children and adolescents are anything but innocent (a message we might recall that Freud considered among his major contributions). The public response to the violence was, of course, to insist that the dead children were, indeed, innocent, which in another sense of the term was true, since not all their victims had victimized Harris and Klebold, if any had. Yet, the celebration of the goodness of the community, school, and victims, also insisted on protecting the appearance of innocence whose falseness was the object of the assault. "We are good," insisted the community in response to the attack, thus indicating that it knew full well what was at stake.

A second example of the attack on innocence, the JonBenet Ramsey murder case, indicates how the two roots of that attack can come together. For JonBenet Ramsey, murder follows a prior (symbolic) destruction of her innocence through her participation as a contestant in a beauty pageant, where six-year-olds were "cosmetically transformed into sultry, Lolita-like waifs."[20] The image of innocence dressed to seduce is itself an attack on innocence. No less than those who bombed the Murrah building in Oklahoma City or attacked Columbine High School are parents such as the Ramsey's engaged in an assault on innocence. Their assault deprived their daughter of her childhood, and of the experience of the true self we associate with children.

Innocence here means not the absence of sexual and aggressive impulse, but the absence of guile, manipulation, and the domination of the personality by the false-self construct.[21] In the effort to destroy this innocence, we can see the work of envy. By forcing the child to seduce the parent, the parent absolves him or her self of responsibility for seducing the child. The parent also promotes and justifies an impulse to punish the child for bearing the parent's projected desires, for example the sexual desire for the child.

We can treat the innocence of children as the absence of sexual or aggressive impulse. But, in so doing we deprive the child not of its innocence, but of its humanity. Alternatively, we can treat the innocence of children as their expectation of, and dependence on, the special bond of parental love referred to earlier as object-related love. To replace object-related love with narcissistic love turns the child into an object for the parent. The replacement of object-related love with narcissistic love is clearly implied in the drama of seduction in which the Ramsey's enrolled their daughter. Love was made to signify the manipulation of desire. This is the loss of innocence in our second sense. It was imposed on JonBenet so that the parents' use of their daughter could be justified as her use of them.

All of this signifies hatred of children, including as its fundamental element the hatred of innocence. This is the same hatred of innocence expressed by the bad fathers in response to Jefferson Smith. To make the child seduce the parent is to take something vital from the child. Whether or not this corruption of the child allows the parent to overcome a sense of responsibility, it assures that the parent's hatred of the child will not be measured against the child's love for the parent, and thus made so much harder to bear. Making the child seduce the parent takes from the child the parent's own (projected) lost feeling of being loved. It is the work of envy, which plays such a powerful role in the phenomena of hatred.

If envy can play such a powerful role in hatred, how can we relate envy, and with it the attack on innocence, to the attack on government? One way to answer this question is to imagine a government capable of providing safety and, when necessary, sustenance to its citizens. The government can, in other words, act as a good object for its citizens, for example, in response to the dependence that is an inevitable part of living in the world. This sustenance can express the community's love for its members. To destroy government so far as it has this capacity (however limited and problematic it might be in practice) is to destroy this source of sustenance, which means to destroy the good object. The attack on innocence, therefore, exactly parallels the goal of the attack on government, which is to destroy what is good so that all will find themselves in a world ruled by the bad object, which is the world of those consumed by hate.

We can also understand the attack on government as an effort to establish innocence by transferring guilt from self to object (government). Recall the central role this transfer plays in the drama of Mr. Smith in Washington. This transfer exactly parallels the attack on innocence exemplified in the JonBenet Ramsey case, where the parents made their child carry the burden of their own guilt by making her seduce them. The government must become a container for the community's guilt if the innocence or goodness of the community (the nation or the people) is to be maintained.

Government Failure

Animosity toward government expresses and responds to its psychic meaning. Yet, hostility toward government is neither a "mere" psychic construct, nor simply the natural response to the reality of government failure. It is a complex structure combining psychic reality and social institutions in a specific way that roots the real failure of institutions in the psychic reality they are made to represent, while making that psychic reality a result of the real and concrete policies pursued by those institutions. That hostility toward government is not a "mere" psychic construct follows from the very real failure of government in United States. Being captured by particular interest, being shrunk to fit an anti-government agenda, government is less and less a reliable source of security for the individual.

The reality of government failure makes it tempting to blame government for the distrust and hate we direct onto it. Where hatred is involved, locating its origin becomes vital. This is because hating without reason makes us hateful, and to be hateful is to be unworthy of love, to be wholly and irretrievably bad. To avoid this judgment, we must relocate our hate outside. We are not hateful, our object is. We hate because that object provokes hate in us by hateful acts directed toward us.

These hateful acts involve betrayal, deprivation, and exploitation. The government betrays our trust, takes our money and wastes it, which means uses it for the purposes of government (building bureaucracy) rather than the welfare of citizens. Then, government fails to satisfy our wants. Thus, one Democratic Congresswoman from Ohio explains the loss of the Democratic majority in Congress as resulting from the accurate perception on the part of voters that "Democrats didn't solve their problems when they were in office."[22] In her book on *Political Anger*, Susan Tolchin concludes that "voters have every right to be angry and are crying out for new leaders and new options that will directly address their problems."[23] Without disputing the significant element of truth in the charge of government failure, it is also important to understand the way in which that charge participates in the psychic drama of government by assuring that our anger toward government originates not in us but in government. We do not hate government because we are hateful, but because government is.

The charge of government failure also colludes in the construction by which the persistence of social problems, even the persistence of individual frustration in life, is understood as the government's responsibility. Lyndon Johnson's Great Society speech offers a compelling expression of this attitude toward government, which sets government up for failure by investing it with a hope organized around the wished for idealized object. This object is always and altogether good in the sense of always and altogether gratifying. By this standard, government must fail. Tolchin notes this when she points out how people hate government "because they expect more than government can possibly deliver, particularly in this era of budget constraints."[24] Budget constraint assures that government will fail not only by the standard set by an infantile wish for a good object, but by any reasonable standard associated with tasks and goals a real government, if adequately funded, might accomplish.

If we reject government failure as the explanation of animosity toward government, how do we account for or understand the prominent place hatred has in the current relationship between the people and the government? Based on the considerations advanced so far, I would summarize the answer to this question into the following elements.

1) The starting point for hatred is the relation with the bad object, which we hate. The object is bad because it fails to gratify, so hatred is from the outset linked to the problem of gratification.

2) When government is made into a source of gratification, as it has been historically, but especially in the post World War II era, the government cannot avoid getting enmeshed in the relationship with the bad object.

3) When a significant proportion of the population experiences the relationship with a primary object as one of abuse or neglect, and therefore of deprivation, later sources of gratification/frustration in life experience significant pressure to become a site for the reenactment of the original relation with the primary object.

4) The need to externalize the internalized relationship with the bad object becomes the need to identify an external hateful object in the world.

5) In the absence of an external threat to the nation in the form of a hostile outside power, the hateful object will be found inside. The search for a hateful internal object has its natural end in government when government has become a main locus of gratification.

I would suggest that these factors working together lead to the dilemma of government as we have come to know it in the United States.

Closed Circles

Social problems are reenactments of psychic realities, which are produced and reproduced by social institutions and social policy. This should make us hesitate to assume that social policy will solve social problems, since the (unconscious) end of policy is to reproduce the conditions that make it necessary, thus to validate the structure of interaction that created the problems in the first place. I do not mean to imply that we cannot (or should not) identify better and worse policies, but only that we should not expect the better policies to be adopted because they are better, so much as we might expect the worse policies to be adopted because they are worse.

In our public experience, the government plays a central but deeply problematic role. It seeks to protect citizens from violent action driven by primitive emotional states spawned by and within the community. At the same time, through its policies, government supports and perpetuates forms of deprivation and oppression that spawn those primitive states and the violence connected to them. The government is the vehicle for the community's sadistic and hateful feelings, targeting individuals and groups (those dependent on welfare, immigrants, criminals) deemed appropriate objects of collective violence. The government, then, is a vital institution devoted to containing destructive forms of aggression; it is also a vital institution for promoting the aggression it must contain. Policies motivated by hatred, because they perpetuate deprivation and violence, assure the need for government to contain violence. Yet, the government is also the object of the community's aggression, and those who seek to destroy the government also act out the community's unconscious agendas.

Consider in this connection how the organization of the criminal justice system around punishment establishes an equation between the motive behind crime and the motive driving the societal response to crime.[25] Indeed, punishment mirrors the mental processes that lead to the violent acts that some imagine punishment will prevent. To see this, consider, once again, the public response to the Oklahoma City bombing. In the hours immediately following the bombing of the Murrah building, the national media took upon itself the task of chronicling the reactions of local residents, friends, colleagues, and family of those killed or injured. Prominent among these reactions were variations on the theme expressed in the lament "I cannot understand how anyone could do such a thing." Most striking in this response to violence is not, I think, the apparent plea for understanding, but the insistence that such phenomena cannot be understood. Admittedly, those interviewed in Oklahoma City might be genuinely perplexed and frightened by an act they, in fact, did not understand. Yet, not understanding refers as much to an active attitude toward the phenomenon as it does to the absence of a convincing theory that might explain it. To say that we cannot understand what someone has done or said is to insist that they and what they have done are alien to us. To understand, or to attempt to understand, is to insist that even the most horrific act is part of what it is to be human.

The same resistance to knowing is expressed in a sticker that began to appear on cars in Denver following the attack on Columbine High School. This sticker reads: "We are all Columbine." What could this mean? The answer to this question will depend on what we consider Columbine to represent. Presumably "Columbine" is meant here to refer to the victims, although Klebold and Harris were also part of Columbine, in some sense as much so as their victims. Yet the form of the statement, with its clear allusion to solidarity with the victims of Nazi atrocities, suggests not only who we are, but also, and perhaps more importantly, who we are not.

To speak of those we can know and those we cannot is to make a statement about our selves, most importantly a statement about who or what we are not. At the center of this statement is the denial of hatred. We do not hate. Those who do hate are not like us. We cannot understand them, we can only defend ourselves against them. This denial of connection with those who hate expresses our denial of connection with the bad object, including the denial of our own badness.

While violence is never senseless, it can be thoughtless, and in this way justify the judgment that it is beyond understanding. Violence stems from what Hanna Segal refers to as the "symbolic equation" in which "thoughts are equated with and become actions."[26] In violence, action replaces words. Indeed, as the "symbolic representations of thoughts," actions "can take the place of thinking in words, if the behavior is never interpreted or translated into words and ideas."[27] Because actions, including violent actions, express feelings and thoughts, they are never senseless. When we insist that they are, we refuse to receive the communication at the level of thought. Rather, we insist on receiving it on its own level: as action rather than thought. Thus we punish the perpetrators rather than understanding them.

Sasha Abramsky describes how a punitive and sadistic prison system transforms those who have merely broken laws into murderers:

> Robert Scully evolved into a murderer while housed at Pelican Bay. There he experienced some of the harshest confinement conditions known in the democratic world. Highly disturbed to start with, he was kept in a sensory deprivation box for years on end.

Psychologists and psychiatrists called in by his defense team believe that he simply lost the ability to think through the consequences of his actions. He became a creature of brutal and obsessive impulse.[28]

Using government as its vehicle, society creates a class of violent criminals that expresses the "social chaos" whose persistence enters into the indictment of government. Because it must sponsor social decay, we can hardly expect government to cure or prevent it. By using government in this way, we assure that our response to violence will perpetuate violence, that government will express the community's persecutory feelings and violent impulses.

The complexity of government's role mirrors the complexity of the community's psychic life. To understand the complex and often contradictory mandate of government will allow us to understand government's failure, and thus the tendency for social problems to fester and perpetuate themselves in the face of a series of policies ostensibly meant to solve them. To understand government's failure, then, we must understand the psychic life of the community.[29] The dilemma of government allows us to see that the community does, indeed, have a psychic life, that the term is no mere metaphor that falsely treats collectives and institutions as if they were individuals, but a way of expressing a fundamental reality of contemporary experience.

5 ABUSE OF POWER

Corruption

In the attack on government, no charge looms larger than corruption. If power corrupts, and if government holds power, then power corrupts government, and government corrupts those involved with it. Distrust of government expresses both the idea that government is a locus of power, and the idea that the greater the power of government, the greater the abuse of citizens.

Corruption has a strong moral connotation. Something is corrupt when it has lost its moral standing. We can see from this how the idea of corruption might find a central place in the attack on government, which is concerned with the distance between the reality of government and its moral ideal. As one candidate for President put it, we must fight "with conviction and courage to rescue God's country from the cultural and moral pit into which she has fallen."[1] In moral language, we corrupt someone by enticing him or her to place desire above duty. Thus, according to Buchanan, the "money men" have "rearranged the primary schedule and rigged the game to protect the party favorites."

Those for whom moral strictures rather than ethical character guide conduct must always struggle against temptation. Confusing temptation for sin, they experience themselves as corrupt. Projecting that self-experience into the world, they see corruption around them, especially in the centers of power. The greater the power, the greater the temptation, the greater the sin. When right conduct means resisting temptation, it requires an intense self-repression. Because right conduct demands self-repression, it provokes anger and resistance, experienced also as a desire to repress others.

To accommodate the tension built into this situation, the energy of desire gets channeled into the sadistic impulse to repress others. In sadism, the moral character finds a desire it need not repress so long as it serves morality. This alleviates the tension between duty and desire. We will find, then, built into the moral position, a secret passageway to desire. Thus, morality, which is duty repressing desire, has a tendency to turn into its opposite: desire masquerading as duty.[2] When desire masquerades as duty, corruption appears in the guise of virtue. We can see, then, how morality keeps corruption close at hand, and why the moral character finds so much corruption in its world.

We can put this another way. The internal repression of desire in the name of morality places an obstacle in desire's path. In so doing, it sets in motion a psychic campaign aimed at finding ways to circumvent that obstacle. This obstacle takes specific shape as the self-reproach that attends any failure to live up to moral standards built into the individual's ego ideal. The agency of the mind responsible for exerting pressure on the individual to comply with duty (an agency Freud terms the superego) can inflict substantial psychic pain in the interest of controlling conduct and directing it away from desire. The problem, then, is to follow desire without provoking the superego in its work of control.

Sadistic attacks on others engaged in pursuing satisfaction of desire are one way of following desire without provoking self-reproach, but there are others. I may be able to convince myself that desire and duty are one and the same, or that I am forced to act on self-interest to protect myself from the immoral and threatening conduct of others. In other words, I might adopt the strategy of the grandiose self for whom what is good for the self is the good: "*l'etat, c'est moi*" or "what is good for General Motors is good for America." Or, I might adopt the strategy of the paranoid self, for whom all seemingly immoral conduct is driven by persecution from outside.

Fred Pine's discussion of Euripide's *Medea* offers a good example of the way a feeling of persecution can relieve the restrictions on conduct normally associated with morality while nonetheless remaining squarely within a moral universe and a moral ideal for conduct. Pine describes Medea's internal experience as "a compound of a sense of injury—a sense that builds to imagined public humiliation—and a sense of righteousness."[3] Medea has been abandoned by her husband, and in revenge she kills her two sons. Medea justifies acts clearly in violation of the moral code by insisting, as violent criminals inevitably do, that she has been driven to these acts by the injury others have done to her.[4] She is not, then, responsible; they are (just as the government is responsible for killing the children in the day care center in Oklahoma City because of the children killed in the attack in Waco).

Medea's state of mind closely parallels the state of mind Hyatt-Williams describes finding in those who commit murder. Murderous patients, he notes "whether they had committed the deed or not, were bogged down in a state of mind in which persecutory anxiety dominated...." Such anxiety is experienced as a response to a threat, which may be internal or external, actual or imagined. The perception of an external threat results in a state of mind in which "aggrievement is rampant and responsibility muted."[5] Of special importance here is the muting of responsibility. The experience of persecutory anxiety offers a powerful solution to the problem of overcoming moral restrictions on conduct.

Guy Adams and Danny Balfour have recently termed the phenomenon just described "moral inversion," which they consider in administrative settings.[6] Organizations are powerful settings for moral inversion since they offer a particularly effective set of mechanisms for circumventing the prospect of self-reproach and psychic pain otherwise likely to result from conduct driven by desire, especially sadistic desire. Indeed, the temptation toward moral inversion is especially strong in organizations, including the organization that is our special concern here: the government.

In organizations, the danger takes a number of different forms. The one Freud emphasizes, and which forms the main subject of Adams and Balfour's analysis, is the transfer of the task of judging conduct from the inner world to the organization and its leader. Freud emphasizes how individuals in groups lose their capacity for autonomous judgment by merging into the group and replacing their individual superego with that of the group. This phenomenon is exemplified when conduct of doubtful moral standing is justified as following orders.

More directly relevant here is a related phenomenon having to do with the distinction between office-holder and person, professional ethics and personal conduct. The office holder has a set of duties, or fiduciary responsibilities, and a professional ethical code. To act as an office holder is to act in the interest of others or of the organization as a whole (in the case of government, to act in the public interest). Outside the office, the person is free to act (at least up to a point) on desire rather than professional ethics. Thus, in organizations, the internal distinction between desire and duty (for Freud between id and superego) becomes an external distinction between office and person. Corruption means using the office to satisfy desires of the person who occupies it. Doing so is what we mean by abuse of power.

Consider, in this connection, the charges recently leveled against Bill Clinton and Al Gore that they used their offices (literally in Gore's case his office telephone) to raise money for the Democratic Party. Whatever the facts of the case, we can see how easy it can be to rationalize use of office to secure reelection (as it was for Richard Nixon), which may be more or less inevitable in the American political system. It might be argued, for example, that securing reelection is, indeed, in the public interest given the danger the opposing party poses to the public well being. What seems to us abuse of power seems to the office holder a way of securing the public trust. And, in any case, everyone does it; so if I don't, I risk losing my office to those clearly more venal than I am.

How great a step is it from such rationalization to the argument that soliciting, or even simply accepting the offer of, sex from subordinates is not corrupt because it helps the office holder do his or her job well. Thus, a head of the National Institute of Mental health remarks about Congressmen: "whenever you have a campaign situation or a situation with a lot of high tension and a lot of power, power is the great aphrodisiac. Sex is one of the great tension relievers."[7] When confronted with the explosive combination of stress and power, the moral standpoint proves itself susceptible to corruption. The irony in this is the response, which denounces weakness of moral character when the intensity of the moral upbringing is most likely the cause of the problem rather than its solution.

Abuse of power is inherently a relationship between the strong and the weak. It depends on a situation in which one depends on another for something vital to his or her well-being. Government offers a setting for such relationships, which reinforces its position within a universe of moral thinking and moral struggle. To understand the animosity toward government embodied in the charge of corruption, we need, then, to consider more deeply the psychic meaning of power.

Asserting Power

A student of mine tells the story of his eight-year-old nephew, who having been abused by a bully in school, came home at the end of the day and beat up his little sister. This is a common story, and writ large is also the story of the conduct of those with power towards those without: violence against those with HIV, violence against outcastes in India, violence of men against women, of parents against children. There is, indeed, much to fear in the powerful.

Why do the powerful attack the less powerful rather than vice versa? Should we not expect the oppressed to attack their oppressors, out of anger at their oppression or a desire to overcome it? As I suggest above, the oppressed do commit acts of violence, but not primarily against their oppressors. Consider, in this connection, the Navajo reservation, where "violence is becoming the norm … more a sport than a crime."[8] Here, the murder rate in 1998 was four times the national average. Much of the violence is brutal and essentially random. One man was bludgeoned to death because "he picked the wrong time to take his trash out." The two young men who stood trial "couldn't come up with a reason for the event but said they were sorry." The oppressed, and certainly those on the reservation deserve to be called that, do commit acts of violence, but not against those who oppress, or might be thought to oppress, them.

Easy explanations are available for all of this. The powerful attack the weak to keep them weak, therefore in their place. The powerful attack the weak because of the corrupting effect of having power. The oppressed attack each other because their anger needs an outlet, and their fellows are available. Whatever the merits of such explanations, they also leave out of account what is arguably most significant about such phenomena, the identification between victim and victimizer.

The part played by identification should be clear for the example of violence on the reservation. Here, violence against others who are like us means violence against ourselves as seen in others. Identification with the victim is powerful, and the attack on the victim expresses not only, or even primarily, hatred for him or her, but hatred for our selves. The role of identification may seem less clear when the powerful attack the weak; but, here too identification plays a primary role.

Anna Freud's notion of identification with the aggressor captures part of the psychic process involved. If we assume that the powerful, like my student's nephew, have themselves been the victims of power, then we can understand their attack on the weak as an attempt to reverse roles in their original humiliation by humiliating others. This means, of course, that their identification with those who have oppressed them is also an identification with their victims, who represent their victimized selves. Their hate for their victims is a hate for a self that allowed itself to be victimized and humiliated.

I will consider identification with the aggressor more fully in the chapter on justice. Here, I am more concerned with the psychic meaning of power, which is bound up with this identification. The secret of power over others is the experience of victimization and thus humiliation, and the need to relieve the shame borne of that experience by transferring it onto others. This same connection between oppressor (powerful) and oppressed (powerless) can be projected by either party into the external world in the form of fear of persecution. Further, once the idea of power as the force used to transfer victimization takes hold psychically, fear of the powerful is not only justified in principle, but represents fear of a projected powerful self. This is the side of power that gets played out in the fear of a powerful government.

Psychically, hatred and fear go together. The more we hate, the greater our fear. This is because what we fear is a projection of our own hate. The intensity of the feelings we have toward an object outside becomes, via projection, the power that object is felt to have to harm us. Because hatred creates (psychically) the powerful for us, the more we hate, the more power we have to fear, and the more power becomes something to fear. Thus, the more intense our victimization and humiliation, the more intense our hatred, the greater the power we attribute to and the fear we have of the hated object. This holds for those who make government the object of hate and fear. The more we hate the government, the more powerful it appears to us, and the more we have to fear from it. Power, then, has a special psychic meaning closely linked to hatred.

In considering this psychic meaning of power, I will take the idea of narcissistic love considered in chapter 1 as the archetype for power over others. It is an archetype in that it contains the essential meaning of power over others, and it is an archetype in that it is the earliest and most primitive form of such power. Narcissistic love is also the archetype of the abuse of power. The absolute dependence of the child on the parent constitutes the parent as a potentially powerful figure in the child's life. Whether the parent chooses to exert power over the child or to limit and direct in other ways is an important matter. Much depends on how broadly or narrowly we define power. I begin, therefore, with a clarification of the idea of power, which I can then apply to the problem of government.

Subjectivity

Narcissistic love subordinates the need of the child to that of the parent. This only makes sense if we can consider the child to have needs of his or her own, that is to say, needs beyond those of mere physical sustenance.

Narcissistic love need not get in the way of the parent attending to the basic physical needs of the child. Narcissistic love has to do, rather, with the way those needs are satisfied, and therefore with the psychic needs that are or are not satisfied in the relationship that satisfies the physical needs.

Up to this point, I have emphasized connection as the psychic need of the child. But, as I also suggest, it is not connection in the abstract that is important, but the quality of the connection, which is to say its psychic meaning. In object-related love, the goal of connection is not the need of the parent for narcissistic gratification, but the child's need to express and develop a sense of a separate existence as having a self (his or her own self) that is worthy of love. In brief, we can say that the child's need for love is the need to feel worthy of love, which is the starting point for the development of a feeling of self-worth (having a worthwhile self). We must deal with power, then, in the context of the feeling of worthiness, and how the use of power attacks and undermines that feeling. In narcissistic love, the parent uses the dependence of the child to undermine any sense the child might develop of the value of a separate self. This attack on self-worth is part of the meaning of narcissistic love, and connects it to the idea of power.

What applies to the relationship between parent and child also applies, albeit in a different way, to the relationship between the individual and the social institution (e.g. government). At this level, I will speak of the feeling of being worthy of love (self-worth) in the language of autonomy. What is at stake in matters of power at the level of social institutions is the capacity to act, or to be the subject of action. I will refer to the primary end on the basis of whose attainment we may judge institutions as individual subjectivity. By individual subjectivity, I have in mind the individual's capacity to act as a subject in his or her life, in relation to things and to others.[9]

In psychoanalytic theory this capacity is sometimes spoken of in the language of the "self" or the "true self."[10] In the words of Christopher Bollas, the true self is "the unique presence of being that each of us is; the idiom of our personality." We experience this "presence" as an internal state, and we express it through our actions, including our interactions with others. Yet, the experience of our (true) selves and its expression in action and interaction are not inevitable. The environment of the true self, both internal (the psyche) and external (the world of interaction and of organizations), may or may not facilitate our living a life expressive of this original vitality, this quality of "aliveness itself."[11]

Our connection with the true self determines the quality of our subjective experience, and the meaning of our actions in the world. The connection with the true self makes experience subjectively meaningful, the expression of a subject who acts. Being the subject of one's own action should be distinguished from being the object of other's action, the agent of others, or the instrument of forces outside our knowledge and control. The alternative to subjectivity is compliance, which expresses domination by another.

Bollas speaks of this distinction in the language of fate and destiny.[12] Destiny refers to a life experience organized around our unique presence of being, a working out in action and accomplishment of the inner sense of who we are. The presence of the true self as the animating principle of life projects gives meaning to life for the individual, which is the meaning of subjectivity in the way I will use the term here. By contrast, fate refers to capricious forces acting on the individual, forces that only by accident allow realization of ends associated with subjective action in the world.

Bollas offers an example of rule by fate when he describes the family experience of one of his patients:

> [Her parents] periodically intervened fatefully in her life by commanding her (and one another) into certain drastically alternative actions, such as suddenly changing schools, clothing styles, households, friends, or vacations. Everything was topsy-turvy. What would mother or father declare next? And these declarations were fateful, as they directly affected the life of the children, who found themselves continually cast into new situations.[13]

In this example, the parents have and exert power over their children. The experience of being the object of the exercise of power is also the experience of having a life ruled not by your own subjectivity (your needs and intentions) but by fate. In relationships involving power, the capriciousness exemplified here plays a prominent role. To be the object of the exercise of power is to be subject to the will, therefore the willfulness, of others. To make power real, the powerful must also be willful.

The effort to control others, or have power over them, has significant meaning to those who use others to deal with their own psychic conflict. This does not mean, however, that those individuals have a meaningful subjective existence in the world. For those engaged in the effort to control others, the connection to objects may involve the most intense experience, for example of anger, fear, hope, and so on. This is because psychic survival, and the hope (or the fear) of attaining (or of losing) a longed for psychic experience, is always at stake in interaction. Yet, the subjective experience built into the exercise of power (the willful control of others) does not express the real vitality of the true self. Rather, it is bound up with the need to transfer the repression of that vitality onto others. Thus, in relations of power, true subjectivity exists at neither pole. Power marks the impoverishment of subjective experience as much for the powerful as for the powerless.

To see this more clearly, it will help to emphasize the connection between subjective experience and the subject of experience. That is, subjective experience refers not simply to the internal quality of the experience, but also to its connection with agency (the quality that establishes the subject of experience). Processes that impoverish subjective experience, even though they are undertaken by the subject him- or herself, diminish the presence of the true self as an active force in experience. Recourse to splitting and externalization has the important consequence of suppressing the capacity for agency, which is the capacity to be a subject of action in the world.

This suppression of agency bears on the individual's well-being so far as well-being refers to a state in which the capacity for individual agency is secure. The experience of well-being depends on the individual's ability to establish secure self-boundaries without which there can be little meaning to the goal of being yourself in the world. Well-being in this sense depends on institutional considerations such as those bound up with a system of individual rights that secure the self in relation to other selves.

If our goal is to secure well-being in the sense just considered, then clearly government has a large role to play, since it is government that secures rights and thus makes it possible for the individual to be him or her self in the world. If this is the case, it follows that those involved in the attack on government have a different agenda, even where they appeal to the rhetoric of freedom. And, indeed, we know that psychically, the project of the attack on government is not to secure liberty, but to deal with inner conflict. Individuals involved in the movement against government are consumed by the task of employing primitive mechanisms for expelling intolerable feelings, which generally means imposing them on others. A semblance of selfhood can be retrieved only in the act of destroying that selfhood in others, since, for such individuals, destruction of self is the activity identified with being subject rather than victim (thing). Thus, the difference between activity and passivity is equated with the difference between domination and being dominated. This construction is then projected onto others, who are assumed also to equate selfhood with domination. As a result of this projection, its container, government, becomes a powerful and dangerous force that must be weakened if not destroyed. Those who are not subjects (do not dominate and destroy) must be victims. We might say, then, that individuals in this condition face a dilemma since destruction of self (in other) is the only way they know to be a self. This means, of course, that they must destroy what it is they most desire, or face its destruction at the hands of others assumed to be similarly organized. Within this construction of the world, difference (different self) is a threat.

Power and Subjective Ends

The term power connects, then, to the impairment of subjectivity. Power also refers, however, to the capacity of a subject to achieve its ends, therefore to the subject's effectivity. Before continuing with the discussion of power as the impairment of subjectivity, let me consider briefly this other aspect of power.

We can, of course, take both subjectivity and the subject's ends for granted, as is the normal procedure in discussions of power. That is, we can assume that the actor is the subject of his or her action, and that whatever ends are pursued through action are the ends in terms of which effectivity is to be determined. This makes effectivity the capacity to achieve ends whatever they may be. Proceeding in this way is not consistent, however, with the notion of subjectivity introduced in the previous section. The fact that we act in a particular way, pursue ends of a particular kind, does not necessarily make us subjects of our action.

This may be because we consciously act for others, as their agents. But, it may also be because the ends we adopt as our own are not really ours, but express our compliance with the needs of others, or their ability to shape our ends in their interest and not our own.[14] Alternatively, our ends may be alien to us not because they serve the interests of others, but because they express our own failed subjectivity, which is to say they express the repression of the true self. It is this last possibility that I will emphasize here.

Given these considerations, we must have two notions of power connected to the idea of effectivity. The first simply connects power to the capacity to attain stated ends, however those ends relate to the self. The second connects power to the capacity to know and achieve subjectively meaningful ends that are our own in that they are connected to the true self.

Power in the second sense has two dimensions, one internal, and the other external. The internal dimension is expressed in the idea of meaningful ends. The individual's ability to define meaningful ends depends on an inner, psychic, configuration, one that integrates, rather than represses, the true self. The external dimension is expressed in the design of institutions that facilitate rather than impede the realization of the self in activity and interaction. Put in Bollas's language, power is the individual's ability to fulfill his or her destiny. To be able to do so is to be the subject of one's life. To be unable to do so is to live a life ruled by fate.

If power understood in this way is problematic, it is because of doubts that arise concerning the possibility of fulfilling a destiny rather than living a life ruled by fate. Particularly for those whose worlds, both internal and external, foster a sense of futility, the idea of subjectivity must seem a cruel illusion. For such individuals, the natural response to those capable of pursuing a subjectively meaningful life is to do what they can to deny them the opportunity, so that hopelessness and futility can be made, or made to seem, an objective rather than subjective reality. This denial of others plays a large part in organizational life, in institutional design, and especially in the ideal of participation to which I turn in Chapter 6. It also plays a large part in the attempt to weaken government, which, if successful, will assure that no one can act effectively as subject in his or her life.

The inner sense of futility can express itself in the effort to undermine others, but it also has another important expression, in the manic denial of limits and frustrations, whether internal or external. Manic denial expresses itself in the idea that all we desire can be gained if only we have the will to do so. Obstacles to attaining our ends may be in the world outside, in the form of others, or they may be internal, in the form of our own desires, feelings, and thoughts. The manic response depends, then, on repression of an unacceptable alternative: the futility of action in the world. As we will see in the next chapter, the movement between fate and destiny, futility and the manic denial of futility, organizes the free market solution to the problem of government. That solution constitutes a way of organizing power that expresses the fear of power in others, and the omnipotent fantasy of the power of the individual.

The manic state connects to power's alternative meaning: the pursuit of ends unconnected to the true self. To see this, we need to consider how severing the link between power and subjectively meaningful ends connects power to domination. Disconnection of ends from the true self means disconnection of action from the individual's "unique sense of being." The absence of the individual element in conduct means the repression of that element, which is also the moment of freedom or self-determination. Notions of power that disconnect it from subjectively meaningful ends must, therefore, connect power to repression. Because it has repression as its end, the power associated with the manic state is obviously a danger to self and other, and it is the sense of this danger that accounts for the flight from power typical of certain democratic ideals.[15]

The two forms of power bear important connections to the distinction between fate and destiny. As I suggest above, the power to pursue and realize our destiny connects in a positive way to subjectivity. This is not true of the power connected to the manic state, which is linked not to destiny but to fate. The power to repress the self is the power to frustrate and deny the individual's most basic aspiration both in self and in others. With regard to others, this is the power to subject them to external forces, which are from their point of view arbitrary. Those who are dominated by others are subject to their will. This subjection to the will of the other can only be real when it contains the element of arbitrary rule. If rule follows a law outside the individual who rules, then it is the rule of that law and not of that individual. This is rule, but it is not domination of one over another, and therefore it is not fully the expression of the power of one over another.

It is the capricious element that identifies power of the second kind. The point is not that rule by another is inherently capricious from the ruler's point of view, though this is certainly an essential element. The point is, rather, that such rule is arbitrary from the point of view of the ruled. And, to some important degree, for rule to be capricious for the ruled it must also be so for the ruler. This capriciousness is expressed in the idea of fate.

This last point brings us back once again to the problem of narcissism. One notable expression of what Otto Kernberg refers to as pathological narcissism is a "chronic overdependence on objects." This chronic overdependence is expressed, as Heinz Kohut emphasizes, in the fragility of self-esteem, which depends on the admiration of others. More generally, self-feeling is contingent on the feeling others hold (and that they can be made to hold) about the self. This kind of dependence on others places them in a position of power over us, since they control what is most important to us, our feeling about our selves. Thus, we can say that the narcissistically disturbed individual experiences him- or herself as situated in a world organized around relationships of power.

If we consider the possibility that the anxiety provoked by existence in such a world can be dealt with by projection, then the experience of being subject to the power of others is also projected on to others so far as possible. The success of this projection will depend on the extent to which the power of others over the subject can be turned into the subject's power over them. Thus, we can express the subjective reality of the narcissistic personality in the language of power, and we can understand something about the psychic meaning of power if we understand better its connection to the psychic demands of pathological narcissism. Once we understand that the psychic reality of pathological narcissism is the reality of power, we can also see how the attack on government expresses the need to put that subjective reality into the external world as a way of relieving the pain it causes when contained inside.

To the extent that power is bound up with the psychic needs of the narcissistic personality, we cannot presume that the problems power poses for subjectivity can be resolved by altering institutions. This is because, so far as pathological narcissism is an important element in the psychic life of the community, those institutions must be consistent with the demands of a personality structure essentially bound up with the inter-subjective experience of power. Institutions must validate the projection of psychic experience into the outside world. When this does not mean the actual destruction of government, it means the weakening of government so it cannot assure the protection of individual integrity, which must be made vulnerable. The goal of changing institutions will not be eliminating the need to deal with the "chronic overdependence on objects," which is the root of the relation of power and domination. Rather, institutions will be molded to fit and express that need. Then, the character of institutions is the result of the prevailing psychic reality within the community.

Powerlessness

While the notion that power involves the capacity to accomplish ends has an intuitive appeal, its connection to the presence of a subject is in some ways problematic. Indeed, the exercise of power when linked to domination attacks subjectivity, and can be thought to have its real end in the destruction of the subject. Thus, subjectively, the end of power is to destroy subjectivity in the other. But, psychically, this destruction of subjectivity in other is a reenactment of a prior destruction of subjectivity in the self. When, as I suggest above, caprice plays a vital role in the exercise of power, the purpose in exercising power is not to attain a meaningful end even for those who exercise it, but to create a relationship whose real end is the destruction of subjectivity. When this happens, power as effectivity exists only in a negative sense.

Saying that power exists in a negative sense introduces the idea of powerlessness, and the possibility that institutions do not instantiate the power (effectivity) of some at the expense of others, but institute a kind of futility (fate) for all. The only difference is in who appears at the active and who at the passive pole of the relationship. While activity is often confused with effectivity, the two are not the same. When our purpose in acting is primarily to deny passivity, passivity rather than effectivity is its real driving force; then, activity is put in service of fate rather than destiny.[16] The manic quality of action denies, as it reveals its root in, passivity, since it defends against the prospect of being moved to the passive pole of the relationship.

The idea of powerlessness is important for understanding the relationship between individual and social institutions. To fix ideas, let me take an example from Mario Vargas Lhosa's novel *The Storyteller*. In this novel, a writer spends six months producing a Peruvian television program called the "Tower of Babel." He is told by the owner of the station that, if he organizes his time well enough, production will take only half his day leaving the other half for writing. He soon discovers, however, that, "in this case, as in so many others, theory was one thing and practice another."

The planning process for each program "went like a charm." The team members "were full of ideas and eager to discover the creative possibilities of the most popular medium of communication of our time." What they discovered in practice was another matter: "dependence on material factors in an underdeveloped country, the subtle way in which they subvert the best intentions and thwart the most diligent efforts." In the end, the great bulk of their time was not spent on creative efforts, but "wasted in an attempt to solve problems that at first sight seemed trivial and unworthy of our notice."

To get the station's van to pick them up in the morning, they "had to go personally to the drivers' home and wake them up, go with them to the channel's offices to collect the recording equipment and from there to the airport or wherever." Even having accomplished this much, it might turn out that the battery was dead or that "higher ups had neglected to authorize the replacement of an oil pan, an exhaust pipe, a tire ripped to shreds the day before on the murderous potholes along the Avenida Arequippa."

When the film was produced, the images on the screen turned out to be "marred by strange smudges." It seemed the filters needed replacing. "But how to go about getting this done? We tried everything short of murder, and nothing worked." They sent memos; they begged; they argued; they even went to the owner-director of the station. "They all agreed with us, they were all indignant, they all issued strict orders that the filters be replaced." But nothing changed; the smudges did not go away.

There were schedules for use of cutting rooms and sound studios. "But in point of fact it was not the schedules but the cunning and clever maneuvering of each producer or technician that determined who would have more or less time for editing and recording, and who could count on the best equipment." Their plans and ideas were inevitably defeated "by all-powerful, omnipresent, imponderables." These all-powerful, omnipresent, imponderables represent fate, whose rule stands in the way of subjectivity. Fate has two vital features: it is powerful, and it is imponderable.

We can, of course, consider the external environment the primary threat to subjectivity, as seems to be the case in the example just presented. And, in a sense, it is, so long as we assume that the potential to develop subjective experience and to realize subjectivity in the world are both vitally dependent on the encounter with the objects on which we depend. But, there is also the matter of the inner world to consider, and how its relation to the world outside bears on subjectivity.

To see how fate and power shape psychic experience, consider for a moment the vignette in the Lhosa novel not as a picture of an experience in the (external) world, but as a picture of the inner world, a fantasy expressive of psychic reality. This world is populated by people marked by indifference toward others, self-absorption, and a degree of (albeit passive) hostility toward the idea that anyone might imagine himself the subject of his life. This world may be real enough for some people in some settings, but it is also a fantasy of powerlessness. No one has power because everyone is doing everything he or she can to frustrate all plans.

What is accomplished in a world where nothing can be accomplished?

The answer is the living death of subjectivity. In this world, each individual (and therefore all individuals taken as a whole, the society) devotes him or her self to the task of denying and ultimately destroying subjective experience and the original vitality such experience expresses. The psychic theme, then, of the individual and of the society is psychic death. The connection between individual and social lies in the necessity that individual loss be made collective, and collective be made individual, the need that the subjective become the objective and the objective the subjective.

Central to this need is the pain the individual experiences at the prospect that only his or her subjectivity has died, while for others the prospect for subjective experience remains alive. Thus, as Gilligan points out, "only the living dead could want to kill the living," just as no one who cherishes and feels his own aliveness, could want to kill another human being." Indeed, "the living dead need to kill others, because for them the most unendurable anguish is the pain of seeing that others are still alive." What applies to the death of the body (murder), applies also to the death of the soul (or, in our terms, the death of subjectivity). Indeed, as Gilligan puts it, "the death of the soul is of far greater concern than the death of the body."[17] For those who are unable to lead a life expressive of an original vitality, the greatest pain is caused by having to see others who are able to do so. The more the world is shaped by the need to avoid this experience, the more psychic reality is made objective social reality.

This is an instance of the alleviation of psychic pain by transferring its cause from the inner world to the outer. The attempt to alleviate pain in this way creates social institutions that assure that the individual's loss is a group rather than an individual experience. Any failure in the oppression of the individual threatens to send the experience of impotence back into the inner world, where the pain it causes cannot be tolerated. The obstacle to establishing the individual as a subject in the world is, then, the need to make that world contain unacceptable aspects of self-experience.

Institutions organized around domination attack subjectivity. Whether individuals within these institutions adopt an active or passive role, the meaning of what they do is the same: repression of subjectivity. Since, in a world of institutions organized around domination, there is no meaningful subjectivity, we can say that there is no power. Alternatively, we can say that the power to deprive the individual of subjectively meaningful experience resides in the institutions, or structures of interaction, themselves, and not in the individuals who are at best their agents. Institutions are, then, built around the idea of repression (of subjectivity).

It is this idea, instantiated in institutions rather than the will or the interests of individuals and groups, that accounts for the loss of subjectivity. We can say, then, that the powerful do not use their power to advance their own interests, or at least this is not the true meaning of the exercise of power. Rather the powerful use their power to make sure that no one can advance his or her real interests (those connected to the true self).

The idea of individuals as agents of institutions plays a prominent role in discussions of power. Thus, Hannah Arendt describes a type of bureaucratic organization "in which no men, neither one nor the best, neither the few nor the many, can be held responsible, and which could be properly called rule by Nobody."[18] In a different context, Karl Marx and Max Weber each describe the capitalist, who we might consider the primary subject in a modern economy, not as a locus of power, but as a mere "agent" (Marx) or "steward" (Weber) of his capital. In these settings, power disappears, and individuals are not effective in establishing their subjectivity in the world, which they lose not due to the domination of others but due to the organization and ends built into institutions.

This turns the main claim of modern society against itself. A modern institution is one in which power gives way to legitimate authority; the individual is not subject to the caprice of others, and is protected as well from the caprice of groups. The claim is made, however, that individuals gain this freedom only by giving subjectivity to overpowering institutions: the market and the bureaucracy. For those who see markets and bureaucracy as the enemies of freedom, the problem of power is compounded, since those institutions historically advanced to combat power become the primary instruments of power. I consider this prospect in greater detail in the next section.

When we define government in the space of power and powerlessness, we focus attention on the problem of deprivation. Is government an agent for those who would assure that no one has power? Or, is government the agent by which society assures so far as possible the effectivity of its members in the world?

It is difficult to answer this question because of government's engagement with both tasks. Government is the agent of the community's collective agenda. When that agenda centers on rule by fate, government becomes the agent of deprivation and oppression. Such a government must not secure the effectivity of others, but rather assure that they are equally deprived. But, government also represents the aspirations of the community to assure the safety of its members as individuals (citizens).

Therefore, government represents the alternative to powerlessness.

The attack on government targets primarily this latter aspect of its mission. Since effective government institutes the ideal of a community of autonomous agents, each capable of acting as a center of initiative, it is the antidote to a world ruled by fate. It must therefore be weakened to assure that all are deprived of the power that would liberate them from the futility of a life ruled by fate.

The Power of Government

We can refer to the use of position for the purposes of exerting power over others as the abuse of power, although in the way we use the term here, power over others and abuse of power have the same meaning. Given this equation, government can only be powerful so far as it can intervene fatefully in the lives of citizens, intervene, that is, in a way that deprives them of subjectivity.

The link between power, rule, and fate tells us much about the psychic meaning of government. So far as we imagine government to be a powerful ruler, the attack on government becomes an act of liberation. This is true whether the goal of that attack is to destroy government, or only to deprive it of its power to rule (for example by replacing government with markets or with participation). On the surface at least, the attack on government, formulated in the language of power, is about freedom. And this is, indeed, consistent with the self-understanding and rhetoric of those who wish to eliminate government, make it smaller, subject it to the will of the people, and so on:

> We know from history that it is a natural tendency of government to seek power, and never to relinquish it. In our lifetime, we have seen government grow to where it consumes 40% of family income. Not long ago, that was called Socialism.[19]

At the same time, underlying the rhetoric of liberation associated with the attack on government is an agenda that would, if successful, assure that power and fate rule everyone's lives. Without government, we are all vulnerable to the depredations of the powerful; we are all potential victims. The loss of government is the loss of a regime of rights that protect the individual from the power of others. This means that the unconscious end of the attack on government is to make the external world mirror the psychic reality of an inner world organized around power and fate.

For those who would replace government with markets, freedom means rule by a world organized to celebrate a predatory narcissism instantiated into law, and turned from vice to virtue. For those who would subject government to the will of the people, freedom means subjection of the individual to the group. These are the two solutions to the problem of government I consider in the next two chapters.

6 THE FREE MARKET SOLUTION

The Invisible Hand

I now turn to a more explicit consideration of the alternative to government associated with the ideal of the free market. The ideal of the free market offers the wished for escape from government, an escape into the private sphere. Indeed, as an historical matter, free in connection to markets refers to their quality of being disembedded from government and family.[1] Disembedded means that the ends of economic activity are now the ends of individuals acting for themselves, rather than members acting for a corporate or collective unit.

Disembedding the market originally implied a policy of laissez-faire. According to this policy, not only was the market to be separated from the state, the state was not to interfere in its operations. The term free market, then, meant not only that the market would be a separate institution from government, but also that it would be independent of government influence. It is this independence of government influence (or regulation) that we today have in mind when we speak of a free market.

Arguments for the free market should not be confused with arguments for the use of markets as a general matter, since we can make significant use of markets in organizing our economies without the severe restriction on government involvement implied in the notion of a free market. To favor use of markets, then, does not in itself imply animosity toward, or distrust of, government.

The free market offers, or is claimed to offer, protection from coercion.[2] It also, then, expresses the fear of power considered in the last chapter. In the words of free market economist Milton Friedman:

The fundamental threat to freedom is power to coerce, be it in the hands of a monarch, a dictator, an oligarchy, or a momentary majority. The preservation of freedom requires the elimination of such concentration of power to the fullest possible extent and the dispersal and distribution of whatever power cannot be eliminated—a system of checks and balances. By removing the organization of economic activity from the control of political authority, the market eliminates this source of coercive power.[3]

Setting out from the premise that government is a locus or instrument of power, Friedman draws the conclusion that less government means less coercion, and therefore more freedom.

Assuming that government is a locus or instrument of power deprives it of any moral standing, except the negative standing associated with the abuse of power. This is, in itself, a significant judgment about government. Once we adopt it, we are inevitably driven to an ideal of limited government. Even were we to assume the existence of public ends we will do best to achieve them, so far as possible, not through the use of government, but by other means. This is the argument Adam Smith puts forward for limiting government. Smith does not deny public ends, but he does insist that government is poorly designed for achieving them because it creates a public power likely to be used for private ends. For Smith, the interests of the nation can be accomplished with minimum constraint on the pursuit of private ends. If this is correct, then the idea of a national interest does not require that a public authority regulate private interest.[4]

For Smith, to accomplish public ends we need an institution that does not constitute a center of power. The market is such an institution. In the market, the individual "neither intends to promote the publick interest, nor knows how much he is promoting it." Yet, while intending his own gain, he is led by an "invisible hand" to accomplish something not a part of his purpose: the maximization of the nation's wealth.[5]

Individuals might not know the public interest; certainly they might not know it as well as they know their particular interests. They might get the public interest wrong. The power of their self-interest might also cloud their judgment about the public interest. The power of self-interest means that the government, or those who occupy positions in it, will likely sacrifice the public interest to it. This makes government a poor bet to oversee the use of resources or the growth of national wealth. Because of this, the less government the better. Smith suggests, therefore, that we restrict the government to tasks connected to public safety, national defense, and those investment projects whose scale is too large to be undertaken by private firms.

The classical economists, among whom Smith is the best known, conceived a system in which we are driven by self-interest to engage in activities conducive to the good of the nation. To gain our interests, we must provide others with the things they need. To maximize our profit, we must produce efficiently and direct our efforts and resources into those lines of industry yielding the highest returns. In doing so, we assure that the wealth of the nation is maximized. Pursuit of self-interest makes us devote ourselves to being frugal, hard working, and efficient, to knowing the needs of others and doing what we must to satisfy them. This is not a hedonistic world of pleasure seeking, but a Puritanical world of self-sacrifice in the interest of profit-making and capital accumulation.

There is, then, an element of self-negation in the pursuit of private interest as the classical economists envisioned it. If to accumulate wealth we must work hard, save rather than spend, and sacrifice present for future, then the goal of private wealth accumulation demands strict discipline, and therefore repression of the self.

We could ask for no better account of the self-negating quality of economic activity organized around private wealth accumulation than that provided by Max Weber in his essay on the religious origins of the capitalist spirit. Weber links the capitalist spirit to the "worldly asceticism" rooted in the protestant ethic. This asceticism "turned with all its force against one thing: the spontaneous enjoyment of life and all it had to offer." The goal was to "subject man to the supremacy of a purposeful will" expressed through the individual's "performance of duty in a calling." This meant building an obsessional character structure in which the conduct of the average man was "deprived of its planless and unsystematic character and subjected to a consistent method of conduct as a whole."[6]

All of this supported the most intense devotion to wealth accumulation, but not for the end of satisfaction in consumption. What appears on the surface as the motive of self-aggrandizement, at a deeper level expresses the most severe self-deprivation.

When the limitation of consumption is combined with this release of acquisitive activity, the inevitable practical result is obvious: accumulation of capital through ascetic compulsion to save. The restraints which were imposed on the consumption of wealth naturally served to increase it by making possible the productive investment of capital.[7]

So long as increasing capital means saving, consumption is the enemy of wealth. If consumption means self-satisfaction, satisfaction must also be the enemy of wealth.

This may have been the case for the petty bourgeois of Weber's essay. It was even true in its way for Adam Smith, who did not shy away from celebrating frugality as the capitalist's virtue. With the dominance of utilitarianism in economics at the end of the nineteenth century, however, the self-negating element diminishes. It is subject to further weakening when John Maynard Keynes advances his famous argument against the virtue of individual saving, which he noted only tended to reduce demand, employment, and output. As Keynes puts it, "our argument leads toward the conclusion that in contemporary conditions the growth of wealth, so far from being dependent on the abstinence of the rich, as is commonly supposed, is more likely to be impeded by it."[8]

Yet, the older argument remains powerful, even in the face of this challenge.[9] The free market argument, when deployed as a part of the attack on government, owes a substantial debt to the worldly asceticism of the protestant sects. In public life, the ideal of discipline and hard work continues to carry the day. Indeed, we might surmise that the challenge hedonism poses to the older ethic serves only to stiffen the resistance of those committed to it.

We can see something of this movement in the words of one aspirant to the office of President, George W. Bush:

> My first goal is to usher in the responsibility era. An era that stands in sharp contrast to the last few decades, when the culture has clearly said: If it feels good, do it. If you've got a problem, blame someone else.[10]

That the rhetoric of repression has in some circles weakened does not mean that the deeper psychic commitment of society to repression of the self has lost any of its power. On the contrary, all the power of this movement gets directed not only at the individual, but also at the institutions of collective life. Thus, government becomes for some a prime target because it is taken to be an enemy of discipline. Indeed, the statement from then-candidate Bush just quoted is preceded by a series of general policy statements aimed directly at government: "Government's don't create wealth. ... We'll be prosperous if we reduce taxes. ... We'll be prosperous if we reduce the regulations that strangle enterprise. ... We'll be prosperous if we embrace free trade."

Discipline establishes the dividing line between the individual (situated in the free market) and the government. The former is subject to the discipline of the market; the latter is not. What the government provides on demand, the market offers only in return for a quid pro quo. Thus, while government combines great power with absence of constraint, the market incorporates a power limited and constrained by the needs and will of others.

The idea of constraint plays a prominent part in the attack on government, particularly in the rhetoric surrounding the federal budget. Insistence on a balanced budget often has its roots in the idea that we must place constraints on government of the kind we experience in our private lives. After all say those who demand a balanced budget amendment to the Constitution, families must live within their means and balance their budgets (which, of course, is untrue); should not, therefore, the government be made to live within its means and balance its budget (which is a non sequitur)? We can ask for no clearer expression of the sentiment to which I have just referred than Ronald Reagan's in his First Inaugural Address:

> You and I, as individuals, can, by borrowing, live beyond our means, but for only a limited period of time. Why, then, should we think that collectively, as a nation, we're not bound by the same limitation?

Underlying the insistence that the government cannot do what the citizen cannot do lies a fear of government, which Reagan expresses further on in this same address:

> We are a nation that has a government—not the other way around. And this makes us special among the nations on earth. Our government has no power except that granted it by the people. It is time to check and reverse the growth of government, which shows signs of having grown beyond the consent of the governed.

What makes government's power frightening is, paradoxically, government's weakness, that is, its inability to fend off the claims of partial interests. Weakness in the case of government means inability to repress self-interest for a higher end. While this weakness poses a threat in a powerful government, it poses no threat at all in the market. On the contrary, what fails in government succeeds in the market. Thus, the government is both too strong and too weak: too weak to be good, and too strong because it is not good. By contrast, the agents in the market (individual property owners) must, if they are to succeed, be strong enough to discipline self-interest to provide for the needs of others; but they are too weak to impose their private failure (should they fail) on the group as a whole.

We can put this point another way. Where the government is one, the market is many. The fear of government derives from the unity it represents; the idealization of the market derives from the differences it incorporates. Unity means power without limit; difference means power dispersed and neutralized. For the older ethic, power combined with the evil impulses of the human soul threatens to undo the repression without which God's work cannot be done. For the newer ethic, power combined with the dominance of self-interest in human conduct assures that government will fail optimally to satisfy private interests. The equation of the public interest with coercion follows from the insistence that unity must be at the expense of difference. This theme of unity and difference is central to the problem of government, and central to it is the idea of self-interest and of a system of self-interest, or market.

Will and Character

The free market, it is argued, organizes the pursuit of self-interest to assure that it eventuates in the growth of the nation's wealth. It does this by requiring that the individual attend to the bottom line, and especially to the growth of his or her capital. As I suggest above, this requires discipline, and therefore self-negation. The agent of this discipline is not, however, outside the individual, but within. The individual disciplines him or her self to the demands of success in the market. Discipline, therefore, lines up with self-interest, and becomes difficult to distinguish from it. Since we discipline ourselves, it must be in our interest to do so.

The force the individual brings to bear on his or her self to assure discipline, and thus success, is the central psychic reality of the market. As we saw above, this is the force of will. In the free market solution, the entire burden is placed on the individual, and on one quality: the quality of will. This brings us to the themes of achievement and individual responsibility so central to American culture and to the American solution to the dilemmas posed by government.

Like Weber, the historian R. H. Tawney traces this solution back to the Puritans.[11] According to Tawney, the essence of Puritanism is will, "will organized and disciplined and inspired...quiescent in rapt adoration or straining in violent energy...".[12] The idea of will summarized a whole conception of the individual and what is expected of him. In this conception, emphasis shifts from the individual's embeddedness in society to the individual's inner life and separate being. Puritan theology made the revelation of God to the individual soul, "not only the center, but the whole circumference and substance, dismissing as dross and vanity all else but this secret and solitary communion." Salvation is made the direct gift of God, "unmediated by any earthly institution." The deployment of the concept of will, and the associated isolation of the individual's relation with God, implied moral self-sufficiency. The Puritan's moral self-sufficiency "nerved his will, but ... corroded his sense of social solidarity. For, if each individual's destiny hangs on a private transaction between himself and his maker, what room is left for human intervention?"[13]

This conception of the human condition leaves little room for any attitude toward those who fail that does not interpret their failure as of their own making, and thus as resulting from inner flaws:

> Convinced that character is all and circumstances nothing, he sees in the poverty of those who fall by the way, not a misfortune to be pitied and relieved, but a moral failing to be condemned, and in riches, not an object of suspicion ... but the blessing which rewards the triumph of energy and will.[14]

As Weber points out, sympathy was driven out by "hatred and contempt."[15]

Tawney goes on to suggest that it is a small step from the idea of individual responsibility to dismantling those protections for the poor that express social obligation. Where individual will and responsibility are all, social obligation can mean very little. This idea, then, casts suspicion on the entire dimension of government concerned with obligation (the so-called "welfare state").

Indeed, many contemporary American politicians appeal to this idea when they take a stand against government programs designed to assure a minimum level of living for all citizens. To accept such an obligation would be to reject the idea that how we are situated in this life must be our own doing, and therefore our due. Again, Newt Gingrich:

> Precisely because our rights are endowed by our Creator, the individual burden of responsibility borne by each citizen is greater than in any other country. ... By blaming everything on "society," contemporary liberals are really trying to escape the personal responsibility that comes with being an American. If "society" is responsible for everything, then no one is *personally* responsible for anything.[16]

The growth of the state must be limited by the idea of individual responsibility. The state appears as a threat to that idea whenever it seeks to recognize and fulfill social obligations since doing so runs counter to the idea that each individual has ultimate responsibility for him or her self.

The history of rhetoric and policy aimed at the problem of poverty provides substantial evidence of the attitude considered here. A main theme in policy rhetoric around the poverty problem is concern for the way in which government policy will increase and reinforce poverty rather than leading people out of poverty. Those who advocate putting people on welfare to work retrieve the old theme of character and moral failing in their interpretation of poverty.

> The idea that any work builds character and discharges social obligations…underlies compulsory workfare programs. Their advocates place priority on any work experience regardless of its quality or pay. Forcing women and children into low-wage, dead-end jobs remains preferable to supporting them with public funds. Clearly even new style workfare cannot shed either the equation of work and virtue or the punitive heritage that has rippled through American relief and welfare practices throughout their long and sorry history.[17]

For advocates of workfare, failure of character is a, perhaps the, primary element in poverty. To work requires discipline; to remain outside the workforce is to exhibit a failure of discipline. But, not only does work require discipline, it also promotes discipline where discipline is absent or insufficiently developed.

Bill Clinton brings together the themes of workfare and responsibility in his 1998 State of the Union Address:

> A strong nation rests on the rock of responsibility. A society rooted in responsibility must first promote the value of work, not welfare. We can be proud that after decades of finger-pointing and failure, together we ended the old welfare system. And we're now replacing welfare checks with paychecks.

In this same address, Clinton refers to America as "a society rooted in responsibility" and goes on to insist that we "must exercise responsibility not just at home, but around the world." He refers to "hard-working Americans," and to "parents who work harder than ever." The themes of the Puritans reappear not only in the rhetoric of a conservative Republican Congressman, but also in the rhetoric of a Democratic President.

There is some evidence that these themes resonate with the public if we consider the strong opposition to welfare spending. In a 1994 survey done by the National Opinion Research Center at the University of Chicago, of twenty areas of federal spending, only welfare and foreign aid were widely opposed, with 62 per cent of those polled judging welfare spending too high. Yet, while welfare spending ranked second from the bottom in support among spending programs considered, "assistance to the poor" ranked eighth. 59 percent reported that they thought too little was being spent on assistance to the poor, and only 16 percent reported they thought too much was spent on such assistance.[18] This suggests that strong opposition exists not to the idea of support for the poor, but to the idea of welfare. Then, to replace the idea of welfare with something else, in this case the idea of workfare, replaces a concept laden with negative connotations, with one bearing more positive connotations. These connotations are more positive in part because they feed into the set of ideals about work and responsibility so deeply rooted in public consciousness.

In this connection, we should also consider Charles Murray's argument summarized earlier that poverty results from public policy. His argument and policy recommendations seem to repudiate the idea that poverty constitutes a moral failing (it is a policy failing rather than a moral failing). Yet, for Murray, policy clearly creates dependence by vitiating the necessity that the individual take responsibility for his or her own welfare. In this sense, if we follow Murray, we can say that government policy makes it unnecessary for individuals to take responsibility for their well-being. What Murray does not do is suggest that solving the problem of poverty requires character change, since for him character is an exceedingly simple matter, consisting, as it does for most economists, in the ability to make rational choices.

The existing incentives are perverse on practical grounds, but could also be judged perverse on moral grounds since they direct the poor into morally questionable conduct. We might surmise, however, that were social policy eliminated as Murray suggests, and each individual forced to have recourse to the labor market, the outcome would then be an expression of individual qualities, including those we associate with character. Then, if we eliminate policy, we return responsibility to the individual. So we can conclude that returning responsibility to the individual should be the goal of policy, which would be achieved by the absence of policy. Then, any who fail clearly do so as a result of individual flaws and not external circumstance.

To say that will is all, circumstance nothing, is to say that the shape of the world depends on the individual's ends and on the magnitude of the (inner) force the individual brings to bear in pursuit of his or her ends. This understanding of the individual's situation in the world recalls the illusion of infantile omnipotence that denies the externality (objectivity) of the world, and refuses to give up the prospect of what Glasser refers to as the ultimate narcissistic fulfillment. Making will the basis of our relation to the world involves a denial of reality exemplified by Bob Dole's insistence during his failed presidential campaign that he can cut taxes 15% and balance the budget simply because he has the will to do so. Making the federal budget a matter of will denies those substantial forces outside the control of government that influence its revenues and expenses. The same reality-denying suspension of higher ego functions is brought into operation when candidates for office insist that, if elected, they will solve such social problems as drug abuse, urban violence, welfare dependency, and so on. Candidates offer to provide the electorate with what it wants without regard to what, in reality, it is possible to have.

Yet, there is also something punitive in the insistence that will is all, circumstance nothing. To see this more clearly, we need to recall what it is that stands in the way of narcissistic fulfillment. The child quickly discovers that the primary obstacle to narcissistic satisfaction is not external, but internal: the child's emerging separate self whose difference from the (narcissistic) parent cannot be tolerated. Thus, the force of will gets bent to the task of self-repression. Repression of self is, however, only a prelude to repression of others, which leads to the struggle of wills and the attempt to impose our will on others. Those who fail in the inner struggle will also fail in the struggle with others. They become object (thing) rather than subject (will). Will is the inner or psychic force marshaled against obstacles to retrieving connection with the object, and thus gaining the promised ultimate fulfillment; and will is also the force marshaled to avenge and displace the experience of loss of relatedness imposed by the object's self-absorption.

What underlies the construction centering on will is the same opposition between reality and ideal that makes government the object of citizens' hostility. Here, splitting has the following meaning: the ideal moment gets associated with omnipotence of the subject as expressed in the effectivity of his or her will; the moment of reality gets associated with the impotence of the subject, as expressed in the rule of external omnipotent forces. The splitting off and suppression of the moment of reality, then, gives the other moment, will, a special meaning in opposition to the reality of other selves, and in isolation from its opposing pole, the objective moment. This special meaning is expressed in the dismissal of circumstance as being of no account.

Recourse to will against reality expresses a defense against the loss of will in the face of a reality within which no creative act is possible. This reality in which no creative act is possible is the relationship with the narcissistic caretaker. In that relationship, the child does not affect, let alone create, its reality, but adapts to or complies with an external force incapable of recognizing the child as a separate center of initiative. Then, the wished for satisfaction in sustaining a relationship is only available at the cost of the repression of the self. The (true) self must be kept from expression in the world, repressed and denied by deploying will against desire. On one side, we have the attitude of omnipotence and the manic state (will controls reality), on the other that of fate (reality overwhelms will), each the mirror image of the other. Fate means willful control of the individual by external forces, originally the narcissistic parent.

If government protects the individual from the willful control of others, secures autonomy by protecting rights, then government is a necessary, if not sufficient, condition for assuring that the individual can be a center of initiative. In other words, government fosters an external reality in which the individual, while not omnipotent, can take initiative and live creatively. The individual lives as him or her self in a larger world of others. Subjectivity exists both within the individual, in the form of effectivity and initiative, and outside the individual as a world of subjects, each also with the capacity for self-directed action. In this world, reality does not oppose the individual as inert object to active (willing) subject, but reality does limit the individual.

In the Unites States, the attitude of omnipotence is the dominant moment; thus will is all, circumstance nothing. This assertion denies, and thus insists upon, a deeper reality, which is the fear that omnipotent forces outside our control (fate) will rule over us. Fear of passivity fuels the movement into action. The need to overcome or deny passivity makes willing an end in itself, rather than the origination of action in an autonomous agent. Since the purpose of willing is to overcome passivity rather than achieve agency, the thoughtful element, which connects action to freedom and reason, disappears. Thus "acts of violence constitute a *direct and concentrated expression of the active will....*" As such, they act as "a mode of activity which permits the individual to *do battle against his inclinations toward passivity and inertia.*"[19]

The construction that isolates the moment of willing has specific implications for how we define character, and thus understand its development. First, character is identified with strength of will. Second, strength of will is measured by the capacity for repression and self-denial. Third, character develops in relations that require us to exercise will. We are required to exercise will when our survival depends on it, which it does when we are opposed by the will of others, or left on our own (cannot depend on others). In this construction, it is struggle, especially struggle of wills, that builds character.

Thinking this way makes neglect and abuse the positive basis of character development, justifying punitive social policies such as those that deprive welfare mothers and their children of public assistance. To maintain our (impaired and divided) personhood, we must struggle against any reversion to dependence on others, where dependence means submission to their will. Here, again, one is either the subject who victimizes or the victim.

The task we call on will to perform is repression. To succeed in this task, we must internalize self-repression by identifying (as the parent has done through abuse and neglect) with the bad object. The badness of the world (circumstance) is no excuse for failure, since the (assumed) badness of the world is what defines the task in the first place. If being good means being successful in the inner struggle against the self, then seeking recourse to external authority for relief from that struggle means seeking to become good without being good (overcoming the bad). We use the government to attain our ends without achieving them, to gain the benefits of virtue without the struggle to become virtuous. This gives added depth to the idea of corruption. Dependence on government enables government to visit its corruption on the individual, who is corrupted by his dependence on a corrupt government. Corruption now means to make dependent, thus to lose your will and, therefore, your autonomy.

Clearly, this construction promotes fear of (dependence on) government. Embedded in this fear is the assumption that government assists us in our lives by destroying what is most important to us: our autonomy. The attack on government forces us to consider more closely the problem of individual responsibility and dependence on others. To counter the attack, it does not help simply to reject autonomy so that dependence can be made more palatable. We gain no ground by reversing the Puritan judgment and insisting that will is nothing, circumstance all. The problem with the rhetoric against government is not its defense of autonomy, but its assumption that will equals character, that strength of will is the measure of character, and that therefore character is something we can best develop in tests of will. This assumption permeates American culture and gets expressed in the lament about the welfare state considered here.

The Rhetoric of Welfare Debate

I suggest in the last section that in American public life the idea that will is the primary object and basis of achievement is a prominent, and at times dominant, theme. I also suggest that this idea expresses a fundamental psychic configuration important to understanding what appears on the surface of public discussion and debate. To provide support for this claim, I will consider once again the rhetoric surrounding the policy debate over the problem of poverty.

A main theme in the history of welfare policy discussion has been the distinction between the deserving and the undeserving poor, a distinction that rests on a moral judgment. The deserving poor are poor through no fault of their own, but as a result of a loss imposed from outside: loss of employment, or, for women dependent on their husbands, loss of a spouse. The undeserving poor, by contrast, are poor because of their own failure, which can be attributed to their flawed character. Thus, the deserving poor do not deserve to be poor, while the undeserving poor are those who deserve to be poor.

This judgment stems from and continues an early distinction between poverty and pauperism closely related to the ideas about poverty that we find rooted in the Protestant Ethic. Thus, the undeserving poor are judged harshly. Indeed, the term undeserving refers specifically to those whose condition results from moral failing, who are poor as the result "of willful error, of shameful indolence, of vicious habits."[20]

Michael Katz points out the close connection between the moral definition of poverty and "the identification of market success with divine favor and personal worth."[21] The early link between the moral definition of poverty and the rise of the free market ideal set the stage for subsequent formulation of policy, and for the rhetoric of policy debate that continues through the last century. Specifically, Katz links the moral definition of poverty with the literature on the "culture of poverty." The culture of poverty idea "placed in a class by themselves those whose behavior and values converted their poverty into an enclosed and self-perpetuating world of dependence." Those placed in this category remained "different and inferior."[22]

On the surface at least, the idea of a culture of poverty did not turn the problem of poverty (or at least of the subset of the poor living in a culture of poverty) into a moral problem, the result of a moral failing. Yet, on another level, it carried forward an essential element of the moral rhetoric of poverty. Katz summarizes this element in the following way:

> We can think about the poor as "them" or as "us." For the most part, Americans have talked about "them." Even in the language of social science, as well as in ordinary conversation and political rhetoric, poor people usually remain outsiders, strangers to be pitied or despised, helped or punished, ignored or studied, but rarely full citizens, members of a larger community on the same terms as the rest of us.[23]

Katz's formulation is an interesting one. Implicitly, it insists that we consider the poor like "us." At the least, it insists we consider the so-called undeserving poor no different than those who are poor due to no "fault" of their own. To get to this point, we must reject the idea that the failing of the poor should be understood in the language of fault, which is the language of virtue and vice, and therefore the language of the moral construction of the world. But, at the same time, we also reject any notion that the poor, especially those who have carried the stigma of the undeserving poor, are, indeed different from those who can make their way in a market dominated economic system.

There is in this insistence that the poor are us a denial that the poor are what they are, which is like us, but also different. This denial of the poor has an odd parallel in conservative rhetoric at the time of the Reagan administration, in which a primary theme was that poverty did not exist.[24] We can, of course, interpret the conservative denial of poverty as a cynical attempt to find justification for cutting government spending on poverty programs by appealing to spurious empirical evidence, which it may have been. Yet, when juxtaposed with Katz's insistence that the poor are us, it takes on a deeper significance. It provides not only a justification for a particular fiscal agenda, but also an expression for a collective psychic agenda: the denial of the poor.

When denying the existence of the poor failed, conservative rhetoric turned to the idea that poverty resulted from government activism, whose result was to sap the poor of initiative by turning them into dependents of the state.[25] Katz's denial of the poor leads in a different direction, toward insistence that poverty is not an individual problem at all, but a political problem: "by individualizing poverty, many American social scientists have aided the mystification of its origins, and obscured its politics."[26] That is, by considering poverty a matter of character, social scientists and politicians have denied that poverty is a political problem. But, of course, insisting that poverty is a political problem denies that it has anything to do with character.

To insist that the poor are us is to insist either that poverty is not an expression of individual character, or, if it is, that the relevant qualities of character are not limited to the poor. The specific quality of character at stake, as we have seen, is the quality summed up in the term will. To deny that poverty results from character flaw means either (1) that qualities of character have nothing to do with whether we are poor or not, or (2) that the qualities of character that lead to poverty (or make it more likely) are not flaws. Put in the language of will, it means that either will is unimportant to character or that failure of will has nothing to do with the capacity to cope successfully with market economy.

Yet, both propositions run up against a difficulty. This difficulty becomes clear enough when we consider the contrasting roles of equal opportunity and community action in the debate over policy to alleviate poverty.[27] Emphasis on opportunity places the burden squarely on the individual, and on that quality of the individual that determines his or her life trajectory. Opportunity only secures the individual against poverty when the individual has the qualities needed to take advantage of opportunity, qualities including those closely associated with will such as the capacity to take initiative in discovering and exploiting opportunity.

Emphasis on community action also places emphasis on will, although in a less obvious way. Thus, for some, community participation would overcome "anomie and social disorganization by energizing previously apathetic and disaffected poor people to act on their own behalf."[28] It is not far from the hope that policy will stimulate people to act on their own behalf to the idea that policy should have as its result a strengthening of will. Thus, whether oriented toward community action, participation, and politicization, or toward providing opportunity, anti-poverty policy has the invigoration of will as a central element.[29]

Competition

Central to the free market solution is the contrast between the one and the many. Because the market contains many individuals, it respects difference; because the government represents a single subject, it always threatens to destroy difference in the name of a particular interest aiming to be the only one. The aspect of the market that defends against the loss of difference is competition. Competition plays a large part in the defense of the market, since it is the quality of the market that assures it will sponsor freedom.

Yet, however much competition sponsors difference, it also acts as a force against difference. It does so because for competition to work, the different actors (entrepreneurs or firms) must share a common goal. Because of this, the link between competition and securing difference is more complex than might be assumed if we look simply at that aspect of competition that fosters multiplication and differentiation.

The term competition refers to the pursuit by more than one subject of a goal that cannot be attained by one without being lost by others, or at least cannot be equally attained by all. Competition rests on two foundations. The first is freedom of opportunity; the second is the dependence of livelihood on exchange. In other words, competition combines the freedom we associate with modern societies, freedom from the predetermination of the individual into a fixed social position, with the danger to the individual implied in making his or her livelihood contingent on success in a struggle with others. The freedom of opportunity associated with competition means the elimination of barriers to entry into industry and occupation other than those of potential for accomplishment as defined by the particular profession (in the case of business, the accomplishment measured by profitability and market share). This freedom underpins the claim that markets assure efficiency and innovation, thus contributing to social ends as they enable individuals to pursue private gain.

This freedom also secures the link between competition and difference, since it not only allows participants the freedom to innovate and distinguish themselves, it rewards them for doing so. When we direct our attention exclusively to this aspect of competition, we see it as a force assuring that no centralized authority can extinguish the freedom of the individual to pursue his or her distinct ends.

The process of competition only works, however, when participants are subject to specific motivation. This specific motivation has two aspects: what the participant can expect to gain and what he or she can expect to lose. Competition is not simply about freedom, then, but also about channeling the energies of individuals in particular directions. In a free market economy, what the individual hopes to gain is the attainment of a state in which the narcissistic illusion becomes real. This is the prospect that self-limits can be put aside, that the obstacles others represent can be eliminated by eliminating others (as in eliminating competitors or taking their market shares). What individuals stand to loose, then, is exactly what they hope to gain at the expense of others, since others share the same hope. In other words, everything of value to the individual (which is to say the prospect of narcissistic gratification, which in this context is indeed everything of value) is at stake in competition. Then, if we note that in the free market, livelihood is at stake in exchange, this is not simply the livelihood associated with acquiring the subsistence, but the livelihood of the self. And, this is not simply the livelihood of the self, which is the possibility of being a self, but the livelihood of a self whose selfhood is made contingent on his or her ability to overcome self-limits and subsume others. The more prominent the role of competition in social arrangements, and especially the fewer the limits on what can be gained and lost in it, the more firmly is loss made the central psychic meaning of interaction. We can think of this drama of loss in the language of greed.

The end of greed is not to gain satisfaction, but exhaustively to contain, consume, or otherwise incorporate something, to have all of it.[30] That to have all of something means to take it away or keep it away from others is an implication of greed. Because of this, we can treat greed not only or primarily as a relation to things, but as a relation with others. The exclusionary quality of greed and of the self-interest connected to it gives us the first hint of the vital connection between greed and loss. Greed expresses the fear of loss and the effort to defend against it. The greedy person is constantly aware of the threat of loss, and because of this is driven to attempt to take from others lest they take from him first. He must keep what he has safe from the depredations of others. Thus, greed exists in a system of greed, real or imagined.

I must withhold from others because I perceive them as a threat to take what is mine from me. What is it that is mine and that I fear I will lose? As a practical matter, of course, greed can attach itself to anything judged to be of, and therefore to contain, value. Thus, the "longing or greed for good things can relate to any and every imaginable kind of good—material possessions, bodily or mental gifts, advantages and privileges…."[31] Yet, greed is only for things deemed of value, and it is the value and not the thing to which the greed is attached. This means that the object of greed is not the various things to which it is ostensibly attached, but something else. Psychically, those apparently varied things to which our greed attaches itself "all ultimately signify one thing. They stand as proofs to us if we get them, that we are ourselves good, and so are worthy of love, or respect and honor, in return."[32] We can see in this a powerful connection to the idea of the value of things, to the accumulation of wealth, and therefore to those economic institutions organized around the pursuit and accumulation of private wealth. What ultimately makes things of value to us is that our connection with them affirms our own worth.

Greed promotes rivalry and fear. It places us in a world of competitors, a world in which our original insecurity about ourselves is made a quality of our life with others. Their presence is now perceived as the source of our insecurity, when in fact it is our insecurity and dependence on the accumulation of things that makes others a threat to us. This is the threat of loss, and we can say, therefore, that desire turns into greed when desire is powerfully bound up with the fear of loss. Then, what appears to be a desire for things is not a desire at all, but a defense against loss. If the psychic meaning of greed is loss, it is the fear of loss of those things that establish the goodness and value of the self, the fear that they will become the property (or properties) of others. Loss becomes especially painful to us because unconsciously it means "that we are being exposed as unworthy of good things, and so our deepest fears are realized."[33]

But greed does not merely express, and defend against, a feared experience, it also provokes the experience it seeks to defend against. Greed attacks the other since insisting that I can be good only if I can possess all that is good means imposing the loss of what is good on the other. More fundamentally, it imposes the loss of a connection with the other. Greed provokes and assures the loss of the other as a source of good things for us. It stands in the way of love. If this is correct, then we cannot treat greed as merely reactive (to the prospect of loss), but must also consider it a causal factor. It is because it fuels the loss to which it is a response that greed seems so primordial.

So much is clear in competitive sports where no sooner has the current champion been crowned than the question is asked can he or she repeat, and then repeat once more. The immediate aftermath of victory is that we must start over, play again, and once again risk everything. But, of course the prospect that the competition will begin anew no sooner than it has ended assures that winning and losing are not so absolute as the comments in the section above would have them be. Competition, then, exists in and through its own contradiction. Everything of value is at stake, and stands to be won or lost. Yet those who win everything must be made to put it at risk and enter the competition anew, just as those who have lost everything will return as hopefuls in the next round.

We can think of the competitive system as a system of the controlled expression of greed. In doing so, we shift attention away from the obvious goal of competition, specific things of value, and see that goal as fending off the loss of things of value. If we consider competition, as I suggest, not from the standpoint of what stands to be gained, but of what stands to be lost, then the purpose of competition is to impose loss on others, to take something away from them, and have it all for yourself.

In the free market, competition, and thus the system of greed, is subject to the least possible control. The problem with competition under these conditions is that too much is at stake. If, indeed, we have everything to gain and everything to lose, then competition must extinguish at least one, and more likely all but one or at most a few, of the competitors, thereby extinguishing competition itself. When this happens, competition no longer sponsors difference, but destroys it. This is certainly the fear we have in face of monopoly, where we are at the mercy of a single supplier.

The psychic meaning of competition, then, is to reenact a drama of loss. If we wish to consider the part cast for government in this drama, we must understand how government involves itself in loss. The government may, for example, limit loss by providing a safety net for participants. Or, it may affirm the inevitability, even desirability, of loss by raising the stakes, removing limits, or participating as a powerful competitor. The stronger the community's need for reenactment, the less government can work to lower the stakes and limit loss. The more the community's psychic life gets organized around loss as its binding force, the more the government will appear as a threat to its constituting psychic reality, and the more government must be limited in its ability to provide security to the individual.

7 THE DEMOCRATIC SOLUTION

Introduction

For those who distrust government, two solutions have been particularly attractive. The free market solution eliminates much of what government does by eliminating the public sector and public life. Distrust of government can also lead in another direction, however, one in which the attack on government is meant to enhance rather than eclipse public experience. This is the democratic solution. The call for democracy, when it expresses distrust of government, operates firmly within the terms of the opposition of government to people I consider in chapter 3. Yet, while the roots of the call for greater democracy are in some ways similar to those of the call for expansion of the private sector at the expense of the public, the solution itself is quite different. In this chapter, I explore the psychodynamics of the call for greater democracy when that is meant to solve the problem posed by government.

The fantasy expressed in the call for greater democracy shares certain important features with the fantasy of Mr. Smith and his experience in Washington considered in chapter 2. When Mr. Smith goes to Washington, he finds himself better suited to govern than those who have made governing their profession. It turns out that their experience and expertise only serve to obscure the real issues, which are simple matters of applying simple values and pursuing simple and well-known ideals. To govern, we require not expertise but moral leadership and common sense. These are just the qualities Jesse Jackson offered the American people in his candidacy for Democratic nominee for President in 1988. "Politics can be a moral arena where people come together to find common ground," and "leadership must face the moral challenge of our day." Armed with faith, Jackson echoes the sentiments of Mr. Smith: "I just want to bring common sense to high places."

The fantasy that governing takes no special expertise plays a central part in ideals that would place government into the hands of "the people." Doing so dismisses any thought that to govern we must undergo a process of learning skills and gaining appropriate experience.[1] This aspect of the fantasy of government by the people links it up with the fantasy, central to the Capra film, that we are prepared for adult life without successfully negotiating a development process appropriate to forming us into adults. This fantasy expresses the "hatred of a process of development" considered earlier. It is not, however, simply a negative attitude toward development, but also the idea that development can be replaced by joining a group of a particular kind.[2] This joining a group of a particular kind underlies certain democratic fantasies that combine the idea that the people can govern themselves with the idea that the people constitute a special group: the democratic community. To understand this better, I will first consider certain characteristics of groups, and especially of the kind of group that offers its members an alternative to a process of development.

Groups

Reference to groups introduces complexities having to do with what we mean when we speak of a "group." For some, a group is a set of actually existing individuals in face-to-face contact. Thus, C. Fred Alford defines the group as "individuals occupying space and time together." Then, for a group to exist, the number of individuals must be small enough and their interactions such as to enable members to come "to know each other as individuals," though it does not ensure that they will do so.[3]

Even for this apparently straightforward group construct, however, questions can be raised about the "groupness" of a particular set of people.[4] What makes them something more than a collection of individuals, establishing them as a whole—the group—that takes us beyond the sum of the parts? The problem becomes more complex as we consider larger groups, especially groups that exist only ideally, never meeting together in one place at one time: nations; ethnic, religious, and other communities; and so on. Such ideal groups are important, though we may wonder if they bear anything in common with the smaller groups, if their groupness shares any significant characteristics with the groupness of those that meet face-to-face. Alford insists that these larger entities, whose members cannot interact directly, are not groups, though they may be "grouplike entities" if they resemble groups. Resembling groups presumably means that certain entities too large to be considered groups nonetheless exhibit group characteristics, and that these characteristics are best explained by reference to real (small, face-to-face) groups.

Uncertainty about the existence of groupness outside the face-to-face setting may result from an overly concrete approach to thinking about group reality. Such an approach makes the reality of the group depend on our ability to find it in space and time. The larger group cannot be located in this way, but exists as a mental construct. This distinction may, however, be more apparent than real, since the reality of the small, face-to-face, group lies not in its temporal or spatial existence, but in its emotional significance for the individual, and thus is as much a mental construct as is the larger group.

The key concept that captures this existence of the group as a mental construct rather than an empirical entity depending on a coincidental presence of the members in time and space is regression. The idea of regression has, since Freud's essay on group psychology, been a powerful one for thinking about groups.[5] Pressures to regress are significant in groups, and, indeed, certain groups only exist through the regression they foster in their members. Does this make the group inherently a regressive phenomenon? Does it mean that individuals who achieve, and somehow maintain, emotional maturity thereby have a relation to reality that prevents them from succumbing to the "myth" of the group: that it exists, and is as (or more) real than the collection of individuals through which it appears?

Linking the notion of groups to regression roots the existence of the group in its ability to provoke and mobilize primitive emotional states, and especially primitive defenses. These include defenses considered in earlier chapters such as the splitting off of unacceptable parts of the self and the pursuit of a relatedness based on identification as sameness rather than the recognition of (different) self. Connection as identification aims to unite the individual with the group self-ideal, often embodied in its leader. Some argue that all true group phenomena operate in this primitive emotional space, exploiting weaknesses in members' self-organization. This argument, however, ignores the possibility that the group can mobilize members' mature emotional capacities, supporting rather than attacking higher ego functions.[6] The group does this by creating the synergy derivative of interaction, and by encouraging the development of reality based goals and ideals, especially those consonant with self-boundaries and respect for others.

If the "group-like characteristics" referred to above in considering entities too large to allow face-to-face interaction express regressive phenomena, then it is unclear why large groups are not groups. Regression in the service of connection to the group is not limited to small face-to-face settings. On the contrary, such regression is notable in certain large groups, where it takes such familiar forms as national chauvinism, racism, and ethnic hatred. Furthermore, nothing in our experience of these larger groups suggests that their groupness is derivative of any links to smaller, face-to-face, groups. In establishing groupness, ideas such as love of country are as powerful as the impact of face-to-face interaction with a real particular other. For this reason, I will take the group to be the entity that exhibits group-like characteristics, whatever its size and however those characteristics manifest themselves concretely.

The regressive pull typically experienced in group life must have significant implications for our understanding of democracy, so far as democracy is about group self-organization, and therefore is treated as a phenomenon of group life. In particular, this way of thinking raises the question of the connection between the call for democracy and the regression constitutive of group life. Is democracy a part of the regression associated with the creation of groupness, or is it a protection against that regression? Linking democracy to regression may or may not make it inherently a "bad" thing; but it must have significant implications for how we understand democracy, and especially its limits. In exploring this problem, and other related problems of democracy, it will prove helpful to consider a distinction introduced by Bion between what he terms "sophisticated work groups" and "basic assumption groups."[7]

Types of Groups

Pierre Turquet summarizes Bion's notion of the work group in the following way:

> The sophisticated work group is a group called into being for a predetermined, clearly defined primary task that has been openly accepted, at least at the conscious level, by its members and at which, again consciously, they have agreed to work. ... In its attitude to primary-task implementation—that is, to work—the work

group is activated by a desire to know: to acquire insights, to discover and understand explanations, and to form hypotheses that can be tested. It will also be concerned with the consequences of its own behavior and actions—not only between individual members of the work group but also with the group's external milieu.[8]

Members of the (sophisticated) work group associate voluntarily, and feel free to resign without their disassociation from the group threatening them in any significant way. This means that neither their identity nor their basic well being depend on the group. We can say, then, that sophisticated work groups do not raise the stakes for their members.

The structure of the work group is derivative of its primary tasks. This means that designating leadership and assigning tasks does not follow the need to establish rank, but the need to get things done and the derivative need to place the parts of its tasks under the control of the appropriate individuals. As Alford points out, "[w]ithout effective leadership, the group itself is incompetent" as are its members.[9] By contrast to the situation in the work group, "[w]hen structure becomes an end in itself, it is most probable we are dealing with a basic assumption group."[10] Structure becomes important in itself when, for example, position in the group along with the power associated with it, rather than getting its job done, becomes the goal. When position and power become the primary ends of the group and its members, we can assume that regression to a basic assumption group has taken place.

A basic assumption group is one in which the existence of the group takes precedence over any reality-linked task the group is ostensibly organized to accomplish. While such a group may organize itself around different concrete assumptions about its emotional life and the meaning that has for its members, these particular assumptions are derivative of the central assumptions that the group is an end in itself and that the individual must be subordinate to the group.

A work, or task-oriented, group is not democratic in the strongest sense of the term. It has a job to do. To do it well, the group must (1) discover and respect the different competencies of its members, and (2) organize itself to get things done, which means assigning authority and responsibility over parts of the task and designating authority to oversee the task as a whole. Yet, a work group works best when it is open and engages the talents and energies of all members in a positive way. To do so, it must enable members individually and collectively to involve themselves in decision-making in areas that call on their experience, skill, and knowledge. We can, then, use the term democracy for this organization of the work group, although it involves acknowledging expertise, authority, and leadership.

Democracy as a group ideal can facilitate or impede getting the job done depending on the type of democratic ideal imposed on the group. To see this, consider the following example. In the mid 1980s, the Chancellor at my University announced a major curricular revision targeted at the Core Curriculum, which is required of all undergraduates and is usually taken during the first two years of college. This revision was part of a broader response to criticism of higher education's perceived failure to assure that students acquired "basic" knowledge in areas such as common culture, science and mathematics, geography, and so on. Whatever the merits of the Chancellor's reorganization of curriculum, and in my judgment they were not great, the widest and deepest objection to his proposal was that faculty were not involved in discussing and deciding on a matter most considered their special concern. The new curriculum arrived as a *fait accompli* produced by the Chancellor working with a small group of hand picked faculty members and administrators. The appropriate procedures that assure faculty decision-making in an area of their special professional competence were ignored. The faculty's expectation that decision-making would conform to the democratic norms appropriate to a University were not fulfilled. Thus, faculty members' professional selves were diminished and offended. The result was anger and demoralization.

The problem of democracy was at the center of this experience. The anger provoked by undemocratic methods of group decision-making was not, however, a response to lack of participation as a general matter, but to that lack of participation involving a denial of professional respect. The issue of democracy was raised, but also circumscribed by considerations of professional competence. The failure of participation meant that decisions were placed in the hands of individuals and groups without the qualifications to make them, that they would be badly made, and that those with the appropriate qualifications would feel diminished and excluded.

A second experience of democracy exemplifies its connection not to getting the job done and maintaining morale in the group, but to regression. In the course of recruitment of an economist for my unit, economists were informed that their judgment of candidates carried no more weight than did the judgment of faculty who had neither the training nor competence to evaluate the qualifications and abilities of potential faculty in this area. This denial and denigration of the professional competence of economics faculty was justified by appeal to democratic norms: to allow any special weight to the judgment of individuals because of their professional accomplishments would violate a norm of equality that underlies democratic process. Using this line of argument enabled faculty lacking appropriate qualifications for judging candidates to avoid any acknowledgement that others might have something of value (competence) that they do not. Indeed, in my unit, this method of coping with, or more precisely defending against, difference is so ingrained that students, including first year graduate students, are included as members of hiring and promotion committees, although they have no professional competence to make important judgments affecting the unit's welfare.

The two experiences just briefly summarized exemplify two different uses of the term democracy and two reasons for demanding greater democracy. One links democracy to professional competence and the organization of a group for the purpose of accomplishing a reality-based task. The other links democracy to goals of group solidarity, making the group itself more important than any job it might be mandated to do. Roughly speaking, the first emphasizes the work group dimension of group life, the second the basic assumption group dimension.

When faced with an external threat or an internal imperative, or when overwhelmed by ideological/political considerations, a work group may become a basic assumption group, or what ought to be organized as a work group can get organized as a basic assumption group. In contrast to the work group, which has a primary task connecting it outside the group, the basic assumption group has a primary task "arising entirely from within its own midst and ... pursued solely for the satisfaction of the individual members of the group."[11] This task may be providing security for the members, dealing with a perceived external threat to the group, creating hope, or providing the members with access to a feeling of omnipotence only available through merger. The primary task of the basic assumption group is inner oriented; the outside world exists mainly to provide a repository for disavowed group feelings. Basic assumption groups require that their leaders personify the group as a whole. This is because, in contrast to work groups, for basic assumption groups the existence of the group as an entity in itself is vital.

Basic assumption groups "are self-contained, closed systems ... they have little desire to know, since knowledge might be an embarrassment, might cause disturbance in the internal harmony or 'groupiness' of the group."[12] Basic assumption groups tend to emerge spontaneously, without effort, their members needing no special training to accomplish the group's primary task. Such groups operate on the plane of myth, often being the groups within society (such as the church) responsible for society-wide mythology and ideology. Basic assumptions represent the spontaneity of shared mythology in contrast with the knowledge and thinking involved in work groups. Since the task is about creating and sustaining myths, there is no question of expertise. On the contrary, basic assumption groups are associated with loss of skills and impairment of higher ego functions. This deskilling is in sharp contrast to the work group, which "seeks in a sophisticated way to protect the skills of its individual members."[13]

Turquet notes that one of the most important targets of deskilling in the basic assumption group is the skill of the leader, including his or her ability to make decisions.[14] The more the leader becomes a part of a basic assumption group, the more he or she gets involved with group anxieties and fantasies. This involvement inhibits the leader's ability to act on the borderline between the group and the world outside, to make decisions in the face of uncertainty, and to maintain the group's connection to an outward-oriented primary task. The loss of higher ego functions in basic assumption groups goes together with a diminishing of the individual selves of the members. The members are not there for their own sake, but to fulfill the group's purpose.[15]

The deskilling, especially of leadership and authority, in basic assumption groups connects them to certain phenomena of democracy. If democracy includes an attack on skill differences, then it binds itself to the basic assumption group. In answer to a question raised earlier, it is a part of, rather than a protection against, regression in groups. Democracy constitutes a basic assumption in many groups, a constituting idea that makes the group something more than a collection of individuals or a system for working together via division of labor.

The key in forging the link between democracy and basic assumption groups is that the appeal to democracy takes decisions out of the hands of individuals, including leaders, and places them into the hands of the group. As I suggest above, the attack on, and deskilling of, leaders characterizes certain democratic groups and establishes them as instances of the basic assumption group. In such cases, democracy removes constraints on decisions other than those having to do with conforming to the group's wishes and goals. These goals tend to be about group self-preservation and advancing the group's basic constituting assumptions. Thus, the quality of groupness becomes essential to making democracy meaningful. It is only the sui generis existence of the group that makes democratic decision-making on the part of the group as a whole the relevant consideration. In light of this, it is not surprising to find cases in which those individuals most susceptible to the need for a basic assumption group are also those most ready to invoke demands for democracy within the group. These are individuals most in need of groupness, and of the regression connected to it.

In the regressed group, democracy is not just about how decisions are made relevant to a defined task, but about defining the tasks themselves. This movement tends to destroy the autonomy of members since it attacks the limited existence of the group around a defined task. Once it is organized in this way, or to the degree that it is so organized, the group becomes a threat to the autonomous or mature individual, just as it is a support for the member's more primitive self, and a stimulus for the member's more primitive needs. Regression to a basic assumption mode of being involves raising the stakes for the member, and may be prompted by any structural or constituting conditions that involve raising the stakes (such as having employment or professional identity depend on group membership). When raising the stakes leads to regression, work cannot get done, or it cannot get done well.[16]

Governing and Democracy

That work does not get done, or get done well, in basic assumption groups can help us better understand a now common lament about government, the lament that it "doesn't work" and needs to be "reinvented." The regression from work group to basic assumption group has much to do with disappointment in, and animosity toward, government. The attack on government is often framed in the language of democracy, as for example when it involves attacking "professional politicians" (as if amateurs are to be preferred), or the absence of "participation," or the way decisions fall into the hands of "experts." This attack is done in the name of the "people," deemed the only appropriate decision-making entity. There are, then, two entities operating over the same time and space: the government and the people. One is an institutionalized structure for getting things done; the other is a mythical group with a fantasized existence rooted in ideals and an idealized past. The former is, or has the capacity to be, a work group (or system of work groups); the latter is essentially a basic assumption group. The attack on government puts pressure on it to regress in the direction of the basic assumption group, which requires that it cease being a government.

There is an important connection, then, between hostility toward government and the call for democracy, since greater democracy, though arguably a cause of government failure, appears on the scene as its cure. In the words of one observer:

> Recent history suggests that when large numbers of Americans become dissatisfied with the workings of their government, they call for more democracy. The more they call for more democracy, the more they get it. The more they get it, the more dissatisfied they become with the workings of their government.[17]

The result is the regression of government from an organization capable of getting at least some of the work done to a basic assumption group that rarely gets anything meaningful accomplished because doing so is not, ultimately, its real purpose.

Part of getting the job done involves division: the division of government into its various parts, each associated with a specific task (national security, education, transportation, commerce, finance, social services, and so on). This division poses problems for some because it removes government from control by, and direct identification with, the people. It makes government less democratic by criteria deriving from the idea that the "people" should directly control its decisions. This direct control assures that the government equals the people equals a basic assumption group. Thinking about democracy this way makes it, or more precisely makes the group organized to realize its ideal, a total structure.

The distinction just drawn between democracy as a total structure and democracy as a way of assuring respect for the individual in a work group involves the matter of boundaries. Democracy may be circumscribed or totalizing. It may be a vital element of group life, or the whole of group experience. It may enliven group life for the individual, or make the group a threat to autonomy. Which democracy has been activated in the group depends on the relation between its basic assumption and work-oriented aspects.

The distinction between circumscribed and totalizing democracy applies not only to democracy in the small, but also in the large. To see this, consider two different uses of the term democracy in the context of nations. According to the first, more circumscribed, usage, democracy refers to that subset of (political) rights that apply specifically to decision-making where outcomes call on the group as a whole or bear on collective life. In this understanding, the notion of a system of justice organized to protect the individual and assure respect for the self-in-other is primary, democracy secondary. Democracy must be sustained by the assurance, provided outside of democratic process, that the integrity of the individual necessary for democracy is nurtured and sustained. This is accomplished by social institutions that develop and secure the "norms of democracy."[18] Within a larger system of justice, democracy applies only to decisions on matters designated within the domain of the group. Outside that domain, democracy is not an issue.

According to the second usage, democracy is not one, limited, part of a system of justice, but its central organizing principle, so that rights other than political rights are understood to derive from, and be justified on the basis of, their role in facilitating group self-determination.[19] Democracy, then, becomes the primary moral virtue, and, indeed, the context in which alone true moral character can develop. Thus Benjamin Barber insists that while citizenship may not be "the highest or the best identity that an individual may assume, ... it is the moral identity par excellence."[20] The same idea is expressed in a very similar language by Warren Magnusson in his book *The Search for Political Space*. For Magnusson, the search for political space is not only about asserting self-interest or imposing domination.

> It is also a moral search—a quest for a place where people can act on their values and pursue their ideals. It thus involves an effort to become human in the fullest sense. ... In the most benign political processes we are compelled to deal seriously with other people's ideals and interests, and this can teach us profound lessons in respect for one another.[21]

If correct, this hypothesis would make political participation in a democratic setting the dominant moral principle. Doing so equates justice with democracy, as is sometimes done by those who use the term democratic to refer not to the subset of political rights, but to the whole of a society organized around the ideal of social justice.[22]

It should not be surprising that this distinction in usage has to do with the relation between the individual and the group. In the first usage, which makes justice primary, democracy secondary, the individual, even as a member of a democratic association, retains his autonomy since he has recourse to rights associated not with the group, but with his being an individual. The individual, then, has rights against the community.[23] In the second usage, which makes participation the primary virtue, this is less the case or not the case at all. Rather than having rights against the group, or rights that secure boundaries between self and other, therefore between self and group, rights bind the individual to the group and are about group membership.

Democracy, Community, and Character

Communal identity refers not to a part of the individual's life and being, for example a professional identity or other particular interest, but to the personality's integrating force. When the identity of each, and with it his or her feeling of personal integration or wholeness, is at stake with the identity of all, then each is a stakeholder in all issues that affect the community. Indeed, each is a stakeholder in all issues that affect any member, since members are identified with each other and the lines separating them into individuals are blurred. As a result, interdependence moves beyond contract and division of labor to establish a unit with the quality of groupness we associate with identification among its members.

Thus, those who believe that being of a particular gender shapes character in ways relevant to all aspects of life, also believe in a communal (gender) identity in this strong sense. Similarly, those who believe, with Marx, that it is the effect of capitalist accumulation eventually to place all workers into a common situation where they have common interests, also believe in a strong sense of communal identity. Communal identity is group identity that determines, even displaces, the members' individual identities.

The democratic ideal is that the separate group identifications will, to a significant degree, be replaced by the more universal identification of equal citizenship. What has been less clear is whether this new identity constitutes a group in its own right. Whether universal citizenship can be construed as a group identity bears on whether the democratic institutions through which citizenship is expressed are constitutive of democratic community. The new identification (citizenship) may or may not, then, constitute a new group (democratic community).

Linking group identification with citizenship has important consequences for democracy. These consequences arise because the basis for group identification—sameness of group members—is now made universal. The result is the modern notion of equality that forms a pillar for many of the arguments about democracy considered here. The strong appeal of democracy stems from its connection to equality of universal citizenship. So long, however, as the quality of groupness is retained, democracy's appeal will also stem from the hope that it will retrieve older forms of group or communal identification in the context of equality. The result of mixing communal identity with the equality of universal citizenship is to make democracy, and the politics associated with it, a group or communal phenomenon. Thus:

> Citizenship and community are two aspects of a single political reality: men can only overcome their insufficiency and legitimize their dependency by forging a common consciousness. The road to autonomy leads through not around commonality.[24]

For some, equating democracy with government applies the egalitarianism of the justice as democracy argument to the organization of government. It envisions governing not as a professional practice, but as something all citizens can and should do. Thus, "[i]nstead of the special institutions of a privileged minority (privileged officialdom, the chiefs of the standing army), the majority itself can directly fulfill all these functions, and the more the functions of the state power devolve upon the people as a whole the less need is there for the existence of this power."[25] This construction follows the constitution of a community in the strong sense just introduced. In it, the state and the people "become one and the same."[26] The result is to limit or eliminate the application of any concept of justice other than that subsumed under popular self-governance. Thus, making democracy coterminous with government applies the equation of justice with democracy to the institutions of government.

Yet, making responsiveness to its constituency conceived as a group or community the primary or only virtue of government raises some important questions having to do with what it is the group is competent to do. One influential answer imagines that participation in group processes fosters an attitude of regard for others necessary for collective life. Participation develops public spirit, possibly even competence to govern, within the polity. As one student puts it, "To participate is to create a community that governs itself, and to create a self-governing community is to participate." Thus:

> In a strong democratic community ... the individual members are transformed, through their participation in common seeing and common work into citizens. Citizens are autonomous persons whom participation endows with a capacity for common vision. A community of citizens owes the character of its existence to what its constituent members have in common and therefore cannot be treated as a mere aggregation of individuals.[27]

Remove participation and you create apathy, ignorance, and the preoccupation with self-interest that not only destroys public spirit, but also creates a fertile ground for irrationality, ideology, and harmful division. Following this line of argument, the group's competence to achieve meaningful public ends, including those we associate with justice, follows from the way groups shape an ethical consciousness in their members. So far as ethical standing is taken to be derivative of group process, justice as a virtue of governance depends on the group.

There is something magical in the thinking underlying this line of argument, which insists that the experience of participation will create a regard for others not otherwise present. The conviction that this will happen does not rest on any explicit model of the development of moral personality or ethical character. It does not appeal to the cognitive and emotional structures and capacities that must develop for the emergence of the orientation toward others it favors. What it does appeal to is the equation of morality and group identification:

> For it is as citizen that the individual confronts the Other and adjusts his own life plans to the dictates of a shared world. *I* am a creature of need and want; *we* are a moral body whose existence depends on the common ordering of individual needs and wants into a single vision of the future in which we all share.[28]

The individual, then, *qua* individual, is an amoral (if not immoral) creature. The other only exists for this individual in the context of democratic participation. This only holds, however, if recognition of the other means recognition of sameness (identification) in the context of the group.

The link to group identity suggests that the argument just summarized operates at the level of morality rather than ethical character. Ethical character is not contingent on group identification, but on autonomy, including autonomy from the group. By contrast, the moral ideal is the ideal of group identity. Communal identity, then, participates in the regression in groups we considered at the beginning of this chapter. This means that the moral ideal Barber advances is a treacherous one in that it demands regression.

Freud suggests that the specific regression demanded in groups is from autonomy to identification. The member gives up autonomous judgment based on an internalized ego ideal in favor of the shared ideal of the group. The group, then, offers the individual a strategy for circumventing the constraints on action associated with the guilt that normally results from violating internalized ethical ideals.[29] In the language introduced earlier, groups offer members the opportunity for the moral inversion necessary for acts of cruelty and violence.

Shifting Ground

Let me now consider an example of the shifting ground experienced in larger societal groups between their basic assumption and work group dimensions. This example is drawn from Guy Lawson's description of the referendum in Quebec on separating from the rest of Canada.

The movement for separation began its campaign in the hands of Jacques Parizeau, the premier of Quebec, a man who believed that an appeal to the voter's financial interest would secure the majority needed for separation. During the early weeks of the campaign, however, the results of this appeal were not encouraging. Three weeks before the vote, the campaign changed hands, with Lucien Bouchard, the leader of the Bloc Québecois, taking over de facto leadership. Now, "what had been under Parizeau a tedious discourse about passports and currency and deficits was transformed into a bitter struggle to forge a new nation."

Bouchard dismissed the ominous economic reports with a wave of the hand. He ridiculed surveys showing that many voters were confused by the referendum question, which was artfully designed to imply that separation might not really mean separation. He ignored statements by Quebec's aboriginal people, who claim vast tracts of the province for their traditional land, that they would separate from Quebec if Quebec separated from Canada.[30]

The transition from Parizeau to Bouchard was a transition from a technician to a man "who understood anger and the power of an image," and who could provoke what Lawson describes as a "hurricane of passion." In the end, there were two referenda, one over economic issues, and one over "ancestry, identity, questions of the heart."

The transition during the final weeks of the referendum over separation is a transition whose absence is often lamented in electoral campaigns in the United States, particularly those involving the office of President. Candidates appear colorless; they lack qualities that might capture the imagination of the electorate, or the capacity to generate excitement and emotional engagement. They are most often professional politicians attempting to appear as something else: charismatic leaders capable of realizing the mythic aspirations of a nation, including its constitution as a basic assumption group. The contempt in which Americans hold "professional politicians" clearly expresses a failure of the political process; but it expresses something else as well. This something else is the wish that social problems could be dismissed with a "wave of the hand," that government not be required to deal with real problems in a realistic way that involves knowledge, skill, and expertise.

In Quebec, to provoke the transition from a vote based on the realistic assessment of the likely implications of separation for everyday life to one that was all about myth and identity, it was necessary to replace the leadership with a man capable of engaging the voter on a more primitive level. This meant injecting issues of oppression and deprivation, which made the election part of a drama of victimization and liberation. Thus, observed René-Daniel Dubois, a leading Québecois playwright, quoted in *Le Monde*:

The Québecois imagine that sovereignty will be their act of birth.... Meanwhile, they do not define themselves as actors, but as victims of the hatred and wickedness of others.[31]

The drama of liberation from oppression cast the Quebecois in the role of victimized minority. Yet, their vision of a separate nation cast them in an altogether different role. Separation of Quebec is about a national identity desired and available only to a part of its population, an identity that excludes Quebec's Anglophone and Inuit populations. The supporters of the referendum, themselves demanding their rights to a nation of their own, are in equal measure adamant in their opposition to claims of others to a nation of their own. Thus, the hoped for Quebec nation harbors seeds of oppression, indeed of the transformation of victims into victimizers. Again, René Daniel Dubois:

> ... The true alternative is this: to be the young man in the white shirt in front of the tank in Tiananmen Square, or to be the driver of the tank. Our myths tell us that we are the young man. The truth is that we are seated in the tank.

This connection between regression and victimization cannot be overemphasized. To transform the group in the direction of a basic assumption group, or to constitute it as such, means to provoke feelings of wrong, of deprivation, and of humiliation. The more these feelings predominate, the less effective the capacity for reality testing and associated higher ego functions. Once the issue of victimization is raised, real practical issues get resolved by a "wave of the hand." The transition is provoked by a mix of threat and promise: the threat of continued victimization if action is not taken and the promise of liberation from oppression if it is, a promise whose darker side is the need to shift oppression onto others.

The referendum is not simply an effort to liberate a people, or to give the people a political-institutional existence as a nation-state. It is the process by which the potential latent within the population to be a people can be realized. This tells us something important about the category "people," which plays such a large role in certain conceptions of democracy. Those conceptions of democracy heavily dependent on notions such as "the people" or "the community" operate in the space of oppression and promise, despair and hope, victim and victimizer, because this is ultimately the space in which a people comes to life.

In the United States, it is the myth of the American Dream tied to the idea of a unique historical purpose identified with the rhetoric of freedom that creates the people, and establishes the reality of the nation. The United States welcomes the oppressed of the world, and offers them hope. To be an American, then, is to accept the reality of the myth of America as the Promised Land.[32] To reject that myth is to be something other than an American. Thus Cornell West, who is an American academic, chooses to identify himself not as an American, but as "a black man trying to be an American citizen."[33] Why is he not an American? He is not, because he denies the reality of the myth that constitutes the American people:

> My wife is Ethiopian. ... She came here because she wanted to. She was trying to get out from under a tyrannical, Communist regime in Ethiopia. She's glad to be in a place where she can breathe freely, not have to hide. ... So I've got to take her, you know, almost like Virgil in Dante's *Divine Comedy*, through all of this other side of America so that she can see the nightmare as well as the dream. But as an Ethiopian, she came for the dream and did a good job of achieving it.[34]

West understands that to be an American, if by that we refer to a people and not a juridical and geo-political entity, you must participate in a people-constituting myth. His rejection of this myth means he is not an American.

Or does it? As it turns out, and as is clearly stated in the passage quoted above, West does participate in the myth, but negatively, as one who belongs to a group that has been and, he believes, continues to be, excluded. He harbors no less a desire for the Promised Land; what he has given up is hope that it will be realized for him. In place of realizing hope, his action is organized around imposing his loss on others (specifically his wife), making them understand how hollow is the dream, and how far from being real in the world. If you reject the reality of the myth for yourself and your group, while still organizing your emotional life around it, specifically around issues of its reality in the world, then you are as deeply implicated in it as those who embrace it in a more positive sense. Understood in this way, Cornell West is very much an American.

Clearly, for West, America is about oppression and liberation, sin and redemption, as suggested by the allusion to the *Divine Comedy*. West goes on to describe America as "a civilization in which there is a problem of evil," a civilization in "sustained denial" of evil.[35] As I suggest above, this is the space in which a people constitutes its reality, in which a population becomes a group.

Equality

Basic assumption groups seek to incorporate a democracy that work groups do not, while work groups are capable of being democratic in ways basic assumption groups cannot. Basic assumption groups are often highly undemocratic. Religious communities and ideologically motivated political organizations, for example, exhibit a high degree of authoritarianism. Equality and participation are expenses these groups can rarely afford. Yet, democracy is often a part of the transition from work group to basic assumption group. Indeed, democracy can act as a constituting basic assumption for a group: the assumption that all are equal and undifferentiated.

Freud's comments on the psychic significance of the group are relevant here. He emphasizes the role of envy in forging group spirit.[36] The suppression of difference within the group, which constitutes the group as a psychic and social reality, eliminates envy only by giving in to it and embracing the implied attack on difference. We envy those who are different from us because we imagine that difference expresses their acquisition of something we lack. Freud draws an important conclusion from this about the nature of social feeling:

> Social justice means that we deny ourselves many things so that others may have to do without them as well, or what is the same thing, may not be able to ask for them. This demand for equality is the root of social conscience and the sense of duty.... Thus social feeling is based upon the reversal of what was first a hostile feeling into a positively-toned tie in the nature of an identification.[37]

Authoritarian leadership, when appearing as pressure for merger into the leader, can develop out of democracy precisely because of the pressure for sameness. In such cases, the equality we associate with democracy is put in service of the need to eliminate difference. In light of this, it might be less surprising to see authoritarian personalities, incapable of tolerating difference, who also imagine themselves democrats. For these individuals, democracy is a weapon to be used in the attack on leadership, an attack necessitated by their own need to dominate, which they defend against by projecting it onto others. In such cases, the more powerful the need to dominate others, and the more intense the impulse to project that need onto others, the greater the need for democracy. In other words, we need democracy to protect us from our own projected impulses.

If democracy expresses a repressed and projected need to dominate, it also expresses a grandiose fantasy of governing. When this fantasy cannot safely be kept within the self, it seeks a safer container, which it finds in the group. The grandiose fantasy of the self becomes the grandiose fantasy of the group. The call for participation, then, expresses the projection of the individual's grandiosity onto others, "the people," assumed to share his or her need to govern, notwithstanding the possibility (even likelihood) that what people actually want is not to govern, but a government that does its job well.

This aspect of participatory ideals is seldom given the attention it deserves. Indeed, we may surmise that the energy behind the demand for workplace democracy, at least in its more extreme forms, originates in the projected narcissism to which I have just referred. Thus, those who imagine themselves to be the advocates of the (oppressed) worker also depict the failings of the workplace as the result of management failure. Doing so implicitly and explicitly insists that the failure of the workplace is due to management and to organizational structure, and can be fixed by changing management culture or the organization of authority (usually involving the elimination of authority). This endows management with a power to do evil comparable to the power to do good that management arrogates to itself. In this respect, its critics participate in management's omnipotent self-fantasies.

One important danger defended against by the fantasy of participation is exclusion (deprivation) and the feelings of envy provoked by it. Understanding the significance of exclusion and envy in fueling certain demands for democracy can help illuminate the significance and meaning of a concept central to the rhetoric of democracy: participation. The idea of participation represents the wished for escape from the world of exclusion and envy. Yet, in practice, participation creates significant opportunity to exclude others by providing a public forum and captive audience for those with a need to dominate.

The Use of Public Space

The more narcissistic the individual, the more driven he or she will be to occupy the public space created by democracy. The more aggressively such individuals pursue the occupation of public space, the more likely those with less primitive emotional agendas will concede public space to them. Here, again, we must bear in mind the tendency for more primitive affect to dominate in groups. Thus, democracy, which appears to be about removing oppression, about the rule of the "common man" (and possibly the common woman), about universal citizenship, turns out to be about the struggle to occupy public space. Understanding the meaning and use of public space becomes important, then, for understanding democracy, which, in principle at least, makes public space available to all.

Hannah Arendt suggests that we use public space to establish the objective reality of our subjective being. Indeed, for Arendt, appearing in public "constitutes reality." Public space makes this possible because it is the only place in which we can be "seen and heard" by others. Thus, "[t]he presence of others who see what we see and hear what we hear assures us of the reality of the world and ourselves...." Arendt goes so far as to insist that "our feeling for reality depends utterly upon appearance and therefore upon the existence of a public realm into which things can appear out of the darkness of sheltered existence...."[38]

In saying this, Arendt equates two potentially different groundings for the sense of being real: appearing for others, and appearing in public. She equates the two because she defines the public space as the space of others, which makes appearing in public equivalent to appearing for others. Appearing in public has this special significance because only the public consists of others: those who are also persons, but differ from us. This moment of difference plays a vital role in enabling the public space to accomplish its peculiar purpose. "Only where things can be seen by many in a variety of aspects without changing their identity, so that those who are gathered around them know they see sameness in utter diversity, can worldly reality truly and reliably appear."[39] For Arendt, the public realm is synonymous with the presence of others, and our reality depends on our recognition by others: those who are not us, and are not subsumed into our persons.

Put another way, reality-constituting appearance must be before strangers. This means, however, that we establish our reality by being known by those who do not know us, which is, of course, the characteristic way we know those who become public figures. We might ask, then, what sort of self becomes real in this way. Since this public self is known by strangers—those who do not know us—the reality of this self is our reality for strangers, a reality as alien to our selves as those strangers are. This is the reality of the false self, since it is for the false self that appearance constitutes reality.

For Arendt, the need to appear in public is not satisfied by having a life outside the family, in society: the world of voluntary associations and private contracts. She argues against any conflation of society with the public. This introduces a significant constraint on our effort to establish our reality by appearing in public. We cannot do so in our professional lives, which give us only the limited recognition of others who, because they are like us, do not fully constitute a public for us. Being in a work group, then, and appearing for others in that setting, must, if we follow Arendt, leave our reality suspect. Yet, this limited society is as public as most of us get in our lives. To be recognized by a limited set of co-workers is as real as our selves can hope to become. If this is not enough, then our world does not afford many the opportunities to establish the reality of their persons.

The ideal of democracy is that appearing in public will not be limited by birthright and attributed status, but open to all. The call for democracy can be a call to transform a part of society, or society as a whole, into a public where no one is excluded, there is no privatization, and all participate. Yet, in a modern society, the more all appear in public, the less any individual can gain recognition by so doing. Just as assuring universal suffrage assures that no one's vote matters, assuring publicity for all would make no one's person truly public. Democracy, then, does not secure the reality-constituting experience of appearing in public for all, but only creates a public in which the many recognize the (false) reality of the few, the difference from pre-modern society being in the way access to this experience is gained. Thus, if establishing your reality as a person requires "appearing" in public, and if, in practice, only a few can appear in public, then democracy constitutes a struggle over personhood, the magnitude of the person being measured by the amount of public space he or she occupies. In this setting, equality (of citizenship) is the root of domination.

The narcissistic gratification promised by public life can be a significant part of the idea of participation for those whose grandiosity impels them to fill the public space originally created to assure that no one is excluded. Thus, the idea that democracy's virtue lies in participation begs the question, which is about the nature and meaning of participation, and about the entity in which one participates. As Alford puts it, "participation is not a good in itself." When participation "is based upon and assumes the suppression of the self" it "can only reinforce the regressed group."[40]

Because sophisticated work groups can exist only when basic assumptions are either inactive or congruent with getting work done, those groups are neither as democratic as basic assumption groups can be, nor as undemocratic as basic assumption groups inevitably become. Sophisticated work groups are democratic if by democratic we mean incorporating respect for the individual member and providing that member appropriate discretion over relevant parts of the task at hand.

Basic assumption groups can be democratic if by democratic we mean that the norm of equality dominates the group, and the group dominates the member.

Democracy has been an important element in the struggle for individual freedom and self-determination. Democratic norms make regard for the individual the basis for group decision-making. Democratic norms also secure tolerance for dissent, and the rights of those in opposition. Because of this, a democratic group finds itself faced with a contradictory task. On one side, to maintain itself as a group, it must subordinate the individual. To accomplish this task, the democratic group must foster that regression in its members necessary to establish the reality of the group as such (its groupness). On the other side, a democratic group is predicated on the autonomy of its members, an autonomy that is threatened both by subordination to the group and by regression in service of maintaining the group's reality as something different from that of the aggregate of individuals.

It is of special importance that we focus attention on the way totalizing democracy is understood to create the group entity. This act of creation places the social order into the hands of the group. Put another way, it makes the self-governing group the architect of society, which can be whatever the group needs or wishes it to be. A conscious act or set of such acts on the part of the group, then, creates society; governance is the act of group self-creation. Imagining that society could be organized this way involves suspension of those higher ego functions associated with acknowledging constraints, in particular the constraints of what is and can be. Put in another language, these are the constraints of reason and reality testing, which are set aside in favor of a self-rule that directs a group will. Thus, the democratic group mirrors the omnipotent fantasy of the regressed individual, who imagines that the world can and must adapt to his or her wanting and willing. We can know, then, that groupness has moved to the fore and democracy been made a part of regression when the group loses touch with the limits and possibilities of its existence within a larger world, including a world of individuals (its own members) separate from the group. This is a world not of the group's own making and, in important ways, resistant to its demands.

The idea of the group will that is so vital a part of the democratic community mirrors at the level of the group the central ideal of the free market, that it liberates the force of individual will to remake the world. The centrality of the idea of will as the maker of reality then forges a link between the free market and democratic solutions to the problem of government.

Spontaneity and structure

At those moments when democracy seems especially flawed, it is sometimes remarked that, if imperfect, it is also better than the alternatives. Yet, to say that democracy is better than its alternatives is to take democracy for granted, to beg the question: What is this democracy that exceeds its alternatives in virtue? Is it the actually existing democracies one might, for example, compare with the so-called "actually existing socialisms" of the now defunct communist world? Is it representative democracy? Direct democracy? Is it the democracy that levels citizens, destroys difference, and denigrates professional competence? Is it the democracy that establishes a narcissistic struggle to occupy public space? Or, is it a democracy that secures individual integrity, respect for professional competence, and protection of the individual from the primitive emotional agendas dominating in some of the groups considered above? Evidently, we clarify little when we note the superiority of democracy to tyranny; indeed, we do not even establish that democracy is not itself a form of tyranny.

The considerations advanced above can be relevant to understanding what sort of democracy is, indeed, better than the alternatives, and what limits democracy must accept if it is to participate in group dynamics that respect the separateness of the members. Clearly, this democracy is not the direct democracy that turns itself into a total system of group domination. Nor is it the radical democracy that makes all individual right derivative of the rights of political participation and group self-governance. To answer the question about the democracy whose virtue exceeds that of the alternatives, we need first to answer the question about the group: What is the end of group life, and the appropriate relation of group to member?

In this chapter, I have explored two markedly different answers to this question. Each bears on our judgment about democracy. The appropriate answer has to do not only with the role of regression in shaping group life and defining group ends, but, more specifically, with the role of primitive defenses and primitive emotional agendas. The basic assumption group shapes democracy to its ends, often involving the use of others to relieve, or otherwise cope with, inner conflicts. This democracy can lay only minimal claim to superiority over tyranny, since it is itself a form of domination.

Only the democracy that organizes a group capable of mobilizing and connecting with member's mature emotional life can establish itself as clearly superior to its competitors. This democracy respects differences, including differences in professional competence, and including the difference in professional competence of those who manage group life itself. Rather than fostering primitive emotional agendas, this democracy would be an important part of the effort to contain those agendas.[41]

Democracy becomes the enemy rather than the expression of individual self-determination when democracy participates in the destruction of boundaries between individuals (e.g. rights) and between the individual and the group. We can understand this problem better if we emphasize one important aspect of what I refer to above as totalizing democracy: its lack of structure. Unstructured forms of governance, because they disdain boundaries, place the individual into a situation of significant anxiety.[42] In doing so, they foster the emergence of primitive emotional agendas, especially grandiosity and primitive aggression. The solution to this problem is to establish forms of governance that incorporate structure, especially to place democratic process into a setting that limits and contains aggression. Administrative structures can accomplish this end, and in this do not oppose, but facilitate attaining, the legitimate ends of democracy.[43]

The idea that structure is important to secure the group against regression is consistent with a hint put forward by Freud in his essay on group life. Overall, Freud's essay does not offer much to encourage us in our effort to imagine the creative possibilities for the individual existing as part of a group. Groups, he insists, are the site of regression, of the "intensification of affects and the inhibition of the intellect." Yet, Freud leaves a small door open. He suggests that there are certain groups that do not demand destructive forms of regression in their members. There are, Freud tells us, groups that operate in exactly the opposite way "and from which a much higher opinion of the group must follow." This opposite opinion owes its origin "to the consideration of those stable groups or associations in which mankind pass their lives, and which are embodied in the institutions of society."[44]

Freud characterizes those groups of which a higher opinion might be formed not only as more stable, but also as "organized" and "artificial."[45] They are not spontaneous, unstructured, ephemeral. Because of this, neither are they authentic groups. Indeed, they are not groups at all, but institutions. Put another way, they instantiate group life, and in so doing remove from it those qualities (of groupness) vital to making group life what it is.

Government is an institution that removes groupness from group life. In other words, government enables us to live together, to acknowledge our mutual dependence and the qualities we share as human beings without putting us into groups. Government can enable us to be citizens of a state and not members of a people or a community. It does so by developing an enduring structure that replaces spontaneous action with a collective thought process.

In his essay on civic morals, Emile Durkheim proposes that we consider the state an organ of collective thinking.[46] In emphasizing collective thinking, Durkheim centers attention on just that quality of government that is vital so far as the matter of resisting regression is concerned. So far as government is a deliberative organ, it assures that thinking intervene before action, an intervention lacking in the conduct of a basic group. Thinking is not something that can be done by a group as a whole, especially by a large and abstract group such as a community. Indeed, it is just this collective thought process mediated through enduring institutions of government that gets put aside in both the free market and participatory ideals.

Of course, structure can undermine the goal of democracy to secure the integrity of the individual, which happens when administrative structures "grow to such an extent that they dominate the society of which they are a part."[47] Administrative structure can facilitate oppression, as was the case in Germany in the Nazi era. It does so in part by relieving office-holders of moral responsibility.[48] So far as the office holder is not an individual, and is not expected to exercise autonomous judgment, actions taken in the name of the office are not subject to the moral restraints that limit action taken by the individual outside the institutional setting. A disparity arises in the space of professional ethics. Only when both the organization and its members embody professional ethics, so that the organization's larger ideals are also those of the professionals who occupy its offices, can this disparity be overcome.

Doubts about the possibility of achieving this goal become doubts that administrative structure can ever avoid becoming an apparatus of repression. These doubts stem ultimately from two connected sources. One is the premise that ethical conduct can only be assured in an egalitarian and participatory community, which administrative organization clearly is not. The second is the related premise that lines of authority must constitute a structure of power, that so far as there are lines of authority, they will be used for the purpose of willful control. This is clearly the case, for example, when the driving force of the individual in the organization is coping with envy, both acknowledged and projected.

Thus, neither administration nor democracy is in itself the solution. Rather we must consider the appropriate combination of the two, or more precisely, the appropriate division of labor between them.[49] Administration in the absence of democracy establishes a capricious power over the citizen, just as democracy, when it takes over all organizational decision making, undermines individual rights and threatens the individual's effort to maintain an autonomous identity in the context of group life.

Overcoming Power and Building Character

The solutions to the problem of government considered in this and the last chapter cover the same ground and respond to the same threats. Both conceive government as a locus of power over its citizens and both consider government a corrupter of character. Both contend that altering institutions can free citizens from the power of government while offering them a setting appropriate to building character.

The free market solution eliminates the danger posed by government's power by limiting government, which we do by replacing it so far as possible with market institutions. The smaller the arena for government action, the less government's power, the fewer the abuses of power. While the democratic solution appears to move in the opposite direction, it can also be seen to reduce the power of government, if we consider government not the process of governing, but enduring institutions of governance. The more those institutions are controlled and even replaced by the will of the people, the less the power of government. While the market solution replaces government with a system of private contracts, the democratic solution replaces government by the people as a whole, the democratic community.

Removing the power of government is seen as the first step to building character. For some, government undermines character by encouraging dependence. For them, will is the essence of character. Will and therefore character are built in a struggle of wills, and dependence is the enemy of will. For those who conceive the problem this way, the competitive market society is not only the antidote to the power of government, it is also the necessary setting for shaping character. For those who emphasize democratic ideals, community builds character, and government is the enemy of character so far as it stands in the way of community, which it does when its institutions displace the people in the act of governing. Whichever route we take to solving the perceived problem of government, our journey takes us onto the terrain of power and character, which are the two main themes in the psychic drama of government.

These two themes express an underlying issue, the issue of deprivation and loss. Overcoming power bears, as we saw in chapter 2, a complex and problematic relationship with oppression, since it can mean attaining the capacity for subjectively meaningful experience in life, or it can mean attaining a state of powerlessness and rule by fate. In either case, however, the issue of power is an issue about the losing and finding of subjectivity in self and other. Power is the capacity to achieve subjectivity and it is the capacity to take it away.

Character is also about the finding and losing of subjectivity. The character built in the struggle of wills is, as we saw in chapter 6, a character built on self-hatred, self-repression, and therefore the loss of self. The character appropriate to democratic community is not the ethical character we considered in chapter 1, but the character of the member, who has, to use Freud's language, given up his or her autonomous ego-ideal for the ideal of the group (and of its leader). Subjectivity is here lost to the member so it can be gained by the group. Building character means loss of self into the group. The issues loss pose for government center around the problem of justice, of citizenship, and of difference. These are the issues I consider in the next two chapters.

8 CITIZENSHIP AND DIFFERENCE

A Better Tomorrow

In his second Inaugural address (January 21, 1985), Ronald Reagan offers an observation on "present-day Americans." We are not, he says, "given to looking backward." This observation is a commonplace of American political rhetoric. Thus, the two major party candidates for President in 2000 express the same sentiment. According to Al Gore, Americans "respond to someone who sees better times—and I see better times."[1] And according to George W. Bush, "Americans always look forward, to the next horizon. In this blessed land, there is always a better tomorrow."[2] All of these references pale when set against the words of Franklin Roosevelt:

> Shall we pause now and turn our back upon the road that lies ahead? Shall we call this the promised land? Or, shall we continue on our way? For "each age is a dream that is dying, or one that is coming to birth."[3]

Like references to moral standing, also prominent in Reagan's communication with the nation, references to the past and future clearly indicate the presence of a powerful psychic agenda. In Reagan's speech, that agenda seems, however, somewhat obscure and confusing. While the tone is set by the comment that we Americans do not look to the past and expect a better future, another theme quickly joins that of progress, one that at first glance seems somehow inconsistent with the idea of leaving the past behind. This is the theme of renewal: the better future is better because it returns us to our past.

Language alluding to the second theme occupies considerable space in what follows. We are told that the system by which the government works for the people, "has never failed us," thus suggesting that what Reagan seeks to find in our future is the system set in place by the Founding Fathers. Shortly after this comment, Reagan tells us that we are in the process of "creating a nation once again vibrant, robust, and alive," thus suggesting that our agenda for the future is to recreate our past. It is time, we are told, to "renew our faith." The President refers to his second term as years during which Americans will have "restored their confidence and tradition of progress." All of this suggests that our task is to find redemption from a fall from grace so that we can be readmitted to the Promised Land.

One way to begin to understand the meaning embedded in this conflicting rhetoric is to distinguish the real from the ideal, and note that in the President's speech the ideal lives in the past and in the future, not in the present. Thus, the central opposition of real and ideal is here drawn in temporal space as an opposition between past, present, and future. The past and future are both good because they are not real, and the present must be made good precisely because it is real, and what is real can always be better than it is. There is, however, more to it than that.

Toward the middle of his speech, after he has sounded his anti-government theme, Reagan turns to the matter of unity.

> Our two party system has served us well over the years, but never better than in those times of great challenge when we came together not as Democrats or Republicans, but as Americans united in a common cause. ... Well, with heart and hand, let us stand as one today: One people under God determined that our future will be worthy of our past.

Only as a people can we reconcile the contradictions of past and future by making our future worthy of our past. Uniting as a people will unite yesterday and tomorrow. The opposition of real and ideal arises out of disunity; we might even say it is the fundamental disunity that must be repaired.

What distinguishes the past and future from the present is what distinguishes unity from division. This suggests that we consider the whole problem of time as one of the sought for merger with the good object, a merger recalled or written into the past and hoped to be retrieved in the future. In this chapter, I would like to explore this theme of merger, of unity and difference, more closely.

Fear of Unity

In his essay on the struggle to establish the nation-state and national identity in developing countries, Clifford Geertz draws attention to the problem of unity and difference that is, in its way, the problem of the state. For developing countries, the problem appears as one of subordinating "specific and familiar identifications in favor of a generalized commitment to an overarching and somewhat alien order."[4] Geertz suggests that the new national identity poses a danger to the individual that he or she will suffer a "loss of identity as an autonomous person, either through absorption into a culturally undifferentiated mass or, what is even worse, through domination by some rival ethnic, racial, or linguistic community that is able to imbue that order with the temper of its own personality."

Ernest Gellner has linked this threat to local communities and local identities to the demands of modern technology and economy. As the division of labor extends beyond the local unit, there emerges a larger cultural unit appropriate to the need to integrate the new political economy. For Gellner, the main point is that "a society has emerged based on a high-powered technology and the expectancy of sustained growth, which requires both a mobile division of labour, and sustained, frequent, and precise communication between strangers involving a sharing of explicit meaning, transmitted in a standard idiom and in writing when required."[5] The culture appropriate to a modern society must be sustained by a political-social unit of adequate size, which is a nation-state.

There must, then, be a greater integration at least in the sense that one high culture stands in place of the many local cultures. Gellner emphasizes the integrating function of this high culture, but he does not insist we imagine it to be universal in any other sense, whatever claims along these lines it will inevitably advance for itself. Clearly, the dominant high culture must adapt to the purpose of integrating a modern society; indeed it may need to be invented just for this purpose. But, for Gellner, it remains a particular culture, and others might have served as well had they risen to dominance. Gellner thus justifies the anxiety about the state expressed by those concerned to protect their particular cultures: it may well be alien to them, and it certainly intends to displace them with something alien.

We can see how loss is built into the problem of nation building. For all but the group whose culture rises to dominance, the emergence of the nation means the loss, to one degree or another, of their particular cultural identity. Even where holding onto cultural difference remains a possibility, the particular culture must lose its salience to a significant degree where it becomes subordinate to an alien culture.

Consider, in this connection, the argument Warren Magnusson advances for local politics. At the center of this argument is the idea that the state embodies a "metaphysic of unity."[6] The attachment of the state to integration, to ever larger units, distances it from the aspirations of citizens to have a space in which they can articulate and advance the particular concerns that arise out of different life situations, "a politics in which human differences are taken seriously." This space is the locality, "the place where people live their day-to-day lives...." The locality is "the site for face-to-face contact, immediate economic and social relations, immediately shared experience and interests."[7]

Its drive for unity, then, is the problem of the state since it alienates the citizen from any meaningful political process that would be responsive to the particularity of his or her life circumstances. The stronger the state, the more alien it must be. Thus, the state must be opposed precisely because it is the site of integration. It must be replaced with local politics, which is the site of difference.

For Magnusson, the association of the state with integration means that we should consider a dispersion of state power to the local community. In so doing, we increase the political space available to the citizen understood as a member of a community. Thus, for him, particularity is a matter of community. But an oddly similar conclusion arises for those who link particularity not to community but to the individual. For them, the problem of the state is also that it undermines particularity in the name of a metaphysic of unity, but their solution is a different one: the free market.

This idea is well expressed by Milton Friedman when he considers the dangers of majority rule. Majority rule expresses a pressure for unity of a particular kind, especially when the majority is that of a large, or overarching, political unit.

> The widespread use of the market reduces the strain on the social fabric by rendering conformity unnecessary with respect to any activities it encompasses. The wider the range of activities covered by the market, the fewer are the issues on which explicitly political decisions are required and hence on which it is necessary to achieve agreement.[8]

The drive for unity in the face of diversity is here interpreted as an expression of the drive for the part to dominate the whole. So far as the whole has no standing in its own right, or so far as the universal moment of human experience is treated as a metaphysic, the drive toward unity is an expression of power over others. It is the way one part of society attempts to enforce its will over the other parts by insisting on a whole expressive of its partial interest, the particular interest masquerading as the public interest.

Thus, the distrust of integration and community is the same distrust of power we considered in chapter 3. This fear of power has parallel expressions in the free market and democratic solutions to the problem of government, depending on whether the particular interest is considered primarily that of an individual or a group, and whether politics is considered part of the problem or part of the solution. In this chapter, I consider the problem of unity and difference as a problem about group identification and citizenship rather than as a concern that might be addressed by free market policy. It is, nonetheless, worth bearing in mind that the problem of difference is also a problem that a free market policy centered on the individual rather than the group is meant to solve.

The Problem of Difference

The problem of difference looms large. The poor differ from the rich, the sick from the healthy. Men differ from women. Americans of Chinese descent differ from those whose ancestors arrived from Northern Europe two hundred years ago. Some differences we celebrate; others we lament. Yet the question remains, Which should we value and which should we resist? Why can we tolerate some and not others?

The problem of difference is, in its way, a problem about citizenship. Differences rooted in identification with certain kinds of groups (most notably racial, ethnic, or religious groups) can conflict with the universality we might assume is implied in the notion of citizenship. This is because the connection to such groups can undermine the recognition of personhood in those outside the group, and thus foster oppression. Whether difference denies or enhances personhood, removes or promotes oppression, challenges or reinforces shared citizenship, depends on its origin and meaning, and, in particular, on how it is rooted in the process that establishes group identity. Groups that impose a shared identity on their members foster the idea that those members differ from others in ways that rest uneasily with the expectations we have of fellow citizens. The complex implications of group identity for citizenship have posed significant problems for government. If connection to government calls on a shared, and thus more universal, identity than that linked to a particular group, it can challenge the hegemony of the group over the member, who is also a citizen. In this case, the group rests uneasily within the larger unit for which the government is responsible. Alternatively, when government becomes identified with a particular group, the government loses its ethical standing.

A characteristic of group identity that can distinguish it from the identity of the individual as a citizen is that the former is often imposed in ways that the latter is not. The imposition of group identity has been most striking for groups we are made a part of from birth because of our gender, race, or ethnicity. Julia Kristeva emphasizes the dangers entailed in reducing men and women "to the identification needs of their originary groups," including the danger that these needs will foster a "hate reaction" directed at those "who do not share my origins and who affront me personally, economically, and culturally."[9] Honoring, or otherwise encouraging, diversity can reinforce originary group identifications imposed on persons placed into membership independently of their will.

While some group identities operate coercively, others operate in concordance with self-determination, facilitating the expression of qualities and talents that emerge out of processes of individuation and self-formation. Kristeva goes so far as to suggest that we gauge the freedom society affords the individual by the individual's ability to choose his or her group memberships.[10] Yet that ability depends on the character of the groups and the way they bind members to them.[11] In thinking about diversity, it matters what sorts of group identities we have in mind. In particular, it matters whether our connection with groups affirms, expresses, and develops self-determination, or represses freedom in the pursuit of group ends opposed to it.

The shape of social and political institutions significantly affects the kinds of groups to which individuals belong and the meaning belonging has for them. In particular, it affects whether belonging threatens or secures the individual's aspiration to an autonomous development. We need, then, to understand how social policy affects freedom through its effect on group affiliations.

Shared Identity

To belong in a group is to have a place in the world, to be identified with that place, and thus to have an identity resting on a group foundation. For certain kinds of groups, belonging is not only one aspect of our relation to the group, it is the prime psychic significance of group membership.[12] Such groups enter into the member's sense of self in a special way. The member's identification with the group takes the form of a shared identity. To belong to a group organized around a shared identity is to know who you are independently of your self, since your self is not so much yours as borrowed from the larger collective entity. This borrowed self is shared with fellow members who are not really different. Within such groups, there are no others.

Consider, in this regard, Frances Fitzgerald's observation about the members of Jerry Falwell's Liberty Baptist Church. Not only do members have a way of dressing that distinguishes them from non-members, but they all seem to think alike: "As an outsider soon discovers, there is no real point in talking to more than one of them on a topic of general interest, for there is a right answer to every question...."[13] No doubt, this is in some ways an extreme example. Yet, thinking and dressing alike are important in establishing a common identity for groups intent on reducing or eliminating distinctions among members. Fitzgerald notes a similar pattern in the gay community of San Francisco during the late 1970s, where "gay men even presented a uniform appearance."[14]

Psychically, this process of identification operates through the formation of the ideal self or "ego ideal." The group has an ideal of the member including for example: physical traits such as size, shape, or skin color; character traits such as suppression or expression of emotion and assertiveness or compliance; preferred vocations; preferred ways of being expressive through music, dance, and literature. For the member, the aspiration to belong means an aspiration to be, so far as possible, the group's ideal. This aspiration implies that the member's ideal self is borrowed from the group.

Belonging provides the member with an external source of security in being. This external source can either supplement or substitute for the member's internal self-assurance. Substitution for the member's self is one of the functions of originary groups. This substitution of corporate for individual self, by undermining difference, forms a collective in which the members do not feel a sense of separate being. This formation of a corporate being affects the member's tolerance of difference. Belonging sets up oppositions between us and them not implied in the differences between persons. "Attachment to the group is at once an act of solidarity and an act of exclusion."[15]

Put another way, underlying matters of difference and the psychic meaning of groups are "merger fantasies." These are fantasies that express the wish to overcome self-boundaries and individual limits to establish a primitive unity (or "oneness") that recalls and recreates, so far as possible, early experiences of connectedness within the family and especially the mother-infant dyad. Merger fantasies can play a significant part in group life.[16] Our relations with others might threaten us either because they disrupt merger fantasies or because they insist on merger. The more our psychic equilibrium depends on the hope, however unrealistic, of merger, the more we are drawn to groups that dissolve the individuality of their members. The challenge that our membership in such groups poses to our own autonomy threatens to become a challenge to the autonomy of those outside the group. This happens because groups predicated on merger understand that the idea of autonomy threatens their domination over their members. Thus, what most frightens members of Liberty Baptist Church about secular education "is not just that the schools teach the wrong answers; it is that the schools do not protect children from information that might call their beliefs into question."[17]

The more our psychic equilibrium depends on autonomy, the more groups that demand merger pose a threat, while those identifications that facilitate autonomy threaten us so far as our psychic well being revolves around the hope for merger.[18] These very different threats have much to do with our tolerance or intolerance of those who differ from us.

Externally imposed identities are given independently of our actions and decisions. Because of this, they must be in some sense original. An original identification claims grounding, usually in nature, that precedes our consciousness of our selves. As Benedict Anderson comments, "in everything 'natural' there is always something unchosen."[19] Imposed identifications link us to the ancestors and founders who, in history and myth, first established the group. Thus, in originary groups, "the dead decide for the living."[20]   This quality of imposed group identifications gives them their tremendous power. They are among the first things we know about ourselves: we are boys or girls, black or white, Chinese or French, Smith, Cohen, or Khan. We cannot know ourselves before we are ourselves since knowing is the activity of a self; yet we cannot become ourselves unless we know the self we will become. Originary groups play on this tension of maturation by seeking to define who we are before we have a chance to do so ourselves.

Early in its development, the self lacks the degree of integration needed to maintain its identity against potentially hostile external impositions. In F. von Broembsen's words, this primitive self "does not have the cognitive or affective resources to resist a hostile, colonizing, definition of itself."[21] This colonization of the self is what I have in mind by an imposed identification. Once colonized, the trajectory of development, especially regarding identity formation, expresses an alien presence within the self that impedes realization of its aspiration to self-determination. This underscores the importance of understanding that imposed group identifications, operating on the child through the medium of the family and the greater culture, must take root early in psychic development, before the individual forms an identity of his or her own adequate to ward off alien self-interpretations.[22]

In originary groups, we are known to all because we are, in important respects, the same. Yet, if we develop, even within such groups, elements of an individual identity, those who know us as members, know us falsely. This way of being falsely known oppresses since it denies our personhood, seeing in us not persons but members. The original identification that places us in a supposed natural grouping is an identification we can never quite overcome. Insofar as we also develop a personal sense of being, we suffer a split in our sense of self. The stronger our personal sense of being, the more our imposed group identification becomes an alien presence within the self. It is inside us, and yet it is not of us. Since it can never be fully reconciled with our aspiration for an autonomous development, the imposed original identification impedes self-integration.

Self-integration does not mean the elimination of difference. An integrated self may have different aspects and capacities expressed in different settings: different emotional states, different talents and skills, different interests and affiliations. Problems arise when these different aspects of identity conflict with each other because they express inconsistent aspirations and ideals, when they are not different aspects of one identity, but different competing identities. Considering the psychic and moral value we attach to achieving our ideals, when they conflict, success in realizing those attached to one identity forces us to judge ourselves harshly for failing to realize those attached to others. Thus, for example, when one identity incorporates autonomy, another compliance, autonomous action provokes a harsh judgment from our compliant self. Then, psychic differentiation becomes psychic division and brings with it the psychic pain of inner conflict.

Failure of psychic integration has damaging consequences resulting from the coercion implied in the development of psychic division. The colonizing forces must repress any aspiration for an autonomous, genuinely individual, development according to a trajectory not previously determined, but yet to be discovered. A part of our identity now works against our desire to be a person in our own right. The opposition between the group and the individual becomes an inner division between the impulse to develop and express a uniquely individual sense of self and the desire to belong to a group. The internal repression of the self in the interest of the group offers fertile ground for the cultivation of an impulse to repress others, to visit on them the denial of autonomy associated with the colonization of our selves made part of our own development. The oppression of others is, by its nature, repression of the self-in-other, which reenacts the original repression of the self in the interests of group connection. Understanding oppression as repression of the self-in-other is vital if we are to establish the link between repression of self and oppression of others, which has a fundamental bearing on the problem of difference.

The family plays a central role not only as our first group, but also as the lens through which our greater group identifications are focused on us. Families bear a name and history that identify members first into the family group and then into the groups to which the family belongs by its own externally imposed identifications. Insofar as families are organized as systems that link members to originary groups, the family relates to each member not as a vehicle to facilitate individuation and identity formation, but as a vehicle to assure that the power of original identifications continues unmodulated throughout life and across generations. The family that knows its members before they know themselves shapes its members to belong to groups capable of repeating the family patterns of knowing self and other. By contrast, the family that learns with the child who he or she is and might be allows the child to mature into a person capable of choosing group affiliations according to whether they fit his or her character.

The way society imagines the development of the child mirrors, and is mirrored in, the way the family relates to the child. In both settings, freedom either becomes a central value or gets lost in the subordination of individual development to group identity. The freedom at stake here is not the freedom to be anything and do anything, but the freedom from imposed group identifications. Under the power of group identifications, the shape of the person into whom the child will develop is already determined by the shape of the group member. Weakening the power of these identifications means that the person into whom the child will develop is not already known either by the larger society or by the family. The freedom that this weakening of imposed identifications affords is, in Erik Erikson's words, the "freedom of opportunities yet undetermined."[23] This is the freedom to develop, which contrasts sharply with the situation in which development is replaced by the process of adaptation to an already given identity.

Nation, Culture, and Community

We can apply some of the considerations advanced above to the idea of a nation if we treat nations as originary groups and national identity as an imposed group identification. Doing so builds a bridge between nationality and the other primary forms of imposed identification. When one is born to a national identity, it seems a natural quality on a par with gender or race. "In this way nation-ness is assimilated to skin colour, gender, parentage, and birth-era—all those things one cannot help."[24] Nations stake their claim to originary status by reading their own origins back in history. Doing so, however, poses difficulties. Anderson highlights the historically recent origins of nations and their biographies, and the strenuous efforts nations undertake to read themselves into antiquity, where they have no roots and do not belong.[25]

While the nation's aspiration to be a natural and original group fails the historical test, this is not the case for another original group with which the nation is intimately involved: the ethnic community. In his study of ethnic groups, Anthony Smith emphasizes history, origins, and myths. The ethnic community exists because of its connection to an origin in the distant past and to a set of cultural practices having the status of traditions empowered by their rootedness in the constituting myths of the group. These considerations suggest how well the ethnic community conforms to the idea of an originary group.

Establishing the link between the nation and the ethnic community supports the nation's uncertain claim to antiquity. Establishing this connection also provides the ethnic group with a political and territorial existence. When this happens, however, the nation falls under the dominance of the ethnic community. This dominance can threaten the purposes of the nation so far as they diverge from those of the ethnic community. This divergence is, perhaps, most vivid where the ethnic community defines itself in religious terms. A nation committed to being a religious community (whatever the religion) cannot at the same time sponsor the freedom of expression associated with the idea of citizenship. Thus the conservative Jewish parties in Israel ask the question: What is the meaning of the Israeli state without its commitment to Judaism? At the same time, the more liberal parties suggest that Palestinians living in Israel as citizens are as much a part of the nation as are Jews. Divergence between the purposes of the nation and the ethnic group implies a tension between nation and ethnic community that raises again questions about the nation as a true originary group. Few nations succeed in establishing themselves as originary groups by connecting themselves to a single ethnic community. The difference between nation and ethnic community appears first in the multiplicity of ethnic groups within the nation. This multiplicity of ethnic groups has different consequences at different times and in different national settings.

Nations sometimes adopt the identity of one ethnic group. This places the chosen ethnic identity in a privileged position. In this position, it can use the state to commit acts of violence against those in other groups. Thus, the connection of the state to particular community assures that it will become a coercive apparatus, justifying the fear of the state with which we are here most concerned. This is always the danger implicit in linking the state to community, especially local community. The resulting violence against and impoverishment of those (subordinate) communities without privileged access to the state express the effort to ground nation in community (in this case ethnic community). Examples of states serving the ends of ethnic or religious violence are ubiquitous, from the last century's war against the native American tribes, to the war in Bosnia. To avoid these consequences, nations have, in recent years, taken up the idea of diversity as a good in itself. The resulting celebration of diversity continues state sponsorship of ethnicity, but without the exclusivity of the state's identification with one ethnic group.

State sponsorship of particular community can place the group above the individual with potentially serious consequences if it marks a "retreat from universalistic values to more ascriptive ones," placing the (individual) citizen into a dilemma.[26] To acquire the benefits of the state, citizens sacrifice the universality of citizenship and adopt the garb of particularity. Identifying with their community carries benefits, but it comes at a price since it demands subordination of individual identity to group identification. Further, so long as the nation is not absorbed into the (ethnic or religious) community, there must remain a tension between the more universal values it embodies and the values of the particular communities whose diversity it sponsors.

When the link between nation and community fails, the nation must develop a separately founded national identity and connect citizens to each other and to the whole on a basis other than common origins. Since this new identity will be shared by citizens of differing ethnic origins, it must be more universal than those identities still rooted in ethnic diversity. The more universal forms of shared identity leave room only for that particularity consistent with the demands of a universally grounded shared citizenship. The new national identity embodies universals such as equality of citizenship regardless of race, gender, or ethnicity, and tolerance of individual difference. Because of this universality, the new identity not only supplements but also challenges the old.

The problem of forming an identity appropriate for citizenship would be complex enough if it meant nothing more than shifting an attachment from one group (the ethnic community) to another (the nation). What makes the problem more difficult is that the nature of the attachment, and not simply its object, changes. Citizenship is a legal status gained, an idea held, and a value to which we become attached; but, it is also a psychic achievement involving formation of an identity consistent with a specific attitude and orientation toward others. Central to this attitude is respect for the self-in-other. Respecting the self-in-other means recognizing that someone different from us is also a person (has a self). This implies that there are different ways of being a self, many of which are as yet unknown, and that respect for selfhood does not mean celebration of a particular, already given, way of life, but celebrating the freedom of each individual to develop a way of life suitable to his or her talents, interests, experiences, and creative capacities. Development of this attitude requires social institutions that facilitate self-development in its different and changing forms.

The appropriate attitude toward others sees us connected to them not because we are members of the same group, or have the same identity, but on a more universal basis that supports difference. Connection with others no longer demands identification with them, but instead recognition of them as equally, though differently, persons. While recognition contains the idea of difference, identification imposes sameness. The appropriate attitude toward others does not form automatically, even where the legal status of universal citizenship is recognized; nor does it form primarily through teaching relevant values, as many today seem to believe. Because it calls on an orientation of self to other, it depends on a specific psychic development that fosters appropriate self-boundaries and establishes the psychic reality of the (legally recognized) separation between self and other.

For the growth of citizenship, the quality of attachment must change. Indeed, this change is what we observe taking place when distinctions rooted in particulars begin to take on more universal qualities. For example, the gender differences currently stressed in political and intellectual discourse override the particularities of community, culture, and in some cases even history to establish transcendent qualities of men and women. Similarly, all those of even partial African descent, whether Nigerian, Brazilian, or North American, claim a common identity that overrides the seemingly insurmountable diversity of culture, nationality, and history. Originary identity loses its grounding in originary group.

This loss of connection between identity and group also applies to the relation between citizen and nation. Insofar as it embodies the modern notion of citizenship, the nation gives up its rooting in the ethnic group calling into question the consistency of citizenship with group membership. Is the modern nation a group, especially an originary or imposed group? Does the effort to make the nation a group, which we associate with building nationalist sentiment, damage its grounding in the idea of citizenship?

An alternative roots the nation not in the group, but in culture. A culture may or may not form into a group. The forming of culture into a group has much to do with the vicissitudes of nationalism. Tsvetan Todorov emphasizes the difference between thinking about nationalism as community (group) and as culture.[27] He suggests that, while attachment to culture "leads toward universalism—by deepening the specificity of the particular within which one dwells ... civic nationalism ... is a preferential choice in favor of one's own country over the others—thus it is an antiuniversalist choice." Culture can provide a vernacular for expressing universals. In this respect, the particular culture is like a particular language, particular in that it is different from other languages, but universal in that it enables expression of the ideas also expressible in other comparable languages. Culture is a medium that, while particular in form, is universal in the opportunities it affords. Civic nationalism, by contrast, sets up the vernacular as a privileged expression for universals. In doing so, it constitutes those who share the culture as a group that denigrates others in a way (modern) culture as such need not. This causes divisions within and between national communities.

Culture as vernacular offers elements out of which identities can be constructed. In the words of one student, "collective identities should be seen as no more than symbolic resources out of which individual identities can be made through specific interactions with others."[28] The construction of identity is here considered the work of the individual. Since identities are not given to individuals, individuals must shape those identities for themselves. Indeed the construction of putatively group identities (for example of ethnicity, race, or gender) now becomes the work of individuals.

When cultural attachment becomes nationalism, however, it moves from a particular that embodies a universal to a particular that replaces the universal in order to exclude other particulars. The nation as a cultural locus is not necessarily a group, while the nation as locus of nationalist sentiment inevitably is. The issue has to do with the role and mode of instantiating culture. Culture can be a context of meaning and practice within which the individual takes on a definite existence, or culture can be an imposed group identification threatening freedom and self-development. Nationalism makes culture an imposed group identification.

When this happens, nation state as an originary group stands opposed to the universal (persons), which is not a group, and to the particular (culture), which is the setting for a personal existence but not a group to which the individual belongs. Todorov suggests that the relations among these dimensions of personal and group life are complex, that national identity simultaneously promotes a universal ethic of regard for others and denies such regard for those who stand to the members as "other."[29] This problematic mix of universal and particular characterizes the dynamic of originary groups, which know members differently from others, and whose knowledge of member and other can endanger the identity of each.

Being related to strangers is an important attribute of membership in modern groups. Anderson and Gellner see it as a defining characteristic of the modern nation, which makes fellow citizens of people who do not know each other. Citizens only know each other abstractly as bearers of rights and obligations, not as particular persons with concrete wants and capacities. In this sense, fellow citizens are known to each other while remaining unknown. This way of knowing differs fundamentally from that used to know members of originary groups. The difference is what I referred to earlier when I distinguished between identification with and recognition of.

To be unknown as a citizen of a modern state rather than member of originary community liberates us from imposed identifications. Each of us as citizen remains his or her own person. Our recognition by others as a citizen leaves significant room for those differences between persons vital to self-determination. Our fellows do not know who we are simply by knowing that we are citizens. Our common culture enables us to know others. Yet, so long as the shared culture does not make us the same, we do not immediately know the others who share the culture with us.

On a psychic level, freedom means freedom from imposed identifications. It refers to the potential within each person for a unique life trajectory expressive not of the demands of conformity to already given identities rooted in originary groups, but of the individual's creative capacities and interests. Psychic freedom begins at home with the relation between family group and child. It then carries over to the societal level, where facilitating freedom means limiting the relation between nation and originary group, and the tendency for nations to form themselves into groups, thus turning culture into a group phenomenon. Countering this tendency requires limiting the state's sponsorship of originary groups. This means facilitating individual difference rather than sponsoring group identity.

Celebrating Diversity and Removing Oppression

Injustice connected to group identifications poses special problems. Discrimination (or more severe forms of oppression imposed on individuals because of their identification with a particular group) wrongs individuals. But the oppression targets the individual only because of his or her group connection, and thus harms the individual as a representative of the group. The intent is to harm the group, and to ignore or suppress the member's particularity. Oppression of group members means suppression of their individuality; it denies that the member is anything more or different than a group member.

Suppression of individuality has implications for the distribution of injustice across group members. Because of their group identifications, discrimination against one member can be felt by others. Members, then, share oppression because the oppression of one is the oppression of all. This identification of the member with the group makes sense, psychically if not ethically, of the idea that special benefits provided to any members of an oppressed group, however they may have been treated individually, right a wrong.

Because of this complexity in group experience, we can speak of wrong done to a group, over and above that done to an individual. Whether this allows us to speak of group rights, beyond those of the members as individuals, is another matter. The wrong done may still be the violation of the group member's individual right and not the right of the group as a whole. Indeed, this must be the case if the wrong done is bound up with treating the member not as an individual in his or her own right, but as nothing more than an instantiation of group identity, in no way different from any other member. If wrong means suppression of autonomy and its expression in individuation, right must pertain to the individual and not the group as a whole. Yet, even if the right is individual, other group members experience the wrong precisely because the wrong constitutes an attack on the group through its member.

Group identification brings a shared, even corporate, selfhood. By blurring self-boundaries, it facilitates the movement of loss from person to person within the group. This experience leads to the conclusion that justice demands removal of the loss not primarily from individuals but from the group. Often enough this means shifting the loss to others, especially to members of those groups held responsible. Once we establish group identity and treat oppression as a group experience, it is no large step to see the oppressors also as a group, and to distribute responsibility accordingly. Then, not only do those group members not themselves oppressed feel the oppression of their fellows, but they also see responsibility in members of the other group independently of their individual involvement. All of this is natural enough when we organize our thinking about the world around the idea that groups dominate individual identity.

Psychically, oppression means imposition of identity and the attachment of a negative valence to the identity so imposed, in particular, the negative valence of inferiority. Oppression of groups means treating members as representatives of the group and not as persons in their own right, while attaching the negative valence to group membership. Celebrating diversity aims to remove oppression by replacing the negative valence of group identity with a positive one. We can, however, question whether celebrating diversity really removes the negative valence, since it makes what is positive about personhood a group trait rather than something the individual can achieve in his or her own right. Celebrating those traits celebrates the presence within the psyche of an imposed identity, fostering ambivalence about, and possibly even hatred toward, the part of the self that aspires to an autonomous development. Placing a positive valence on group identity places a positive valence on the repression of the individual's autonomous self. Celebrating diversity, then, removes one aspect of oppression, the attribution of inferiority, while reinforcing the other, reduction of the individual to his or her group identifications. While the conscious intent of those who advocate multiculturalism may be to encourage tolerance of difference by encouraging coexistence of many cultures, the underlying meaning and significance of the celebration of cultures can be something else entirely. This something else is the adhesion of identity to the originary group, and the formation of identity appropriate to belonging in that group.

The problem is compounded when we recall how group identity, and especially national identity, can be connected to oppression. In chapter 5, I consider how the effort to establish Quebec as a nation depended on an appeal to oppression, and an explicit willingness to oppress others (the Anglophone and Inuit populations). The connection between group identity and oppression leads to the celebration of oppression common in groups. Examples of this celebration of oppression include remembrance of experiences of group defeat (the Holocaust, Wounded Knee, and so on). Since the group cannot sustain itself without holding onto its experience of oppression, which binds the group together, it can never mourn its loss, but must instead find ways to reenact it, and therefore also to reestablish it in the psychic life of each generation.

These observations on the psychic meaning of originary group identification pose problems for the effort to secure the rights of members of oppressed groups. We cannot assure that members of those groups are protected without protecting their right to belong to such groups, and to share group-defining characteristics. Under these circumstances, protecting the individual demands protecting the group. Yet, so far as the struggle to remove oppression reinforces group identification, removing oppression can also reinforce oppression.

Privatization of public obligations tends to create a vacuum into which groups linked to ethnicity, race, culture, and religion enter. Measures aimed at weakening the state are also measures that strengthen originary group dependence, and therefore identification. Thus, for example, measures designed to eliminate welfare dependence may shift dependence from public to private rather than eliminating it, which is what some critics of the welfare state explicitly hope for. While some imagine that doing so will force the individual to cope with his or her own problem in the individualist spirit of the market, this assumes that individuals have the capacity to do so. But, if all individuals had this capacity, the welfare problem would not arise, at least not in its present form. Thus, the appeal to the market as a crucible for shaping character turns into a way of expressing sadistic impulses towards those unable to make their way in a market environment. The market leaves such individuals vulnerable to exploitation and oppression by other individuals and by groups. The group saves the individual, but at the cost of his or her individual identity. Only government can offer security to the citizen without demanding that he or she become a member of a group.

Government failure forces individuals to have recourse to the group in time of need. Doing so can intensify the forces building social fragmentation among partial group allegiances and group antagonism by replacing dependence on the state with dependence on the group. Originary groups thrive on the insecurity individuals feel about their ability to establish an identity in their own right. Measures that enhance the security of individuals are measures that diminish the hold of originary groups over them. Providing what security the state can provide and muting the rhetoric of diversity will contribute to freeing individuals of dependence on originary groups. Yet, in the end, we must not lose sight of the psychic dependence that remains after the other forms of dependence (especially material dependence) have been removed. While removing other forms of dependence can contribute to alleviating psychic dependence, removing the latter remains a task for which the state is ill suited. The problem devolves onto the family, and it is in this arena, where the influence of the state, while real, is not strong, that the question will ultimately be resolved.

Ambivalence

Those, such as Reagan and Buchanan, who seek unity but also fear it, involve themselves in the issues raised here in a particular way. The ambivalence they express suggests the ambivalence we feel when identification with the good object means loss of separate, and therefore different, self. When this happens, what we most profoundly desire is what poses the greatest danger to us: loss of self into a group identity. In the public arena, this ambivalence takes as its objects the government and the nation. Here, identification with the good object means attachment to a common culture, which makes the nation a group and national identity a matter of group identification. The group contains the good object, and it is only in connection with the group that we can be good.

This situation requires a morality of exclusion and fosters conflict with those who are not group members. Thus, it poses a threat to others, and conflicts with the universalistic ethic expressed in the idea of citizenship. At the same time, group identity threatens the autonomy of group members, who become good by becoming other than themselves. The contradiction is mediated, though not solved, in various ways, such as combining free market policies with nationalistic rhetoric (Reagan), or protectionist policies and cultural unity with enhanced power for local government (Buchanan).

These various combinations simply express our ambivalence toward integration, an ambivalence we can only overcome by giving up the hoped for merger, and with it the hope for the ultimate narcissistic fulfillment. In its place we can gain a life organized around a separate and different, therefore limited, self. In relations with others, this has the significance of giving up identification in favor of recognition. Seeking recognition rather than identification opens up the possibility that we will thrive where the nation is not a group that embodies what is good, but a setting that enables us, so far as possible, to be our selves, and shape a life expressive of our original vitality. Then, identification with the nation will not make us good, nor will difference make us bad.

Typically, national unity is conceived as a matter of common culture, and thus of group identification. When formulated in this way, unity must inevitably pose a threat to the individual, and to subordinate groups facing absorption into a national culture. Fear of unity then derives from fear of merger and loss of separate identity. The rhetoric quoted at the beginning of this chapter only intensifies the threat to the individual and to outside groups. It raises the stakes by offering narcissistic gratification at the expense of autonomy.

9 DEMANDING JUSTICE

Our Search for Justice

As we approach the climax of Frank Capra's drama about an innocent man (Mr. Smith) in an evil world (Washington), we realize that the head of the political machine is about to commit an act before which all his manipulation and graft pale into insignificance. He is about to make an innocent man pay the price for the guilt of others. And, in this worst of all acts, he will enlist the government (specifically the Senate) as his accomplice. The government, which we expect to be the steward of justice, will assure that the innocent are punished for the crimes of the guilty.

This same fear permeates the Goldman family's account of the trial of the man (O.J. Simpson) accused of the murder of their son, Ron. As the family's story unfolds, it becomes clear that their search for justice is a mission to assure that innocence and guilt will be clearly and appropriately assigned by that system empowered on earth to do so: the system of justice. In their search for justice, they encounter a powerful obstacle, an obstacle that lies at the heart of the emotional significance of justice.

The force that threatens to obstruct justice for the Goldmans is privilege, specifically the privilege bestowed on the wealthy and the famous. Their search for justice, then, becomes a battle against privilege. The battle against privilege is, for them, a struggle for recognition, not simply of the rights of the victim to justice as retribution, but of the virtues of the victim, virtues that seem to be lost in the attention bestowed on the guilty. Thus, the Goldmans link privilege to neglect; to privilege some is to neglect others. The emotional force most evident in the Goldmans' search for justice and battle against privilege is their hate for the man accused of the crime and for all those who would help him escape justice. The themes of their search for justice, then, are privilege, neglect, and hate. For them, justice means vindication of the innocent through punishment of the guilty, and the triumph of virtue over privilege. These are the themes of justice as the Goldmans imagine it; and in this, their viewpoint, while idiosyncratic in some respects, closely parallels the ideal of justice that dominates contemporary public life.

As we follow the Goldman family's account of their "search for justice" the issue of privilege quickly moves to the forefront. "It seemed clear that Simpson was accustomed to receiving special treatment, not only in the community, but from the police and the courts as well."[1] This theme dominates the early sections of the Goldman's book as the family expresses its fear that justice will not be done because of the defendant's special status as a celebrity. They found it "absurd that Simpson would be allowed to turn himself in the following morning at ten o'clock," noting that "only if you are a celebrity or wealthy" do you get to "turn yourself in."[2]

The family multiplies its complaints about the special treatment accorded Simpson because of his celebrity status. Fred Goldman (Ron's father) reports his surprise when he first saw Simpson in court wearing an expensive suit, when he expected to see him "wearing orange prison overalls or whatever prisoners normally wear." Goldman was also disappointed to discover that Simpson was not "restrained by handcuffs and shackles." Worst of all was Simpson's demeanor in court, where he could be found "smiling at what he seemed to consider an adoring crowd, sauntering toward the defense table."[3]

The family is outraged at this special treatment that extends into Simpson's life in jail.

> From the beginning of his incarceration … the defendant had badgered the county for special privileges. As a result, the star prisoner showered more often, slept later, and enjoyed ten more hours of free time than other inmates. He had an exercise bike for personal use. He spoke on the telephone and seemed to be allowed to watch television whenever he liked.[4]

The family is appalled when it finds out that Simpson's "celebrity status would make it difficult for a jury to sentence him to death."[5]

The significance of the family's preoccupation with the special treatment received by Simpson becomes clear when we consider the second theme: neglect. On one level, the primary purpose of the book is to counter the attention paid to the celebrity involved in the crime, and shift that attention to the unknown victim, Ron Goldman, and, by extension, his family. "I explained [to reporters] that it was agonizing for us to hear our son referred to as simply Nicole Simpson's friend, and I concluded, 'He has a name. His name is Ron.'" When approached by Barbara Walters for an interview, the family reports that they "reserved comment on the guilt or innocence of the man who would be tried for Ron's murder. It was Ron whom we wanted to discuss." The family feared that, as time passed, Ron would be forgotten. They wanted people "to know who the real Ron was, and where he came from." On CNN, the defendant was prominently featured, but "Ron was ignored." As the trial unfolded, the "victims faded into the background."[6]

The family felt strongly that inadequate attention was paid to their concerns. Their letters to the judge received no response. The promised update sessions from the Prosecutor were often canceled or ignored. A main theme of the book is the sense that Ron, his family, their interests, needs, and concerns were neglected as attention was directed toward Simpson and his team of lawyers.

If we consider the book not so much a factual account of a family's way of coping with a tragic loss, but a fantasy on a theme of neglect, a peculiar quality of the narrative begins to make sense. We are struck in reading the book by the space in the narrative occupied by Ron's birth mother (Sharon), a character of no apparent importance to the matter of justice for Ron. Her role, as it turns out, is to highlight the theme of neglect and abandonment. Fred Goldman offers the following account of his ex-wife as caretaker for his children, including Ron.

> Immediately after our divorce, Sharon had custody of the children and I had full visitation rights. Then I learned from Ron's grammar school teacher that he was acting up in class and not doing as well as he had been. Knowing that divorce can be hard on kids, I pushed for all of us to get some counseling. Sharon balked at the idea, but eventually agreed to attend some of the sessions. In our early conversations with the counselor, Ron and Kim complained about Sharon's lack of attention. She bailed out and refused to continue the process.[7]

The father subsequently took custody, with the mother having visitation rights, which were seldom utilized. Sharon reappears during the story of the trial, always as a bad mother. Though she has abandoned her family, she nonetheless claims rights during the trial: the right to media attention as someone who has suffered a loss, and the right to sue the defendant for damages in civil court. She is thus both neglectful and rapacious, both qualities typical of bad objects. As the bad mother, her failings serve to place the virtues of the father, and of the family she abandoned, in sharp relief. She simultaneously highlights the theme of neglect and the virtues of those neglected. This neglect of the virtuous is central to the idea of injustice put forward in the book. In this, Sharon plays much the same role as that played by the press and the courts, which pay special attention to the criminal and not the victims, who are abandoned and forgotten.

For the Goldman family, the search for justice becomes a search for attention. This helps us understand the self-absorbed quality of the narrative. We are told, in word and in tone, that this is a good family, a family whose members care about each other. We are told more than once how Fred took over caring for the children who had been abandoned by their mother, and how Ron also took over the care for his sister (Kim). While we are briefly informed of Ron's abandonment and mistreatment of Kim, and of his financial and personal irresponsibility, these moments disappear into a tale of warmth and caring.[8] We have, then, a good family that has been badly treated, even persecuted, by an uncaring world more interested in celebrity than justice.

The theme of neglect and abandonment leads naturally to the theme of hatred, and members of the Goldman family find much to hate, and much justification for their hatred. Foremost, of course, is O.J. Simpson. The family writes that "[b]eing in jail did not seem like adequate punishment for this man." And, Ron's sister Kim declares, "with venom in her voice" that she wants "to see the murderer suffer and choke and I want to be the last face he sees before he dies. But Simpson was not the only object of the family's hatred. The defense team is described as "the most conniving, slimy, deceitful, unethical, immoral, lawyers in the country."[9] A more important object of hatred, of course, is Sharon, who is more intimately attacked than either Simpson or his lawyers. Viewed as a whole, we cannot avoid concluding that the emotional driving force behind the family's search for justice is hate.

Those who hate often do so in the name of justice. The connection between justice and hate raises important questions whose answers bear on the psychic meaning of government. How does the demand for justice express hate? And, what burden does the link between justice and hate place on government? Justice has many meanings and implications not all of which involve it with hate.[10] Yet, clearly the ones that do have a special importance for the role of government. They place government in a dilemma since it must be responsible for justice. When justice is linked to hate, the government must become involved in the community's hatred. When it does, it may become the agent of hatred, acting out sadistic collective agendas. But, in doing so, it cannot avoid also becoming the target of that same hatred.

There is irony in the denouement of the Goldmans' search for justice. The man they are certain committed the crime against their son and brother, and against whom the evidence is, in their judgment, overwhelming, is found not guilty because the jury comes to distrust those who have collected and presented the evidence. The jury distrusts the prosecution, and thus the state, which the prosecution represents, because of its suspicion that racial prejudice led the police to fabricate evidence. In the eyes of the jury, and to some extent the public, it is the defendant who must be protected against those who would convict him because of his race. The outcome, then, expresses a response in justice to centuries of injustice and oppression. It is now the defendant who must be protected against the privilege exercised for centuries by the white majority. Thus, the very principle the Goldmans most vigorously assert, that justice should protect virtue against privilege, works against them, and confounds their hopes for and expectations of justice. The Goldmans are deprived of justice so that justice can be done. We are left with the questions: Who are the privileged, and who are the victims of privilege? Who must justice serve? In this drama, who plays the role of Mr. Smith? Is it O.J. Simpson who is made to bear the guilt of others because he is black? Or, is it the Goldman family that is made to bear the burden of the crime because they are not?

Demanding Justice

When Simpson is acquitted, the Goldman family insists that justice has not been done. They have the case retried in civil court, where the accused is convicted and fined. This is only the most spectacular instance of a drama played out in courtrooms across the country every day. In this drama, the victims of brutal crimes confront the accused, sit through sometimes lengthy trials, attend and speak at the sentencing hearings when a conviction is attained, and insist on the most onerous punishment, which they equate with justice. The family members, together with the court, insist that those convicted admit their guilt and express remorse. Sometimes they do, although their sincerity can be questioned. "Fake it if you have to, but show some remorse, some sadness " For the family members, justice seems a personal matter. Thus, as the "Trial of the Century" unfolds, the Goldman family laments that "this was a case of the State of California versus the defendant, rather than the Goldman's and the Browns versus the killer."[11]

The court also assumes that the family has a special interest in justice; it assumes that in some sense justice is for them. The family members demand justice to put to rest the trauma of their experience. They believe justice will ease their pain, and make life more bearable. Demanding justice means insisting that the community place responsibility on the appropriate party, gain admission of responsibility from that party, have the criminal experience the pain of remorse and suffer a loss in his or her life comparable, so far as possible, to that imposed by the crime on the victim.

The demand for justice can be heard not only from crime victims and their families, but also from those who are, or imagine themselves to have been oppressed. Members of a racial minority are systematically deprived of economic opportunity, and as a result have lower incomes, less education, more unemployment, and less hope than do those whose opportunities are not constricted in this way. Over time, partly due to the political activity of minority groups, partly due to changes in the prevailing institutions and ideas, the injustice of discrimination and oppression can no longer be ignored. Members of the minority group demand justice. Part of their demand for justice is a demand for preferential treatment ("affirmative action") that in its own way discriminates against those who have previously been favored. Demanding justice again involves shifting a burden from those who have historically been made to carry it to those who are thought to be responsible.

While affirmative action can be defended on different grounds, one of the most basic is that of justice. As a matter of justice, affirmative action seeks to right a wrong by providing opportunity for those who have been denied it in the past. Yet, those who benefit from affirmative action and those who were and are most disadvantaged may not be the same persons. Indeed, those in a position to take advantage of the opportunities afforded by affirmative action are able to do so because they were not so deprived in their lives that they failed to develop abilities, aspirations, and, of course, relevant job skills: minority businessmen rather than the unemployed, academics rather than cabdrivers. We recognize disadvantage not only in the lack of opportunity but also in the failure of hope. Affirmative action does not mean much to those without hope.

This observation leads some to reject affirmative action, or at least its grounding in charges of righting a wrong. It can also lead to accusations that defenders of affirmative action, including those advantaged by it, are engaged in a cynical grab for benefits by exploiting the plight of others within their own group. I do not think this interpretation is inevitable, but to get beyond it we need to understand something about the way in which the plight of differently situated group members is shared. If it is shared, then it matters less whether those who benefit are the same as those who suffered the original oppression. This taking on of another's deprivation is not, of course, limited to fellow group members, but it has a special salience in the context of groups. The sharing of deprivation by those not deprived or not so seriously deprived bears on the matter of claims for redress based not on personal but on group experience. To understand and evaluate these claims, then, we need to understand something about the movement of deprivation and loss across persons and across groups.

In a market-centered, private enterprise economy, some make unimaginably large amounts of money, while others barely get by. These disparities are so dramatic that we may wonder if income differences are consistent with fairness. Some respond to these differences by demanding a more just institutional arrangement in which differences in welfare are not allowed to become so great. Demanding justice means demanding greater equality.

But it can also mean something more. It may contain an idea about income differences that makes them unjust not simply because of their magnitude but also because of how they arose in the first place, and what they imply about the distribution of dignity and self-esteem. Those with less may believe that those with more got that way by depriving them of something rightfully theirs, or that this deprivation is a vital part of the attraction in having great income. That is, it may seem that having a large income is only beneficial so long as others do not, because it therefore places the wealthy in a particular relationship with others. Inequality means deprivation if it leads to status differences in personhood that carry the significance of denigrating those with less in order to enhance the self-esteem of those with more. Many students of political economy have been in the habit of treating inequality as prima facie evidence for exploitation.

That is, they see inequality as a result of the better off taking advantage of the worse off. Then, the demand for justice requires us to redistribute wealth and income from the rich to the poor.

Perhaps there is meaning in the statement that inequality implies exploitation, as there is in the statement that special benefits to members of oppressed groups who were not themselves disadvantaged right a wrong, or that victims and their families have a personal stake in retribution. If there is, it rests very heavily on the idea that oppression, deprivation, and loss can be transferred from person to person and from group to group. The idea that loss can be made right if it can be moved to another, at least so far as the other can be held responsible, is a central idea in demands for justice. It is the idea I explore in the following pages.

In each of the cases summarized above, the government plays a primary role. The government takes responsibility for justice and is its agent. When justice means shifting a burden from one individual or group to another, the demand for justice demands that the government shift that burden. Whatever hate is involved in demanding justice, then, is channeled through government, which, as the agent of justice, becomes the agent of hate.

Agency

We do not always distinguish between shifting the pain of oppression onto others and having those who have caused that pain take responsibility for it. When injustice means being held accountable for harmful acts that are not our own, then relief can include assuring that those who are responsible carry the burden of the harm done. This assurance includes the element of shifting of responsibility, or, if you will, placing responsibility where it belongs. Doing so expresses a commitment to the idea of agency, the connection of actor, action, and consequence. This is an important part of respect for subjectivity. Yet it often gets mixed up with something different, which is the transfer of loss onto others.

We can distinguish the two according to the differing psychic experiences involved in them, specifically according to the different type of pain they call for. The pain associated with holding those responsible for the consequences of their action is guilt, while the pain associated with the shifting of oppression onto others is humiliation. While guilt expresses concern for those who have been harmed, humiliation expresses the need to destroy (the self of) those who have done harm. Thus, justice may be linked to concern for others or to their destruction. The former is a justice linked to love, the latter a justice linked to hate.

The most powerful accusations of injustice seek to identify those responsible for taking from us something in which we are psychically invested: our property (theft), some or all of our capacities (harm to our person), or our connection to another person (harm done to a family member or friend). Justice here means punishment. As I suggest above, punishment, taken as a personal matter, imposes, or attempts to impose, our loss on those held responsible for it. While punishment is often spoken of in the language of guilt, it more often expresses a need to humiliate and destroy than to repair.

The term justice used in this way presumes that someone is or can be held responsible, that the loss can be placed under the heading of deprivation, and that the burden of the loss can and should be moved so far as possible from victim to perpetrator. Justice is about loss and how, or by whom, it will be felt. This holds psychically whether the issue is about special treatment of group members or about punishing a criminal. In connecting loss to deprivation, we place the entire matter into the arena of agency. That is, we take loss to be the result of willful action, either our own or another's. Doing so is not inevitable. We can as easily take our loss to be a matter of fate, or of objective processes, whether social or natural, and we can do so whether there is an identifiable agent or not. The victim of a crime need not see in the criminal the real agent of his or her victimization. The first step, then, in turning loss into a matter of injustice is seeing it as a matter of agency.

The second step is placing that agency outside. Faced with loss understood not as fate but as the result of will, we can move toward guilt or toward blame. Deprivation and injustice presuppose that our loss is the result of agency and that the agency is not our own but another's. If our guilt is powerful enough, and the pain it causes us for our loss therefore also powerful enough, then we must find someone else to blame, someone else to carry our guilt for us.

That guilt plays a significant part in the victims' response to their situation would seem to invert the normal perception of loss, since it makes the victim the agent of his or her loss. Yet, as we have seen, this is precisely what happens to the child in his or her relationship with an abusive or neglecting parent. By taking on the badness in the relationship, the child secures a better world. The cost of doing so is that the child takes on a bad self, and with it responsibility for the failed relationship with the parent.

The child is, then, guilty for what has been done to him or her. Not only does this secure a better world, it also makes the child an agent rather than victim, so that however bad he or she becomes, the reward for badness is to negate the feeling of passivity so central to the idea of victimization. The bad self is, at least, an active self. Later on, this bad self can be projected into the world, which makes the problem of locating guilt complex, but vitally important.

The importance of guilt cannot be overstated. Psychically, guilt represents a loss in positive feeling toward the self that comes with an inner conviction that the self has been bad, or, in a more permanent setting, is bad. Demanding justice, when linked to provoking remorse, means demanding that those responsible feel badly about themselves. If they do not, then the badness alive in the relationship cannot be fully removed from the victim, who knows subjectively that there is badness and that it must rest at one pole or the other. Within this psychic context, admissions of guilt and expressions of remorse are the vital currency of justice. Justice is about who is bad in a context where who is bad cannot be separated from who feels bad. The implied movement of blame and thus loss of self-love between self and other is one of the most primitive and fundamental of psychic processes. Because it is primitive, it carries great emotional significance.

To understand the demand for justice, we must understand this movement of agency between self and other, along with our desire to place responsibility on someone, to insist that our loss was willed, to seek remorse or at least admission of guilt, and then to seek punishment. Similarly, to understand the demand for justice, we must understand the desire to see deprivation as something imposed on us by others, whose responsibility demands that they make good the loss. The considerations just introduced suggest that to clarify the problem of justice we must first establish a foundation in an understanding of the more general problems of deprivation and loss.

Oppression

To understand deprivation, it helps to consider the motivation of those who inflict damage on others. Linking motive to wrong links wrong to will and responsibility. The intent to do harm is, in this respect, important. To understand wrong and justice, we need to know what sort of harm is intended.

It would be easy enough to answer this question in material terms, an answer that removes the situation from psychic and inter-psychic life and places it into the economic. Thus, some attempt to explain crime as a response to material need, and the oppression of workers as the result of avarice. This line of explanation suggests that no harm is intended; or if harm is intended, the intent does not really matter very much. Thinking this way allows us to sidestep any question of motivation that might involve the development of a relationship between criminal and victim or oppressor and oppressed. Because of this, sidestepping matters of intent will not help us to resolve the problems raised above concerning justice and injustice, which clearly involve a complex relationship incorporating harm and the intent to do harm. If we assume instead that crime and oppression are meant to establish a relationship, that in this sense harm to the victim is intended, we open the door to an explanation of justice as rectification.

We need, then, to distinguish between a purely economic connection in which the relation of person to person or of group to group is not important in itself but only instrumentally, and an inter-psychic connection, in which the relationship is what matters, indeed, in which the relationship itself is the harm intended. What, aside from material ends, do we stand to gain by depriving others?

The simplest possibility would be that one party seeks to gain what the other loses. This would be the case if the self-worth of one were made contingent on the loss of self-worth by the other.[12] There is in this an implication about human dignity, that somehow it cannot be shared, or perhaps more accurately, that, subjectively, one only gains dignity by taking it from others, and that one loses it when others have it. Put in a slightly different language, rather than seeing selfhood as something that can exist simultaneously, though differently, in me and others, I treat selfhood as an exclusive property: I can only have it if I can exclude others. Excluding others means either suppressing them or suppressing what makes them other to me, which is their difference from me.

In treating our selfhood as exclusive in the sense just introduced, we insist that our individual qualities, or those of our group, are necessary to being a person. Those with other qualities, who differ from us, are made non-selves rather than different selves. But non-selves need not be accorded respect for their dignity as persons. And, because of this, making others non-selves (or lesser selves) makes them suitable for use as objects rather than for recognition as subjects in their own right. The group definition of self as conformity to group identity leads more or less inevitably to oppression and exploitation of those outside.

Making contingent characteristics of particular group members necessary to being a self not only justifies oppression, it can also make those outside the group a danger to its corporate self. They are a danger so far as they are different and yet claim to be selves. In the group, where all share the same self, this danger is eliminated at least in principle (it cannot be eliminated in practice, which makes this sort of group difficult to sustain). Outside the group, members seek to eliminate this danger by oppressing others, denying and denigrating the differences that mark out another self.

The attack on difference originating within the group also fuels the feeling of danger from outside. The danger from outside is real in that confrontation with other selves calls into question the status of the fragile group self. But, the external danger is also imagined, in that it is a projection of the group's destructive impulse onto those outside. Protection of group solidarity depends on the group's ability to place its hatred outside, but this binds group solidarity to its existence within a dangerous external environment.

If justice demands respect for others, the fear of difference makes justice difficult to achieve. We need, therefore to know more about this fear if we are to understand the demand for justice. The fear of difference originates in the most basic of human relationships and in the frustration of the most basic of human aspirations. I turn, then, to a brief consideration of that relationship and those aspirations in order to establish a firmer basis for understanding the demand for justice.

True and False Self

In chapter 5, I suggest, following Donald Winnicott, that human beings begin life with a vital feeling and capacity (the true self) capable of developing into the core of an autonomous and creative personality. To become real and fulfill its destiny, this vital feeling must develop from impulse and potential into a concrete and substantial way of living. For this potential to be realized, the vital feeling must go beyond a mere internal sensation and become real in the world. Put another way, the internal potential must become real for others if it is to be real for us. This becoming real for others depends on their acceptance and affirmation of its expression in the form of the child's primitive selfhood. This affirmation is what we mean by a connection with the parent.

The danger the child faces is that this connection will fail, and, in failing, the vital feeling will be sent back inside. Since it cannot exist for others, it must be kept away from them. Then, in order to sustain the connection to the world outside, the child must seek affirmation for something other than his or her core of selfhood. Failure of the original connection leads to pursuit of a different basis for connection. Rather than the parent connecting to the child's emerging self, the child attempts to connect with the alternative offered by the parent. This means, in effect, that the child must adapt to the parent rather than the parent concerning him or her self with nurturing the child's developing unique sense of self. Winnicott uses the language of compliance and creativity to capture this difference in trajectory of development.[13] Creativity is the expression in life of an original vitality. Compliance is the adaptation to others that means forsaking vitality in favor of being what the other needs to sustain his or her mode of life.

This shift from adults meeting the child's needs to the child meeting those of the adult is of great importance. It means that to be in the world is to adapt to others, rather than to be your self. We can see here the birth of two closely related ideas: (1) that in a relationship there cannot be two different selves and (2) that relating means need satisfaction. Put in a narrower language, we see here the first stage in the emergence of a condition in which connection means serving the needs of others or being served by them. In this world, the child's self develops on the basis of compliance with the way of being and the needs of the parent. Winnicott refers to the self that develops on this basis as the false self.[14]

For our purposes, it will help to recast the process briefly outlined above in the language of morality. Doing so highlights the force that develops behind the attack on difference, whose psychic and moral meanings are inseparably connected. To make this link we need only recall that the primitive meaning of good and bad is nothing other than connected and disconnected. Being good means being connected to, that is gaining the affirmation of, the parent. Being bad means being disconnected from, or rejected by, the parent. When good and bad in this sense are bound up with compliant and autonomous, we have a moral world ruled by obedience and conformity with the attendant denial of the true (that is creative) self. This moral world is a fertile ground for hatred.

Being good means adapting to the parent and repressing the true self; expressing the vitality of the true self means being bad. To lead a life expressive of the true self, then, must bring disconnection, at least so far as we seek to do so in a world dominated by those who have had to forsake their true selves and adapt in order to survive. This disconnection is the rejection we associate with the suppression of difference, and explains much of the fear of difference alluded to above. Before returning to the fear of difference, however, we need to explore further some of the implications of the distinction between the true and false self.

Winnicott develops his notion of the true self with reference to how the infant and young child experiences living a life, with emphasis on the idea that a life can only be lived if it contains and expresses the child's original vitality. For the infant or young child, this vitality exists in a form appropriate to the character of the child's life experience, an experience dominated by the immediacy of impulse and physical connection to the world, rather than one mediated by thinking, ideas, and impulse control. Vitality is expressed, then, through the child's whole person, with special emphasis on the body; thus "the spontaneous gesture is the true self." The point is that the child's self is not yet expressed concretely in the shape of projects, talents, skills, experiences, beliefs, ideas, and so on. Thus, on one level, the true self exists here as something wholly concrete, the bodily expression of vitality as a virtually physical experience; yet it is also something wholly abstract, since it exists not as a concrete lived life, but as the mere potential for a life to develop.

Development means that the true self takes on the concrete qualities of a lived life. But this development is not inevitable. For reasons Winnicott associates with the emergence of the false self, the trajectory of development may leave the true self behind, where it remains little more than the potential and impulse it was for the child. The true self gets stuck in the concretely physical but abstract, because only a potential, form when it must be hidden from the world in which alone life can be lived and a self become the core of a real particular person.

The true self is sealed within so it can survive. But, even there, it is at risk. This is because the relationship with the parent, protected by the removal of the true self from the world, gets internalized as a part of the child's developing self. This internalized relationship replicates as an internal matter the expectation that life be led in adaptation to a fixed external world and without the creative element associated with the spontaneous gesture or true self. The result is a psychic division between the true self and the internalized relationship.

Recall, in this connection, Mervin Glasser's notion of a "Core Complex" introduced earlier. The Core Complex develops out of a relationship with a parent in which the child's separate self cannot be tolerated, and therefore must be repressed. The prospect of merger with the parent impedes the development of (separate) identity and, while seductive to the child, is also experienced as a threat to the child's existence as a person, the threat of annihilation of the child's identity. This seductive/destructive relationship with the parent enters into the psyche of the child in a particular way. The parent colonizes, rather than facilitating the development of, the child's identity. Colonizing places a difference-denying relationship into the child's developing psyche.

Since colonizing establishes an alien presence in the psyche, it means the child's identity develops under a hostile influence. The influence is hostile in that it denies and denigrates the impulse toward any real self-development apart from, therefore different from, that of the parent. This psychic division is fertile ground for the development of the hostile-destructive impulses referred to above in reference to group dynamics, and helps account for the intolerance of difference that we observe in individuals and in groups.

The notion of a Core Complex speaks directly to the question: Why do people have so much difficulty tolerating the difference between self and other? Intolerance of difference originates in the formation of the false self, and the internalization and repression of the child's original vitality, or true self. This repression is implied in the Core Complex, as it is in the internalization of all relationships that deny, denigrate, or otherwise suppress the child's effort to form an identity of his or her own.

While the parent represses the child's true self and colonizes his or her psyche, the child also internalizes the relationship with the parent. That relationship is both threatening and seductive since it offers connection at the price of sacrificing separate identity. Internalizing, or the active (though not necessarily conscious) participation of the child, follows from the dilemma that the relation with the difference-denying, therefore repressing, parent creates for the child. As I suggest above, repression carries a moral significance in that it is part of the process that determines the placement of badness. In this relationship, either the parent is bad for mistreating the child (in this case, by punishing difference), or the child is bad for provoking mistreatment. Of these two options, the latter is more tolerable to the child because it assures the parent's goodness at a time when dependence on the connection with (therefore the goodness of) the parent is crucial to the child's survival, both material and psychic.

The child's dilemma in dealing with a bad relationship with a parent sets a pattern relevant to the subjective meaning of justice and injustice. That meaning also involves the movement of badness from one pole to the other: from criminal to victim and then back to the criminal, or from oppressor to oppressed and then back to the oppressor. Demanding justice takes on emotional intensity when it gets connected to the primitive situation in which relationship is about the placement of the bad feeling about the self.

Repression of the true self in light of the danger posed to it by the world, both internal and external, establishes the psychic meaning and reality of the experience of oppression in the world. The stronger the internal structure of repression, the stronger the experience of the external world as a repressive place; and, of course, the more oppressive the world, the stronger the internal structure of repression. Thus, repression begins as a relationship of self to other in which the other fails to recognize, or even attacks, the true self. This relationship gets internalized as a repression of the true self. This internal repression gives meaning to the relations with others that subsequently develop.

The internal repression of the self is of special importance in understanding the demand for justice. To see this, consider how the problem of oppression appears if we ignore the internal repression of the true self, and assume instead that the inner world remains receptive to the individual's vital being even if the external is not. Then, to enable individuals to develop ways of life expressive of their true selves requires nothing more than removing external obstacles.

Those who resist removal of these obstacles must do so not to act out their own internal repressive structures, but because of the material benefits they gain by having those obstacles in place. To return to the language used above, oppression is done not for itself but to gain a material benefit; the relationship of oppression does not matter in itself but only as a means to an external end. Then, whether we can lift oppression depends on whether we can imagine and create institutions that assure that all gain (or possibly none gain) to replace institutions in which some gain what others lose.

Generally, doing so means that those who benefit from the current arrangements, through which they oppress and exploit others, must be made to give up their benefits. Because of this, they are not likely to favor the change to a system in which it is not possible for some to gain at the expense of others. Those who currently benefit, then, are the obstacle to change referred to above; and, presumably, those who do not benefit (who "have nothing to lose but their chains") are the agents of change. Thus, the notion that oppression is exclusively an external matter, and not a psychic structure shared, if in somewhat different ways, by oppressor and oppressed alike, implies that eliminating oppression is an external struggle between oppressed and oppressors.

In this construction, the struggle over oppression is a relatively simple matter, at least in principle. Yet, even if we accept the plausible notion that those who benefit materially from oppression are loath to give it up, we still need to consider the implications of the idea that oppression is as much an internal structure as an external reality. Clearly, once we treat the matter in this way, identifying the agent for change becomes significantly more difficult and complex.

If repression is an internal matter, then the purpose of the relationship that oppresses is to enact externally an internal reality. The relationship is as much end as means. The repression remains in place as an internal matter long after it disappears as an external one; indeed it reappears as an external matter because it persists internally. To understand not only the demand for justice but also the prospects for a more just world, we need to consider further the internal structure of repression set in place with the repression of the true self.

The Fear of Difference

The retreat of the true self from a dangerous world, both internal and external, means that the vital element of the person's being does not live in the world; it is not instantiated in projects and activities. By failing to act in the world and become real there, the true self cannot meld with the lived experiences that are what it means to be a person.

What becomes real instead is a false self, which, however, is always experienced by the person as in some respect unreal. It may seem real in that it exists concretely in the world as a life experience consisting of projects and activities; it is, however, unreal in that it fails to actualize the vital element of what it means to be alive. Using Erik Erikson's language, it is a reality that does not actualize.[15] No matter how lively our false self seems to us and to others, it lacks any real vitality.

The unreality of the false self makes it fundamentally unsound. Since it does not express any real vitality, the false self cannot fend off doubt about its actuality. The person, then, must expend his or her energies in defending the false self as a self, even though it is not. Any differences between persons, even seemingly minor differences of taste and interests, threaten the false self because they tap into an internal doubt about its reality. The power of the false self is measured, then, by the fear of difference. The fear of difference makes the person's activities and projects burdensome chores and anxiety-ridden efforts to stimulate and maintain in others a false idea of the self.

Let me focus attention for a moment on contingent differences, differences in taste and style of life, even professional goals and interests, qualities that need not in principle carry any valence of good or bad, right or wrong. Yet, they often do. And, when they do, it becomes impossible to treat difference as contingent and individual, or to tolerate differences however contingent. The language of true and false self suggests that, in accounting for the added meaning taken on by contingent difference, we look not simply at the differences themselves, but at what they signify about the person.

The self may be the animating principle of our lives, embodied in but not reducible to a matrix of activity, ideas, tastes, and so on. Or, it may be replaced by that matrix whose meaning for us is not that it represents our vital being, but that it gains the regard of others. The matrix succeeds only so far as it, like our emerging false selves in childhood, gains acceptance at the expense of vitality. Rigid adherence to the apparently contingent makes sense in this light since the seemingly contingent has been made necessary to being in the world. There is a vital distinction, then, between contingent differences that express the (true) self and contingent differences that take the place of the self.

Recall that an internal danger to the formation of a separate and different self develops as a result of parental colonization, and that parental colonization involves both hostility toward the child and the offer of merger to which the child is drawn. In this context, difference constitutes a threat to merger, and therefore to connection with the parent and all that connection promises. If the internalized hostility toward the self is projected onto others, their effort to be different selves cannot but be perceived as (1) a threat to connection, and (2) a prelude to an attack, since others now are believed to contain the hostile, colonizing, impulse that cannot tolerate difference.

In some ways the treatment of the expression of self in contingent differences as equivalent to, or a stand in for, the self reflects the child's eye view of the world in which the universal only exists as the particular. So, when we see adult intolerance of difference in contingent qualities, we really see a child's structure of meaning in an adult context. When an adult makes selfhood as such contingent on a particular way of being a self, he or she confuses the particular with the universal. Particular contingent qualities become universal and inevitable: being different from us (particular) means being bad or wrong (universal). This structure of meaning implicates difference in the placement of badness.

The key to the process that results in failure to distinguish universal from particular lies in the nature of the true self as a potential. The true self is not a self at all, but the potential to be a self, a potential whose presence from the outset makes us incipiently persons. The true self is Winnicott's way of referring to the potential to be autonomous or self-determining. Universal refers to the capacity or potential, particular to its realization in a concrete form of life. The term universal refers to that shared or general quality of selfhood that can exist in different concrete ways of life. Since it is not restricted in principle to any one way of life, it is universal. Yet, this potential or capacity shared by all who lead a life expressive of real selfhood cannot exist in the abstract but only in and through the various ways of life that give it a particular shape.

If, however, there is only one particular shape or appropriate way of life, then the moment of freedom embodied in the true self as a potential gets lost. If there is only one appropriate way of life, then there is no choosing or deciding, no determining a life trajectory according to the individual's interests, skills, and satisfactions. The true self, which is also the creative principle in life, cannot exist if the way of life is already determined independently and externally. Then, that particular way of life does not contain the universal (freedom) as its animating principle. The person does not express or create, but rather conforms, which is what it means to lead life according to a predetermined scheme.

When a way of life is developed to express the true self, then the particular endeavors and satisfactions that constitute it also embody something universal, a creative principle. But, when the true self retreats from the world, the person's particular endeavors and satisfactions cannot express his or her creativity and freedom. They express nothing about the self. In the deepest sense, they have no meaning since real meaning is tied to a connection with the aliveness we can only feel in connection with a creative self.

When, in response to this condition, we insist on its necessity, this becomes the necessity of the contingent endeavors and satisfactions that stand in place of our lost vitality. This is an insistence on the necessity of the loss of true self and the imposition of that loss on others, an imposition implied in the idea that ours is not *one* way of being good, but *the* way of being good. Since our lost vitality is a lost freedom to live creatively, which means to create a (concrete) self, imposing our loss on others means depriving them of their freedom.[16] Oppression of others, then, originates in the repression of self.

Equating the self with its contingent qualities implies that to be a self means to have those qualities. But, if the contingent and particular is the expression of the potential self, then we can see ourselves in others who differ from us. What we see in others is the potential self, the element of freedom or vitality that makes the contingent a form of being a self. The failure of the true self places an obstacle in the path of recognition of others, since it means that their difference from us prevents us from recognizing ourselves in them.

We can use these ideas to develop a notion of the meaning of justice and injustice. As it turns out, however, they lead us in two different directions, toward two different notions of justice. The first centers on removing those obstacles to leading a life expressive of an original vitality, the second centers around the circulation of loss. The first is the justice of love, the second the justice of hate. Thus, injustice can refer to the community's failure to secure the differences between persons. Justice, then, refers to the process by which the community reestablishes the (violated) boundaries between persons that signify their differences one from another. This is the justice of love. Alternatively, justice can refer to the movement of loss from self to other. This is the justice of hate. A community organized around the justice of hate institutionalizes the treatment of members of certain groups as non- or lesser persons because they are different. It denies that a self can be other than it is for those who are willing and able to comply with prevailing modes of being.

The Circulation of Loss

Let me return now to the question of why relationships develop in which human dignity cannot be sustained at both poles. The simple answer to this question is that the archetype of human relating, that between parent and child, is often a relationship whose purpose is to suppress autonomy (the child's true self in its aspiration to form a life in the world). As an archetype, this relationship becomes the real basis for all future interaction; it is repeated and reproduced throughout life. What this means is that relationships do not deny human dignity at one pole in order to establish it at the other; rather, they deny human dignity at both poles, with one being the active moment the other the passive.

This quality of oppression is missed when we interpret it as a relationship of loss (for the oppressed) and gain (for the oppressor). It is, instead, a relationship of loss at both ends, though one participant plays the active role. Since, however, this act of bringing about loss in the other does not retrieve anything, it must be repeated; and in this repetition, its true meaning emerges. In this true meaning, the relationship is not one whose end is to gain a lost self by depriving the other, but to affirm the inevitability of loss through its reenactment.

Imposing loss on others makes our original loss our own act. In this sense, it enables the oppressor to gain autonomy, but only that autonomy whose meaning is loss of self. The same holds in a different way for the oppressed, who gain autonomy by making their oppression their own act.[17] The more being victimized takes hold within the person's psyche, the more it can be a way of retrieving lost agency. But, the agency retrieved is not the agency lost since the former is centered on loss while the latter is not. It is, nonetheless, important to understand the impaired agency of the victim since it plays its part not only in the struggle against, but also in the perpetuation of, oppression. Within a structure of victimization, the self is not gained, since what is sought is not the self, but control over the process by which we have lost it. Freud observes this phenomenon in the child, who in "passing from the passivity of experience to the activity of play...applies to his playfellow the unpleasant occurrence that befell himself and so avenges himself on the person of this proxy."[18] Control over the process of loss means becoming the agent of loss. Victimization is a passing along (or an attempt to pass along) an experience rather than an original experience in itself. The state of being victimized creates a kind of disequilibrium that drives the victim to attempt to victimize others. This makes oppression the result of victimization and victimization the result of oppression.

The moving force in this circulation of loss is the idea of being bad and the associated feeling about the self. Since justice is about the community seeking to put the badness where it belongs, it necessarily runs into problems. Because the badness can never really settle anywhere, its movement, rather than establishing equilibrium, simply keeps it alive within the community. Oppression, like money, circulates from person to person, being of greatest value in its alienation, gaining strength in movement rather than being extinguished by it. This circulation is both the harm done when we do wrong and the rectification we seek in the name of justice.

Deprivation and Persecution

In chapter 6, I emphasize the role of the Puritan idea of will in shaping the attitude toward government in America, and in providing support for the free market ideal. There, my concern was exclusively with the Puritan idea and its psychic meaning. This left out of account the life experience connected to that idea, which, as we know, was an experience of persecution. American attitudes toward government do not simply originate in an idea transported from England to a more favorable soil in the New World. These attitudes also originate in a specific experience not uniquely tied to the Puritan doctrine. This is the experience of dislocation and dispossession. It is not only the idea that the Puritans carried with them to America, it is the experience of persecution for having that idea, and of the deprivation that persecution entails.

We need to emphasize this experience, because it is an experience in which justice, as I have here characterized it, plays a primary role. In other words, for those nations such as the United States, whose people were significantly affected by persecution and oppression, the issue of justice must loom large. Like the Quebecois, American's have an identity shaped by the idea of oppression. Emphasizing the experience rather than the idea allows us to connect the experience of those who came to America to escape religious persecution with that of others who came to escape repression in its different forms. It also allows a connection to the experience of those forced to emigrate by enslavement. This makes the connection between American culture and deprivation that much more powerful.

In saying this, I do not mean to suggest we simply equate the experience of those whose coming to America was an experience of persecution (slaves) with those who came to escape persecution. Yet, these two opposite experiences have something important in common: they make dislocation and persecution a central theme of the experience of America. America is not only the land of the Puritan ideal, then, but also the land of all those sharing an experience of persecution, dispossession, and deprivation. America is the land of the dream that all those with the experience of deprivation must have in one form or another. This is the dream that they have found their way home, that their beliefs and their culture, which provoked an original dislocation from their homes, will become the basis for integration into a New World. Deprivation, rather than marking us with a loss we can never make good, will become, in America, the basis for attaining exactly what we have lost: a sense of wholeness and connection.

America is not, of course, alone in this experience. Other nations are equally or more profoundly rooted in dislocation, and experience much of what I have described here.[19] In all such cases, the experience of loss and deprivation gets built into national identity, as it is into individual identity. A paranoid psychic situation mirrors a paranoid culture. This leads, in turn, to the pressure to recreate the experience of loss, especially to make reenactment of loss the function and meaning of public life. Public speech is required to resonate with the inner experience, as it does in America when it gets taken over by the rhetoric of self-discipline and responsibility, the attack on welfare dependence, and the expression of a punitive attitude toward criminals. Thus, public policy and institutions are constructed to instantiate the idea of deprivation in order to validate the original loss often experienced several generations in the past.

The dream that loss can be put right animates two vital expectations of American public life: the expectation of justice, and the expectation that we can overcome through acts of will. Both the ideal of justice and the idea that anything is possible deny limits. The deepest limit they deny is the limit imposed by loss. One assumes that loss can be made right, and looks to justice as the process for doing so. The other sees no loss as vital, none that cannot be overcome if forcefully enough denied. The myth of justice (that loss can be put right) and the myth of willing (that no limit is real in the face of the will to overcome) shape the relation of the citizen to government. The citizen demands of government that it assure the justice of recovered loss, and that it recognize no obstacle to the will of the people, who can remake the world to fit its ideal.

For government to assure the justice of recovered loss means, of course, that the government act as the agent that transfers the loss onto others. By imposing loss, for example through a punitive system of criminal justice, the government becomes the object of hate. We hate our government as we hate those who originally impose loss on us; indeed, our government becomes the repository of the psychic meaning and image of those who deprive and oppress.

The experiences just considered set in motion forces that shape a national self-construct, or collective self. At the heart of this construct is a defense against the feelings of inadequacy that inevitably result from an original experience of dispossession and persecution. To compensate for these feelings, the group combines a grandiose sense of its purpose with a paranoid orientation to the world outside. Thus, as Gingrich and others have suggested, the Creator put America (and Americans) on earth for a special purpose: to defend liberty and the autonomy of the individual. To become the most powerful country in the world is not an accident, but the result of action aimed at achieving that result, realizing in the world of affairs the grandiose fantasy of the self that compensates for underlying feelings of inadequacy.

A paranoid element is implied in this partly because it requires the externalization of the disavowed, inadequate, and depreciated aspects of the self onto other groups or nations. The paranoid element also develops because action in accordance with the grandiose fantasy places others in a threatened position to which they respond with threats of their own. By provoking a hostile response, the projection is made real (validated in the world); the fantasy is made to take the shape of reality.

It would seem inevitable that a country that takes in those who have been persecuted, and in so doing celebrates persecution, must place itself into a persecutorial world environment. It must do what it can to assure that its people will reproduce the experience of persecution not only as its victims, but also as victimizers. The highly charged theme of persecution becomes the psychic center of the collective self-construct. Identification with the aggressor assures that the community will persecute others, and that it will justify doing so by allusion to its own persecution, thus simultaneously identifying with persecutor and victim.

Redemption through Suffering

Those who are the victims of oppression seek to find a meaning in their loss that can turn loss into its opposite. This meaning is the same meaning we always seek in repression of self: the building of character. Suffering, which is to say loss of self-esteem, makes us better persons. And, indeed, it can be said, given the concept of character as something built in struggle, that without suffering there can be no character. In the words of Jesse Jackson, "suffering breeds character."[20]

The earliest, and still most vivid expression of this idea is the Book of Job in the Old Testament, a story I will consider in greater depth in chapter 10. Job is a good man who is made to suffer so that the Lord can demonstrate His powers to Satan. Job's suffering is a test of faith, but not only of his faith. It is a test of mankind's faith in, and fear of, God. Is faith in God something bought and paid for by worldly rewards, as Satan insists? While Job remains unaware of his part in the struggle between God and the Devil, his suffering has a higher purpose. The degree of his suffering and humiliation is also the measure of his importance. Yet, Job does not know this purpose, and this lack of knowledge is what tests his faith, which for him must stand in place of understanding.

In public life, when prompted by suffering and loss, we reenact the story of Job, of a suffering without meaning that must be given a meaning commensurate with it. Thirty days after the attack on Columbine High School in Littleton, Colorado, President Clinton addressed students and staff there. Like Job, the victims at Columbine suffer, but do not know why:

> In the Scriptures, St. Paul says that all of us in this life see through a glass darkly. So we must walk by faith and not by sight. ... None of this can be fully, satisfactorily explained to any of you. But, you cannot lose your faith.[21]

And, like Job, the suffering is not without a higher purpose, in this case to build a better future, one that does not include suffering such as this: "Because of what you have endured, you can help us build that kind of future, as virtually no one else can." Indeed, suffering has bestowed a remarkable power on its victims: "You can reach across all the political and religious and racial and cultural lines that divide us. ... You can give us cultural values instead of a culture of violence." This would no doubt seem a tall order were it not for the power of suffering. For, those who endure suffering, as Job did, and do so without losing their faith, have the power of goodness to bring to bear on an evil world.

As the President emphasizes, the power for goodness is the power to unite. Suffering, then, is also linked to the theme of unity considered in the last chapter. Jesse Jackson offers us a powerful expression of this connection in his speech before the Democratic National Convention in 1988. In that speech, he rehearses the long-standing them of Presidents and Presidential hopefuls, "the genius of America is that out of the many we become one." He goes on to tell us what it is that brings us together, where we will find our "common ground." We will find it "at the plant gate that closes on workers without notice;" at the auction where "the good farmer loses his or her land to bad loans or diminishing markets;" in schools, where teachers are poorly paid and students deprived of the financial support they need; and in hospital admitting rooms, "where somebody tonight is dying because they cannot afford to go upstairs to a bed that's empty waiting for someone with insurance to get sick." In other words, we find common ground where we find loss and deprivation.

Jackson offers us a metaphor for the connection between loss and unity, when he speaks of America as a patchwork quilt. America, he informs us, is not "a blanket woven from one thread, one color, one cloth." Instead it is a blanket woven of many colors and cloths. It is the blanket his grandmother made from pieces of old cloth "barely good enough to wipe off your shoes with." She sewed together these pieces of old, useless, and discarded material into "a quilt, a thing of beauty and power and culture." And so must the Democratic Party bring together farmers, mothers, gays, blacks, Hispanics, even conservatives. All those who have been discarded and devalued must become worthy by coming together on "common ground." The common ground is loss and suffering; and it is on this common ground that loss will be made right, and, through faith, those not worthy "to wipe your shoes with" become part of a moral crusade.

Suffering is loss, and loss means a diminution in our sense of self-worth, of physical and emotional wholeness. When suffering takes on a higher meaning, loss is made up. What has previously diminished us now ennobles us. What previously pulled us apart now brings us together. The theme of wholeness is striking in the response to the attack in Littleton. If loss brings us together, it makes us whole; if the loss occurs in a context of division, we look to it as a healing force.

If loss does not heal us, then it has no meaning aside from the diminution of our selves. If we cannot tolerate this prospect, which is of course also the prospect of old age and death, then we must find in our losses a higher purpose. The more we suffer, the more grandiose the expectations we are entitled to have for ourselves, since the greater the loss, the greater the ground that must be made up. Unless this ground is made up, we cannot think that justice has been served. What was before a community like many others, normal, if not average, is remade by tragedy. Thus Clinton goes on to insist: "This is a very great country. It is embodied in this very great community, in this very great school, with these wonderful teachers and children and parents."

The rage of those who suffer must find a suitable target, and it must take on an acceptable form. Today, the rage of the victims must be externalized, typically through a search for liability. Law suits are filed against the schools, against the makers of guns, against the makers of violent video games. Someone must be made to pay so that the accounts of honor and self-esteem can once again be balanced. Where prior to our suffering, we may have had a life, now we have a mission. We organize ourselves around this higher calling; we engage the battle against evil. We must find evil outside if we are to fight it, and force upon it responsibility for our loss. The greater the loss, the more powerful the evil we must fight to achieve justice.

Mourning Loss

If demanding justice means shifting loss from self to other, it contains its opposite. This justice of imposed loss plants the seed of oppression. But, if justice means respect for others, and thus giving up the imposition of loss, then justice makes demands on us we cannot easily satisfy so far as the psychic meaning of our lives centers on imposed loss. To meet the demand of justice, we need to find a way to give up the loss whose circulation we demand justice bring about. To achieve justice means to mourn loss rather than imposing it on others.

We can deny loss, or we can accept that the lost object is no longer available to us. Mourning is the process by which we accept loss. Refusal to accept loss stands in the way of mourning, which becomes blocked, incomplete, or chronic. This expresses the organization of emotional life around defenses against mourning. Paradoxically, refusal to mourn makes loss the emotional center of our psychic lives. It can also make loss the main organizer of interaction with others and with institutions, including government.

Refusal to mourn can take a variety of forms. When we insist that the loss can be shifted from self to others, it takes the form of demanding justice. When the demand for justice means refusal to accept loss, it represents a form of chronic mourning. Justice does not always have this meaning, but the justice linked to hate with which we have been primarily concerned does have the psychic meaning of loss that will not be mourned.

Refusal to mourn can also take the form of attachment to a wished for state to be gained in the future (the "Promised Land"). Then, what has been lost will be regained, so we need not, indeed must not, give it up. Here, to mourn means to abandon hope. Those who mourn must, therefore, be driven from the group whose existence depends on keeping hope alive. For those who live in hope, loss must be neither accepted nor made good in the present. The return of the lost must be kept in the future, since only if it remains in the future can we live in hope. As Bion points out, "only by remaining a hope does hope persist."[22] Hope fulfilled is hope lost.

We can also refuse to mourn by treating our loss as a gain. Within twenty-four hours of the attack on Columbine High School, one Denver newspaper featured the headline (in two-inch type): THE HEALING BEGINS. Healing refers to the repair of damage. Healing is complete when the damage is fully repaired, and we can go on as if the damage had never occurred. To replace mourning with healing circumvents the mourning process. We have seen how the same process transforms loss into gain, since suffering makes us whole. The story of Job is a story of loss that is only a prelude to gain, loss with a higher purpose.

When loss takes on a higher purpose, we cannot give it up, but must instead celebrate it. Memory of loss plays a large part in this celebration of loss. When we are told never to forget, we are told not let go of the experience. Here, memory does not refer to a mental image (however imaginatively constructed) of our actual experience, since those who did not have the experience must still remember. Thus, we are told to remember the Holocaust whether we had the experience or not. Here, to remember means to hold on to the psychic meaning of the experience, to internalize the experience through identification with those who actually had it. To remember in this sense does not diminish us, but makes us better. This means that identifying with loss makes us better than we could otherwise be, which reinterprets loss as gain.

Making loss into gain prevents us from mourning, and reorganizes our lives around loss. Then, mourning would destroy the psychic meaning of our lives, and threaten us with a loss of identity. We celebrate oppression and loss when we formulate a grandiose fantasy of the oppressed group as the repository of the good, in Clinton's terms as having a special healing power for society. Then, paradoxically, those who are not oppressed are the ones who have really suffered the loss.

Refusal to accept loss expresses the quality of our relationship with the object. Accepting the loss of love or of a loved object is no easy matter when it has the significance of the loss of self-worth.[23] When that object contains something vital to us, so that its loss is the loss of (a vital part of) our selves, then we must find ways to avoid the mourning process. To say that the object contains something vital is to say that we have used it as a container for parts of ourselves. We are connected to the object simultaneously by projection (it contains projected aspects of the self), and by identification (we see it as we see ourselves). We cannot mourn when we have too much of our selves invested in the object.

Thus, the loss of a homeland we see as the physical embodiment of our national group means the loss of group identity. Such a loss cannot be accepted so far as what we value in ourselves is our group identity. We are good because we are part of a group that is good; that group is good because it is attached to a homeland that is good. We can never really give up our homeland because to do so is to give up any hope of ever being good. Instead of giving up the homeland we have lost, we imagine how we will return to it in the future, take it back from those alien people who have driven us from it. Or, instead of mourning the lost homeland, we imagine how we can recreate it in a new land. Then the myth of the homeland (that it is all good) becomes the myth of the New Jerusalem.

The loss of a bad or ambivalent object also causes difficulty. As we have seen, the badness we take on to restore the goodness of the object and make it worthy of love means that the rejection we felt from that object becomes internalized. The rebuke we assume is implied in loss becomes an attack on ourselves, an internal critique that leads away from mourning and toward the state in which the loss of love becomes a permanent condition. This is the state with which I have been concerned in the foregoing discussion. It may lead away from mourning and toward melancholia as Freud suggests, but it may also develop in another direction. The outcome depends on whether the aggression bound up with loss gets directed toward self or others.

When it is directed toward others, refusal to mourn takes the form of hate, and of attachment to the hated object. The hated object contains the projected bad self, so its loss threatens the projection of the bad self, which protects the good object. We can no more tolerate the loss of the hated object used to contain our bad self than we can the loss of the loved object that contains our good self. Hatred, then, constitutes a further alternative to mourning, one often implied by the forms of chronic mourning already considered. Aggression against others blocks mourning for the loss to the self.

Anna Freud, in her discussion of identification with the aggressor, considers the link between aggression toward others and the vicissitudes in the development of the capacity for self-criticism and guilt. She suggests that, developmentally, intolerance of the superego toward others precedes severity toward the self. The child "learns what is regarded as blameworthy but protects itself by means of this defense [projection] from unpleasant self-criticism."[24] Eventually, this criticism, which at the outset seems intolerable and must be redirected away from the self, can be tolerated and directed back toward the self. Some people, however, do not complete this process, and, as a result, remain highly aggressive toward others. Freud goes on to suggest that this might represent an abortive melancholic state.[25]

It is a state in which, because of the seriousness of the danger to the self or the weakness of the self-feeling, even a temporary loss, such as that implied in criticism, cannot be tolerated. Indeed, the seriousness just referred to is that the loss of love will not be temporary but permanent, for the adult, not a temporary feeling of guilt or sadness, but a permanent depression. Faced with this situation, rather than accepting our loss (mourning), or turning it against ourselves (depression), we act aggressively toward others, seeking to put it onto them. We make others the object of and receptacle for a feeling too powerful for us to tolerate internally.

The intensity of the aggression reflects the intense pain experienced in the original loss, first of the connection with the parent, later of self-love. Aggression, then, defends against the remembered experience of loss. Retrieving hope, then, means retrieving the pain of loss. To mourn a loss we must first acknowledge that it is ours. The remembered pain blocks this first step, assures that aggression takes the place of mourning, and that the structure of repression persists.

On the psychic level, this is a personal problem. The solution lies in developing a new relationship within which the old pattern is not repeated so the original loss can be acknowledged. But this solution on the psychic level has little relevance to the problem of justice, which is a problem of the community as a whole and its institutions.

Government and the Mourning Process

We have already seen how government can get entangled in the various strategies used to avoid mourning. When government acts as the agent of the individual or group intent on shifting loss from self to other, government becomes the agent of hatred. It does so by acting out the community's punitive agendas toward those deemed in conflict with its constituting myths, including those myths that block any acceptance of the reality of the diminished self.

We need to bear in mind that the self that lives in the world constitutes a diminished self when set against the narcissistic ideal or grandiose self. The latter can shape reality by force of will (whether individual or group) and thus need never accept the finitude we associate with loss. When government becomes the sponsor of a collective grandiose self (as it did for example in the President's address to the students at Columbine High School), the government acts for the community to prevent acceptance of loss.

This would seem to link the government with the good object, and thus defuse animosity toward it. Drawing such a conclusion leaves out of account what is most salient about the grandiose fantasy, that it denies reality. The grandiose fantasy constitutes an unattainable ideal, while the government represents a connection to reality. We can say, then, that when Clinton expresses the community's grandiose fantasy, he speaks not for government, but for the nation. When he fails to realize the community's narcissistic ideal, he represents the government failing the aspirations of the nation and its people, who ask: "If this is such a great nation, why do such bad things happen?"

10 THE CLOSED SYSTEM

The Leviathan

The most vivid and powerful metaphor we have for the state comes from Thomas Hobbes, who refers to the ideal state as the "Leviathan," a mythical sea creature of awesome power. The Lord invokes Leviathan to make a point about His power on earth. This happens at the end of the Book of Job, after Job has been used in Satan's challenge to God.[1] When the Lord suggests Job as an example of goodness and devotion, Satan points out how easy it is to be good when you are blessed by God, as Job has been:

> Hast not thou made an hedge about him, and about his house, and about all that he hath on every side? Thou hast blessed the work of his hands, and his substance is increased in the land.[2]

Take these blessings away, says Satan, and Job "will curse thee to thy face." So, the Lord puts all that Job has under Satan's power. And Satan visits a series of curses upon Job, who loses everything he has: his wealth, his family, his physical well-being.

The story of Job is the story of loss. Having lost everything except his life, will he also lose his faith? Will he question God's will or the justness of God's acts? Will he turn his anger against the Lord? Job's anger is, indeed, great, though its target is uncertain, as he turns it primarily against himself. Job curses his life, and wonders why he has been made to suffer. He wishes for death. Finally, Job speaks with God "in the bitterness of [his] soul."[3] Job laments the loss of his prosperity and honor. Where before he was honored, now he is held in contempt. Job rebukes the Lord: "He hath cast me into the mire, and I am become like dust and ashes. ...

Thou art become cruel to me....”[4]

After all his curses and protestations of injustice, Job finally acknowledges the power and wisdom of the Lord, and his own sin in questioning that power and wisdom. "Behold, I am vile; what shall I answer thee? I will lay mine hand upon my mouth."[5] Now the Lord invokes the Leviathan to represent His power on the earth.

> His breath "kindleth coals.... His heart is as firm as a stone.... When he raiseth up himself, the mighty are afraid.... The arrow cannot make him flee.... He laugheth at the shaking of a spear.... Upon earth there is not his like, who is made without fear. He beholdeth all high *things*: he is a king over all the children of pride.[6]

Seeing now the power of God in the Leviathan, Job humbles himself before God:

> I know that thou canst do every *thing*, and that no *thought* can be withholden from you. ... I have heard of thee by the hearing of the ear: but now mine eye seeth thee. Wherefore I abhor *myself*, and repent in dust and ashes.[7]

In response to this declaration, God bestows upon Job even greater wealth and good fortune than he had previously lost. Job becomes someone among men by becoming nothing before God.

The parallel between the story of Job and the constitution of the Hobbesian state goes beyond the shared image of awesome power in Leviathan. Pride and humiliation, displaced rage and power, and most of all the response to loss and the demand for justice, animate both the story of Job and the modern theory of the state in its Hobbesian form. As Leo Strauss points out:

> It is not mighty power as such which is the tertium comparationis between Leviathan and the State, but the mighty power which subdues the proud. The State is compared to Leviathan, because it and it especially is the "King of all the Children of Pride." Only the State is capable of keeping pride down in the long run, indeed it has no other raison d'etre except that man's natural appetite is pride, ambition, and vanity.[8]

Let us consider in greater depth the idea of the state as the king of the children of pride.

According to Hobbes, the need for the earthly state, the Leviathan, follows from the nature of man, central to which is the "perpetual and restless desire of power after power that ceases only in death."[9] For Hobbes, power is intimately bound up with honor and dignity. Power is manifest in honor, the lack of power in dishonor. It is the eyes of others that make us great or small. Pride, ambition, and vanity are the natural inclinations of men.

The restless pursuit of power after power has two connected roots. First, power when linked to vanity must be measured relatively. To be honored by others is a sign of power; so to honor others is a sign of their power. The more I honor you, the greater your power and the less my own. The second root of the limitless quest for power follows from this, and lies in the fear that what power I do not have others will have, and their having it means my losing it. Man "cannot assure the power and means to live well which he has present without the acquisition of more."[10]

Competition for honor and riches leads to contention. Where no one has a natural right to more and all are equal, the competition for honor and wealth has no limit, and the implied contention leads to the state of war. For Hobbes, equality breeds diffidence. When "two men desire the same thing," as they must if they desire honor, "they become enemies."[11] The only way out of the state of war is for all men to give over their power to the commonwealth. This transfer of power creates the Leviathan, which is, indeed, the creature of the powers of all men alienated from them and constituted as a force standing over and against them. Having created this alien power through the alienation of their powers, men can now pursue their private ends of wealth and honor in the eyes of other men, just as Job, having become nothing before God, can gain honor among men.

Central to this idea of commonwealth is the original image of man centering on the endless pursuit of honor. This endless pursuit of honor is ultimately driven by the fear of loss, just as the endless pursuit of honor creates the circumstances in which it is only reasonable to fear loss. Since my gain is your loss, and covetousness is the rule of the day, loss as much as gain is the end. While Hobbes formulates the problem as a problem of the pursuit of gain, it could as easily be formulated as a problem in the pursuit of loss (for others), since to gain honor means to impose its loss on others. The structure of the argument follows the pattern we considered in our discussion of competition in chapter 6. As we saw there, what underlies the circulation of loss is greed. Though Hobbes does not speak of greed by name as the driving force in the society of men, we can see how greed is that society's organizing principle, and the principle that explains the eventual recourse to the Leviathan.

When Hobbes focuses his attention on the pursuit of honor, he makes it clear that what we have to gain or to lose is esteem in the eyes of others. The Hobbesian world is populated by those who are, in Kernberg's phrase, overdependent on external objects. To lose wealth is to lose a connection to goods whose value also establishes the value of those who own them. To lose goods means to lose our connection to the good, on the basis of which we feel ourselves to have worth. Where greed rules the world, each of us is threatened by the desire of others to have all of everything that is good. The prospect of loss driven by the depth of the experience of loss fuels an aggressive-defensive greediness.

While the Leviathan is an ideal for Hobbes, it is the negation of the ideal for those who see government as a threat. This negation is the loss of autonomy, which expresses the great fear of those who would limit or destroy the state in the name of liberty.

> The defining mark of the state is authority, the right to rule. The primary obligation of man is autonomy, the refusal to be ruled. It would seem then that there could be no resolution of the conflict between the autonomy of the individual and the putative authority of the state.[12]

The critique of the state based on the idea that its authority is the enemy of liberty shares with the Hobbesian ideal a concept of the state as a center of power. The difference lies in the judgment about the necessity for that concentration of power as the means to curb pride and the war of every man against every man Hobbes insists follows from the explosive combination of pride and equality. For our purposes, the close affinity between the Hobbesian ideal and the object of critique of the state is important since both draw attention to the connection between the state and power. The Leviathan, which for Hobbes offers the only solution to the problem of liberty in a world of greed, is, for those who distrust government, the problem for which a solution must be found.

Hobbes's Leviathan is the power of the parties to the covenant that creates the state concentrated into a single ruler. It is therefore the result of the alienation of autonomy. It is less obvious how alienation constitutes the Leviathan of the Bible, but if we recall the link between power and rage emphasized in chapter 5, we may begin to see a connection. Given the rage Job must feel at his loss, and given his inability to direct that rage at God, the agent he feels is responsible, we must expect to find his rage not in its original form, but in an alien shape. This alien shape is the Leviathan. First, Job redirects his rage at himself (he wishes for death), then into the constitution of a powerful external force. We might say, then, that to cope with his suffering and loss, Job conjures up in imagination an external power for good, the Lord, and an external power for destruction, the Leviathan, as repositories for his good and bad impulses. In so doing he attributes agency to his loss, which is an essential moment in the demand for justice to redress grievance. The power of Leviathan is Job's rage at the injustice of his suffering projected into the world. True, God creates the Leviathan; but it is Job who creates God, without whom his suffering would have no meaning.

While Leviathan represents the power of God on earth (in Hobbes's phrase, the mortal God), it is also linked with Satan, who expresses the power of God as His opposing force. Leviathan's qualities are those of the devil (it is after all a serpent), and it has been invoked as part of a struggle between God and Satan. If the Leviathan is the embodiment of projected rage, it contains all of man's destructive impulse. It is man's own destructive force made into an object of his fear. This is, indeed, what many consider the danger posed when the state is separated from the people and set against them as an alien and powerful force.

For Hobbes, as for Job, the destructive force is pride and the state-Leviathan is the king of the children of pride. The problem is that to give up pride is to become nothing. The loss of self-esteem, or the threat of its loss, invokes rage. But, for Hobbes, it is ultimately the limitlessness of the desire for honor that makes holding onto one's honor so problematic. In other words, it is not the desire for honor as such that causes the trouble, but the greed built into making honor something that can only be gained by imposing its loss on others.

Safety as the Negation of Freedom

Job has reason to doubt that God is a good object for him. As we know, God uses Job for His own ends. If this is love, it is of the narcissistic rather than the object-related sort. Worse even than this, God not only fails to protect Job from Satan (the bad object), but gives Job over to him for the expression of Satan's not inconsiderable cruel and sadistic impulses. For Job, God and Satan are bound together.

God insists that, in spite of His treatment of Job, Job must continue to look upon Him as a good object. In so doing, God places Job in a double bind, one typically resulting from ambivalent parenting. And, as children must, Job does everything he can to preserve and protect the putative good object, assuming, as Fairbairn tells us, that it is better to be a sinner in a world ruled by God than to live in a world ruled by Satan, although for Job the two worlds are hard to distinguish. To protect God, Job debases himself. In other words, to continue to love God, Job must hate himself. If Leviathan is the king of the children of pride, it is only possible to escape the rule of this king by giving up pride.

The Hobbesian state, like the Old Testament God, is all about the repression of the self that replaces pride with humility. Also, like the Old Testament God, the Hobbesian state is a projection of the rage provoked by the repression of the self. Only a repressive state can prevent men from destroying one another in the great battle over honor. Repression is the price of peace and prosperity. The repressive state is the expression via projection of a society organized around repression of the self.

We can say, then, that for Hobbes the end of the state is peace and prosperity, as well as a kind of safety for the pursuit of wealth. This is not, however, the safety that offers support for freedom. Because of the dominance of pride in the motivations of men, freedom and safety stand opposed. But, freedom without pride means very little. Indeed, the feeling of self-worth is the central meaning of freedom; so, if we insist that feeling is a threat to others, and thus to safety, we cannot be safe in a world free to value the self.

Hobbes's message is that in the modern world only government can secure the individual from deprivation and loss, but only a government that is itself the repository of what has been lost. The attack on government has the psychic meaning of promoting individual loss into a collective psychic experience, embedding loss in the collective consciousness. It is meant to make us all unsafe, to heighten anxiety and paranoia, to make us susceptible to violation of our personhood.

When government is placed into the emotional space of hatred and loss, it becomes a locus of power, which it must be if it is to absorb the projected anger and hatred of its citizens. But must government become an alien force and thus a danger to society? The answer to this question depends on what it is that must be governed, the unit of governance, and the relationship it bears to government. Whether government becomes the container for anger and hatred, and thus, both in fantasy and reality, a locus of power, depends on the nature of the community, group, or association that is to be governed. Most importantly, it depends on the quality of that unit's subjective life.

The image of government as Leviathan expresses the dominance of psychodynamic links between citizen, community, and government. In Fairbairn's language, it expresses the absorption of government into the community's closed system. In doing so, it excludes the possibility that the community will establish a relationship with external reality. This exclusion, then, assures that the government will be the creature of the community's fear and longing. When this happens, government cannot act as a work group dedicated to accomplishing vital reality-linked tasks for citizens taken individually or collectively. The problem of connection to reality, and of what reality might mean for the community as a whole, then, is the problem of effective government. The problem of connection to reality gets expressed as a matter of the way we understand the unit of governance. The nature of the unit of governance defines its boundaries, and thus the nature of a reality that might exist outside that unit, and to which it must relate.

Closed Systems

A problem arises when the relationship between community, government, and reality takes on the character of the "closed system" we considered in the Introduction. The government made subservient to individual wants, as it would be under a free market ideal, or made subservient to the group, as it would be in a democratic community, is a government absorbed into a closed system. In the first case, it is the closed system of the individual, in the second case the closed system of the community.

As a closed system, there is no external reality to which the community must relate. As a part of this closed system, government exists as an expression of psychic need. It can, then, do nothing to alleviate the destructive conflicts that dominate the community, to extricate itself from the community's projections, or to assist the community in establishing its internal organization on a footing less subject to the control of primitive affect and primitive defenses.

As Fairbairn suggests, the closed system is highly resistant to change because it fosters what he refers to as a "static internal situation." We have, then, "self-contained situations in inner reality, which persist unchanged indefinitely, and which are precluded from changes by their vary nature so long as they remain self-contained."[13] Without the influence of external reality, the system resists change, seeking instead to reproduce and reaffirm itself by maintaining relations not with external objects, which is to say objects outside its subjective control, but exclusively with internal objects. What appear as external objects (for example, other persons) are related to as containers for internal objects, so that the relationship with them can be internalized and kept consistent with psychic need.

For the individual, change requires "a breach in the closed system of internal reality."[14] A breach in the closed system comes about through the intrusion of a real object (the analyst) so far as that object can take on significance for the individual without losing its standing as a part of external reality. The analyst, then, represents reality for the patient, and, so far as he or she is able to do so, change is a possibility. We can say, then, that change, which here means breaching the closed system and fostering its movement in the direction of an open system, depends on the existence of an external object (representing an external reality), and the ability of that object to take on significance.

The solution Fairbairn offers for the individual has no ready analogue at the level of the community. Indeed, it is not even clear what external reality means at this level, not to mention who might represent it for the community, and thus sponsor a breach in its closed system. If no agent exists to represent external reality for the community, this does not mean that change as a general matter cannot take place, but only that the change from a closed to an open system cannot take place. Much can change, but the fundamental psychic reality cannot. As we have seen, this fundamental psychic reality is the reality of loss and its reenactment, with the attendant organization of collective life around hatred, imposed loss, the celebration of oppression, and so on.

The problem defies solution when we insist that communities create their own reality, which makes it the government's job to serve as the community's agent in this act of creation. Then, there can be no hope for the movement considered here, and we must expect instead what Fairbairn refers to as "frozen dramas," which are exactly what we have considered in our discussion of the psychic meaning of public life.

When we consider more closely the possibility that there might be an external reality for the community, and an agent responsible for mediating its relation to that reality, we cannot avoid considering the possibility that government might act in this capacity. For government to mediate a relation to reality of this kind, it must be able to act on the community as a force separate from it. The possibility that the government might mediate a relation to reality makes it a primary target for those parts of the community committed to maintaining it as a closed system. Their goal is to absorb the government into that system, thereby weakening its ability to represent external reality.

We may be tempted at this point to imagine an external reality for the community in the form of other communities. Yet, if this is all we have of external reality, then there is really nothing outside community, though there might be something outside the particular community. When the external reality consists wholly of other communities, then the government of each will find itself limited to acting for its particular community in relations with others. This means it cannot negotiate a relationship with a reality outside of community, which leaves open the question of how we can conceive external reality for community.

In answering this question, it will help to consider further the implications of Fairbairn's notion of an open system. As we have seen, an open system maintains a connection to something Fairbairn refers to as external reality. The reality to which Fairbairn refers here does not consist primarily of objects defined in physical space, as outside the physical boundaries of the individual. Rather, external reality refers to objects existing outside psychic space. To be sure, psychic space involves physical boundaries as a vital element. Yet, it is the psychic separation that determines the openness of the system. An object is not separate in this sense when it contains projected parts of the subject. As we have seen, the use of the object as a container for parts of the self secures it within the subject's inner or psychic reality. External reality, then, refers to the existence of objects outside the system of psychodynamic links, or connections organized around projection and identification.[15] If an object can exist outside our psychic reality and yet take on significance for us, then we have a relationship with a genuinely external reality.

Beyond its separateness in this sense, all we need say here about external reality is that it exists for a bounded self. The self is bounded so far as it holds inside its different aspects (love and hate, good and bad, and so on). We can also say, therefore, that external reality exists for an integrated or whole person in the sense we have used that term here. This holding inside of the good and bad, hateful and loving, means acknowledging what is of the self (its own feelings and self-states) and what is not.

Establishing self-boundaries is what we mean by self-determination. We can say, then, that external reality exists as the other side of self-determination.

Developing a commitment to this reality of the bounded and integrated self, which also establishes the separation between psychic and external reality, is an achievement for the community. This achievement has the same meaning as the separation of the individual from the group. The individual separates from the group by retrieving his or her identity from the hold the group has over it. We can see, then, why the community resists acknowledging any reality outside its closed system, since to do so it must give up its domination over its members and allow them to develop into separate individuals. So far as the member develops into a separate individual, the government has a reality outside the community to which it can relate, and so far as the government seeks to connect with this reality, it becomes an advocate for the individual, if necessary against the community.

It would be more accurate to say, however, that the government becomes an advocate for the principle of individual autonomy than that it becomes an advocate for the particular individual. Or, we can say that it becomes an advocate for the particular individual so far as his or her autonomy is at stake. The distinction is something like the one Rousseau draws between the will of all and the general will. As Rousseau puts it, "the latter regards only the common interest, while the former has regard to private interests, and is merely the sum of particular wills...."[16] We need only add that the "common interest" here refers to the ideal of self-determination, which is to say of the bounded and integrated self. If the government is made to serve some particular, already existing, set of individuals with their particular wants and needs, it cannot stand outside whatever psychic reality spawns those wants and needs. But, if the government serves the more general or universal interest of self-determination, then it stands outside the closed systems of the community and its members.

For government to represent reality to the community, there must be a subjective reality separate from the community to which the government can relate. But, there must also be a reality of government separate from the community. This means that contrary to the free market ideal, there must be a government, and contrary to the democratic ideal, that government must remain separate from the people. Government establishes its reality in this sense by establishing itself as a set of institutions protected to some degree from group control. As Freud suggests, the key is the articulation of an institutional structure that mediates the relation to the group rather than becoming absorbed into it.

As I suggest in chapter 7, the absence of structure is an invitation to the exercise of power. Since power expresses regression, structure works against power. It does so in part by shifting the ends of the organization away from dealing with anxiety to the particular tasks that must be done if citizens are to get on with their lives in a creative way. Conceiving government as a work group whose basic task is facilitating individual autonomy, protecting self-boundaries, and securing so far as possible the external conditions for integration protects government from absorption into the community's closed system. It implies a structure of decision-making, division of labor, and use of expertise; it limits regression, and reduces the likelihood that government will operate as a center of power.

Conclusion

It would be comforting to imagine that structure is the magic bullet against regression and the transformation of government into a locus of power (the Leviathan). But, this assumes the existence of an agent to design the structure of public institutions capable of resisting absorption into the psychic reality considered here. But, who will remake the government by an act of will into a form that assures its ability to establish a relation to a reality outside of community? Assuming the community can do so confuses the solution with the problem. To imagine that government will do so ignores the way its structure is shaped by and molded to group ends, including those of regression.

Diagnosis of the problem, then, does not lead in any simple and easy way toward a practical solution. It is no doubt tempting to suggest alterations in institutional design that would improve the prospects that government will do its job, and the comments in the last sections of this chapter clearly point in that direction. But, they also fall short by a substantial margin. New policy suggestions, even good ones, play the same role in the public realm as does problem solving at the individual level. They assume that problems have not been solved to this point because of a failure of imagination, clear thinking, or because of what those in power stand to lose. All of this ignores the psychodynamics of failure, especially how failure is urgently needed in personal and in public life.

I will, therefore, go no further than the tentative suggestions of the last sections in offering solutions by way of institutional design. If problem solving takes us in the wrong direction, what alternative can we pursue? I think the answer to this is that we might offer a better way of understanding the dynamics of public experience. Indeed, we might offer a way of thinking about public experience that makes sense of what otherwise seems senseless, and makes fully human what would otherwise seem alien, a truth that is in here rather than out there. By doing this, we take the first step toward establishing a relationship to reality that can move us beyond the dilemmas that express the hold of psychic reality over public life.

AFTERWORD

A Note on Method

Since Freud, psychoanalysts have been in the habit of referring to clinical case studies as data, thereby suggesting that the presentation of case material can provide evidence in support of general propositions about mental life, and not merely examples that can make those propositions more vivid and concrete. It would be easy enough to ridicule this habit, as some have, and demonstrate how far from evidence and data, as those terms are normally used, this material falls. Yet, it is equally hard to imagine any other sort of material that could be offered in support of claims advanced about those aspects of mental life with which psychoanalytic theorists are concerned.

Something like this also holds for the claims advanced in this book regarding psychic meaning and public life, except here not even clinical case studies are available. We do, of course, have quantitative data in the form of survey research bearing on the matter of perceptions of government. Such data can be suggestive, and I have referred to it at times in the foregoing discussion. Yet, for reasons I hope have become clear, the limits of survey research for revealing psychic meaning are severe. These limits have mainly to do with the nature of psychic meaning, especially the limited access people have to it. This limitation in access calls into question any research methodology that relies heavily on self-reporting, as surveys must inevitably do. I consider a particularly relevant example of this problem in chapter 4, where I take up the matter of public hatred. In thinking about hatred, we may wonder how widespread it is. But, given the nature of hatred, and therefore the difficulties that stand in the way of people acknowledging their hate even to themselves, we can hardly assume that surveys of public opinion will provide meaningful answers to questions such as: What percentage of the public hates the government?

The alternative is to use what I refer to here as fantasies, broadly defined. Under this heading, I consider such apparently diverse phenomena as theories about government, communications from elected officials to the electorate, and film scripts. I use this material in a way somewhat analogous to the way clinical case studies are used in psychoanalytic theorizing. I say somewhat analogous because the nature of the material and of our relationship with it precludes use of the primary method employed in the clinical setting: free association. This makes interpretation of the material speculative to an even greater degree than is the case for clinical case studies. Appeal to available evidence concerning public psychic life runs into two additional problems shared with the traditional use of clinical data to validate general propositions. First, the incidence of the phenomena in the world cannot be systematically linked to the evidence offered for them. And, second, to an important degree, the evidence has been created through a process of interpretation.[1]

What should we make of these problems? Should we let them discourage us from using interpretation of fantasy as our primary access to psychic meaning? Should they lead us even to question the reality of psychic meaning, which is something we only find when we have already decided it is there? So far as our model of inquiry insists on a purely objective method of validation, we must judge inadequate the types of evidence available for supporting arguments about the nature and meaning of psychic experience. The difficulty with applying this model to psychic life, whether individual or collective, is that it prevents us from using our most powerful and valuable piece of equipment: our subjective experience of the world.[2] The problem is how to use subjective experience in a way that does not drain our conclusions of any inter-subjective validity.

The fantasy material to which I refer all has substantial subjective impact, and it is our sensitivity to that impact that allows us first to grasp the message it contains, and then to interpret that message as to its psychic meaning. This sensitivity is a result of the operation of a number of factors including predisposition and training. It is also the result of the fact that we are all human and have, however impaired it might be, a subjective experience of the world. The sensitivity to which I refer connects us as humans living together with a shared collective experience having a profound meaning and emotional resonance. I take these to be the essential elements in the matter of substantiating claims about collective psychic life.

We may take the key element in the above account of evidence and interpretation to be the reference to subjective experience as a part of what it means to be human. By subjective experience, I have in mind the experience of being a subject of conduct or, in Kohut's words, a center of initiative. That this is part of what it means to be human I take to be more in the nature of a definition than an empirically verifiable hypothesis. In other words, I take it that the development of psychic meaning and psychic reality follow necessarily from the demands of subjectivity. There could be no subjectivity were there no special reality appropriate to it, which is the reality Freud refers to as psychic reality.[3]

The vital element that links psychic reality with subjectivity is the necessity to control awareness. For initiative to come from within, what is inside cannot simply reflect, or otherwise be wholly subject to, forces originating outside. Control over awareness means limiting access to the inner world.[4] Doing so makes subjectivity a possibility since it makes the mind the source of its own reality. Limiting awareness is another way of speaking about establishing dominion of the mind over its experience in its world by securing a world specific to mental experience.

To limit awareness is to establish a boundary between what is internal and what is external. Without this boundary, we cannot speak of a distinctively inner or psychic experience, and therefore of psychic reality. Of course, our experience of this boundary is as much in its violation as in the respect we and others provide for it. But, violation of the boundary only underscores its importance, which is to protect psychic or inner experience, and therefore subjectivity.

Limiting awareness has been a major concern of psychoanalytic theory. Most often, of course, this concern has been with the way limiting awareness impairs self-experience and therefore subjectivity. Thus, we have the well-known idea that the goal of psychoanalysis is to make the unconscious conscious, which would expand rather than limiting awareness. Yet, even the "mechanisms of defense," as Anna Freud terms them, many of which prevent the unconscious from becoming fully accessible, only limit awareness to secure subjectivity, the premise being that impaired subjectivity is better than none at all.[5]

In the limit, the impairment of subjectivity that results from the effort to protect it can lead to the virtual elimination of all psychic life and psychic meaning. In the foregoing account of psychic meaning and public life, we found the attempt to destroy psychic meaning playing a large role. The destruction of psychic meaning is linked to subjectivity in a number of ways, most notably those suggested by Anna Freud's discussion of identification with the aggressor.[6] So far as we are the agents in the destruction of our own subjective lives (as well as those of others) the destruction of subjectivity is also its expression. This act of destroying subjectivity to protect it is also part of the meaning of identification with an internalized bad object, which Ronald Fairbairn emphasizes.

The proposition that the mechanisms of defense are deployed to protect subjectivity will not seem obvious to readers of Freud's essay. There, she puts forward the view that defenses operate to block the expression of instinctual drives. When expression of these drives would violate prohibitions originating outside, but internalized as the superego, or impair survival in an external world on which we depend, they provoke anxiety. Defenses are, then, defenses against anxiety associated with the pressure of instincts in a world where they must be subject to control.

I will not here consider the validity of this interpretation except to say that it still leaves something out, which is a full discussion not of what is defended against, but of what needs to be defended. It is clear enough, at least, that for what Freud refers to as "superego anxiety," the object to be defended is not the physical person, but a particular psychic state, one we might refer to as self-love, or, in the language of Freud's structural model, superego approval. Self-love, however, refers to that emotional investment in the whole person Loewald, following Kohut, associates with the idea of having or being a self. In this sense, we can say that what must be protected is the self, or, in other words, our psychic being. What is at stake in our use of the mechanisms of defense is, then, our psychic being, however it may be impoverished by the effort undertaken to secure it from danger.

The emphasis in psychoanalysis has not all been, however, on defensive maneuvers. Winnicott's notions of transitional space, creative living, and the true self all incorporate the idea that a mental space must be secured against the dominance of external factors. Indeed, the distinction between creativity and compliance central to these notions rests on the presence of a boundary of the kind considered here.

We can think of psychoanalysis as the study of psychic reality, especially of its boundaries, of how they are or are not secured. This means that psychoanalysis is the study of subjectivity. There is no question in this of demonstrating the existence either of subjectivity or of the reality specific to it (psychic reality). It may exist or it may not, just as an economy may or may not exist, and therefore the concepts appropriate to understanding an economy may or may not apply.[7] Neither is it a matter of validating empirically the concepts appropriate to psychic process, concepts such as identification, projection, and repression, since these concepts are simply possible elements in the struggle for the survival of subjectivity, and therefore the preservation of psychic reality.

While offering empirical evidence for the existence of psychic reality is not at issue, this does not relieve us of responsibility for validating specific interpretations of specific instances of collective psychic experience. Consider in this connection, the interpretation offered by Leland Pogue of the Frank Capra film I consider at length in chapter 2. Pogue suggests that the lead character in the film (Mr. Smith) acts as if he lacked certain knowledge to which it is wholly implausible to assume he has not been at some time exposed. Pogue deduces from this that the character has "forgotten" something he once knew. Since for him to have forgotten this knowledge in the usual sense of the term is equally implausible, Pogue concludes that the knowledge has been repressed. The character's act of forgetting can be understood as a way of limiting awareness, and is therefore done as part of a strategy to protect subjectivity. The problem of interpretation is to uncover the threat to subjectivity embodied in the knowledge that the character has made unavailable to himself. On this, Pogue is perhaps less clear than he might be. He nonetheless points us in a useful direction, and thus sets the process of discovery of psychic meaning in motion.

Before considering a specific interpretation of Mr. Smith's mental lapses, we might note that any interpretation offered that appeals to processes such as repression will only be convincing to those who already consider psychic reality a vital part of human experience. Obviously, we could not disprove an account that leaves psychic reality out, and instead insists that Mr. Smith is forgetful, ignorant, stupid, or that he suffers from some organic brain disease. It follows that any attempt to offer supporting evidence for an account of behavior in terms of psychic meaning presumes from the outset that we are considering an instance of subjective experience, and that it is the specific nature of a psychic reality for which an account must be provided.

Even with this presumption, we are limited in this case by the fact that we cannot ask the character in the film to offer associations relevant to revealing psychic meaning since, of course, the character does not really exist.[8] Neither, of course, can we do the sorts of tests needed to determine if he is indeed suffering cognitive impairment of the kind that would lead to the behavior exhibited in the film. We can, however, bring together material offered in the film we judge connected to the experience of forgetting, or in some way associated with it. We can, in other words, seek out

Mr. Smith's associations as they become available in the film's dialogue.

Bringing together material associated in this way is only relevant so far as a basic principle applies, which is the principle that proximity implies connection. Thus, in chapter 8 I note how Ronald Reagan in one of his Inaugural Addresses goes from a discussion of the relationship between past, present, and future, to a discussion of how we must work together as a nation. I conclude from the proximity of the issues, that they are in some sense the same issue. I suggest that temporal difference represents for Reagan a disunion that must be overcome.

That proximity implies connection also expresses the prior conclusion that psychic reality exists and imposes itself on our conscious experiences. Obviously, alternative explanations cannot be excluded on empirical grounds. Perhaps the speech is meant to do no more than offer a series of disconnected comments on topics the President and his advisors deem relevant. Why instead assume that proximity implies connection? Again, I think the answer has to do with the link between subjectivity and psychic reality. Subjectivity is the connecting link in human experience; it is what makes that experience whole. If there were no connections between thoughts, there would be no real thinking, and if there were no thinking there would be no subject who integrates, however imperfectly, his or her mental life through thinking.[9] So, if thinking is the essential activity of a subject establishing dominion over an internal world, perhaps as a prelude to asserting a degree of dominion over the world outside, there must be connectedness in thoughts. If there is not, then there is impaired subjectivity, as expressed in the disorganization of the thought process.

The conclusion just drawn is not overthrown by the observation that in the case under consideration the link is left unstated, and perhaps unknown. Here again, the matter of what we allow ourselves to know and what we withhold from awareness is essential. That a link is not known does not make it any less vital. On the contrary, the force used to withhold it from awareness may measure exactly how vital it is. The considerations advanced up to this point do not rest on any ability to validate hypotheses about the world, but merely on the conclusion that subjectivity implies a specific sort of mental experience, one of the type studied using the concepts of psychoanalysis. We may still, however, want to know what specifically is going on for Mr. Smith and Mr. Reagan.

It is at this point that a specific hypothesis comes into play, one that may or may not be valid. With regard to the Reagan speech, I offer the hypothesis that what is at stake is the effort to bring together the ideal and the real. The discussion about working together is really a solution to the problem of temporal disjunction, which is the problem of merger with an ideal object. With regard to Mr. Smith's lapses of memory, I offer the hypothesis that he is limiting awareness to protect a fantasized relationship with an ideal father. I treat the character as part of a fantasy of the film's director (Frank Capra), and offer limited evidence to support the possibility that the director might have had a relationship with his father appropriate to the fantasy.

Within the context of the Reagan speech or the Capra film, hypotheses such as those put forward here can be validated in the usual way, by appeal to evidence from the text. Even assuming that they are valid in this sense, what sort of conclusion can we draw from them about public life? I think that two conclusions merit consideration. First, the continuing popularity of the film suggests that it has a place in the broader public consciousness, and that the fantasy it contains opens a door not merely to the psychic reality of those who produced it, but also to the psychic reality of the millions who have viewed it over the years. The same can be said for the fantasy in the Reagan speech. In a rough sense, we can assume that the popularity of an elected official, or a candidate for office, measures the popularity of his or her fantasy.

There is, however, a second conclusion that is worth considering. However popular the President, his fantasy is not everyone's, and however popular a film, neither is the fantasy it contains everyone's. There is room in public life for more than one fantasy. We may make a rough guess about the relative incidence of the psychic experiences expressed through public fantasies by attempting to gauge their popularity or the popularity of those who articulate them for us. How many people voted for the President? How many saw the movie? How many adhere to the theory? But, of course, some who voted for the President may not share his fantasy, and some who saw the movie may have found little resonance in the fantasy it contains.

While answering questions about the incidence of a fantasy in the world may be important, doing so is not my primary propose here, which I take to be uncovering psychic meanings and not judging how widespread are the specific psychic experiences those meanings express. The interpretation of the film allows us to understand the psychic meaning of a certain type of public experience. We can see evidence of the fantasy at work in different settings, which can encourage us to assume that similar processes are at work there, and that our interpretation will be of some relevance. I do not claim then that the analysis of the film reveals the psychic meaning of government in America, since to do so would be to assume that there is only one such meaning. I only claim that it reveals a psychic meaning I have reason to believe is important.

I would only add to these notes on method one comment. While it is important to understand the psychic meaning of public experience, and therefore to have valid interpretations of public fantasy, the validity of the particular interpretations offered here is not the most important consideration. More important than defending a particular interpretation is the matter of facilitating access to psychic meaning, particularly since, where matters of psychic meaning are involved, more than one interpretation may be valid. Psychic reality is complex and multi-layered. Because of this, a particular interpretation, however valid on the evidence, may not exhaust the possible meanings embedded in a particular fantasy. I have, in general, chosen those interpretations that fit together into a larger picture of public experience, one centered on matters of finding and losing subjectivity. I take this to be a picture of something essential in public life, but I do not take it to be a picture of all that is vital there.

ACKNOWLEDGMENTS

This book began with a brief note I published on the subject in a newsletter I edited for the Colorado Society for Psychology and Psychoanalysis. This brief note was then turned into a longer paper for presentation first at the Tenth Annual Conference on Psychoanalysis and the Public Sphere in London, and subsequently at the Colloquium on Organizational Psychodynamics at the University of Missouri in Columbia, Missouri, the Colorado Center for Psychoanalytic Studies in Denver, and Columbia University in New York City. I am grateful to participants for their contributions to the maturation of the project. I would particularly like to thank Fred Alford and Jim Glass for their comments on an earlier draft of the manuscript of this book. Neither the paper nor the book would have been written had I not had the opportunity to study psychoanalysis at the Colorado Center for Psychoanalytic Studies. I am grateful to the students and faculty of the Center for a significant part of my education in psychoanalysis. I am also indebted to Pam Wolfe for her editorial work on the manuscript, and to Daniel Whelan and Thorsten Spehn for their research assistance.

Parts of chapters 1, 3, 6, 8, and 9 previously appeared in *Psychoanalytic Studies* (1999, www.tandf.co.uk), *Administrative Theory and Praxis* (1998), *The Good Society* (1996), and *The Journal for the Psychoanalysis of Culture and Society* (1999).

ENDNOTES

Introduction

1 Cass 1999, p. 67.

2 "Every nation has the government it deserves," Josephe de Maistre, *Lettres et Opuscules Ineditis* V.1, letter 53 (1851), in the *Oxford Book of Quotations*.

3 Lapham 1997, p. 9.

4 Hyatt-Williams 1998, p. 69.

5 Volkan, 1994, p. 32.

6 Fairbairn 1958, p. 381.

7 King and Stivers 1998, p. 29.

8 Lear 1990, p. 52.

9 Loewald 1980, p. 123.

10 Loewald 1980, p. 351.

11 Murray, 1984, pp. 154–5.

12 Murray 1984, p. 227.

13 Laplanche and Pontalis 1973, p. 314.

14 The use of fantasy to understand collective experience is emphasized in Kets de Vries and Miller 1984, chapter 2.

1

1 Borger and Kulman, 1996.

2 See Hegel 1951; Erikson 1964, p. 222.

3 The link between morality, inner conflict, and self-repression fits well with basic elements of Freud's structural model, which makes the superego a central player in the moral drama of the mind. In this model, the superego is responsible for assuring moral conduct. It embodies ideals, and has the capacity to punish us by causing psychic pain when we fail to live up to those ideals. However, rather than beginning with the implications of superego formation for moral conduct, I will begin with a related psychic and inter-psychic situation emphasized by Erik Erikson (1964, p. 231). This is the situation that leads to what Ronald Fairbairn refers to as the "moral defense" (see Fairbairn 1943). In this situation, being good

247

and being bad take on their original and fundamental psychic meaning.

4 Kernberg 1995, p. 63.

5 Fairbairn 1952.

6 This formulation to some extent evades the issue, since we need to know something about the nature and content of the relationship so we can know whether the parties find the relatedness it offers satisfying or not. I consider this problem further on.

7 University of Denver Web site, March 1999.

8 Richard Koenigsberg points out that the "wish to maintain the purity of the nation" is fundamental among nationalists (1977, p. 10).

9 Winnicott distinguishes between true and implanted (or false) guilt. A healthy child has a sense of guilt that stems from the development of personhood in and through the recognition of the wholeness of the other. Some children, however, fail to achieve integration of self and recognition of the integrity of the other. Failure to achieve the sense of wholeness of self and other precludes the development of an inner or personal source of guilt. Children who fail in this task must, then, be taught a sense of right and wrong since they will not develop it for themselves (Winnicott 1955).

10 Hyatt-Williams 1998, p. 10.

11 Morrison 1986, p. 352.

12 Morrison 1986, p. 362.

13 Kernberg 1986, pp. 216–7.

14 Hyatt-Williams 1998, pp. 112–3.

15 Kernberg 1986, p. 217.

16 Shame and the effort to displace it onto others drive more extreme forms of aggression (Gilligan 1996).

17 Rothstein 1986, pp. 313–4.

18 Winnicott 1965.

19 See Chasseguet-Smirgel 1985.

20 Ronald Reagan, Second Inaugural Address.

21 George W. Bush, campaign speech, June 12, 1999.

22 Al Gore campaign speech, June 16, 1999.

23 See Grunberger 1979.

24 Jacobson 1964, p. 66.

25 See Hegel 1951, Erikson 1964, Dworkin 1977, and Levine 1988.

26 See Moran 1993.

2

1 "Mr. Smith goes to Washington," Columbia Films 1939, screenplay by Frank Capra and Sidney Buchman from an original story by Lewis R. Foster ("The Man from Montana"). Text is from Movie Scripts Online.

2 This sentiment is clearly expressed by Reagan in his 1981 Inaugural address.

3 The idea of Saunders as a mother figure feeds into an oedipal interpretation of the film.

4 Pogue 1994, p. 162.

5 Jeff's considerable anger is on display early in the film when, in response to ridicule in the newspapers, he makes the rounds of bars to punch out the reporters responsible.

6 Leland Pogue emphasizes Jeff's desire to avoid adult responsibilities (Pogue 1994, p.158).

7 The merger accomplished here can be considered an Oedipal triumph, since the son wins the woman from the dark father who is destroyed in the process. The implication is that the son does not develop into an adult living in an adult world (Pogue 1994, p. 183).

8 Bion 1961, p. 89.

9 Capra 1971, p. 3.

10 Capra 1971, p. 9.

11 Capra includes a scene in the movie based on a personal experience. In a moment of panic about making a satire about government at a dark time in the nation's history (the brink of war), he visits the Lincoln Memorial to gain the confidence to persevere with the project (Capra 1971, p. 260).

12 Gassner and Nichols 1943, p. 651.

13 When released, the film caused considerable controversy, attracting both praise and harsh criticism. Its vindication is also the vindication of the fantasy.

14 Frannklin Delano Roosevelt, Second Inaugural Address, January 20, 1937.

3

1 Flanigan and Zingale 1998, p. 12.

2 Flanigan and Zingale 1998, p. 12.

3 Quoted in Tolchin 1996, p. 9.

4 Pew Research Center 1998.

5 Flanigan and Zingale 2000, p. 12.

6 Pew Research Center 1998.

7 Pew Research Center 1998.

8 www.gallup.com/poll/indicators/indtaxes.asp (March 2000).

9 Smith 1995.

10 Flanigan and Zingale 1998, p. 11.

11 See Gingrich 1995, p. 30, and Lipset 1990.

12 Or, possibly, we can place our trust in the goodness of some of the people: working people, women, people of color, and so on.

13 First Inaugural Address, January 20, 1981.

14 University of Michigan, May 22, 1964.

15 See Hegel 1977, pp. 111–118; Winnicott 1971, chapter 6; Benjamin 1992.

16 Freud 1959, p. 37.

17 For communitarians, this loss of self is often expressed in a stringent norm of equality whose purpose is to secure the group at the expense of the individual.

18 See Caporaso and Levine 1992, chapters 3 and 6.

19 Gingrich 1995, p. 31.

20 Speech delivered on March 2, 1999 in Manchester New Hampshire.

21 Robert Mathews quoted in Dees 1996, p. 141.

22 Dees 1996, pp. 3, 9.

23 Richard Koenigsberg suggests that we see in the attitude just described the working of a coherent fantasy about the nation, a fantasy in which the nation is a "living organism" which has been infected by a disease whose agent is the hated group. Then, the problem is how to go about curing the nation of its disease by removing the group that is its source (Koenigsberg 1977, p. 15). He goes on to suggest that we understand the carriers of the disease as the "projection of a malignant internal object" (p. 16), so that the struggle to remove the hated group from the external world plays out an internal struggle with the malignant object.

24 See Hegel 1977, pp. 119–138.

25 Gingrich 1995, p. 39.

26 Clarkson 1996.

27 Quoted in Gilbreath 1995.

28 Bellant 1995.

29 *New York Times*, October 8, 1995, p. 24.

30 Bellant 1995.

31 Gilligan 1996, p. 189.

32 Talk show host Chuck Baker quoted in Dees 1996, p. 119.

33 William Pierce, author of *The Turner Diaries*, quoted in Dees 1996, p. 139.

34 Gingrich 1995, p. 105. Observers of the American political scene may have doubts about whether the direction in which the Speaker's policies devolve power is working American families.

35 Glasser 1992, p. 495.

36 We may also consider a link to homophobia as a reaction to a homosexual wish for fusion with the father to avoid "engulfment by the mother" (Glasser 1992, p. 498).

37 Similarly, for Mr. Smith, it is the inadequacy of the (real) father that blocks his development into a man and fosters, as an alternative to development, the regressive fantasy of merger with the mother.

4

1 Pew Research Center, 1998.

2 *Rocky Mountain News*, June 6, 1997, p. 5A.

3 The term outrage refers both to the hateful act and to the response to it.

4 Winnicott 1971 and 1988, 69–87. Here, I have reversed Winnicott's use of language to make relating incorporate recognition of other.

5 See also Benjamin 1992.

6 Freedman 1980.

7 Kernberg 1995, p. 64.

8 I consider the meaning of power in the next chapter.

9 See Hyatt-Williams 1998.

10 Hyatt-Williams 1998, p. 66.

11 The attack on government associated with advocacy of radical democracy also removes the state as a protection for the individual, leaving him or her subject to the whim of the people, which is to say of those individuals who speak, or claim to speak, for the people. The threat that radical democracy can pose to the individual parallels that posed by the attempt to destroy government in the name of the nation. On the democratic alternative, see Levine (1998).

12 A. Freud 1936.

13 We need to distinguish here between the innocence of child and adult victims. The former become the objects of violence because they are, indeed, innocent, the latter because they are not. No adults outside the group can be innocent since they must contain group projections of bad objects.

14 Louis Beam quoted in Dees 1996, p. 174.

15 Dees 1996, p. 174.

16 See Dees 1996, p. 176.

17 Hyatt-Williams 1998, p. 68.

18 Gilligan 1996, p. 11.

19 Sanai 1999.

20 Giroux 1998.

21 An alternative notion of innocence is the one associated with Mr. Smith, for whom innocence means identification with the good object by repression or destruction of the bad object. Here innocence is linked with naiveté.

22 Quoted in Tolchin 1996, p. 102.

23 Tolchin 1996, p. 128.

24 Tolchin 1996, p. 18.

25 Gilligan 1996, p. 184.

26 Segal 1998, p. 34.

27 Gilligan 1996, p. 61.

28 Abramsky 1999, p. 32.

29 The language Emile Durkheim uses to describe the purpose of the state captures the link explored here between government and the community's psychic life (see Durkheim 1958, p. 49).

5

1 Patrick Buchanan campaign speech, March 2, 1999, Manchester, New Hampshire.

2 This is however a distorted, even corrupt, form of desire since the satisfac-

tion sought is in the form of denial and deprivation.

3 Pine 1995, p. 109.

4 Gilligan 1996, pp. 11–12.

5 Hyatt-Williams p. 31.

6 Adams and Balfour 1998.

7 Quoted in Kessler 1997, p. 39.

8 Weyerman 1998.

9 Levine 2001.

10 Kohut 1977, Winnicott 1965.

11 Bollas 1989, p. 9.

12 Bollas 1989, pp. 31–6.

13 Bollas 1989, p. 45.

14 Lukes 1974, chapter 3.

15 I have argued elsewhere that power is also connected to the ideology of change that dominates organizational life in the modern world (Levine 1999).

16 On activity as denial of passivity, see (Koenigsberg 1977, p. 22).

17 Gilligan 1996, pp. 32, 96

18 Arendt 1986, p. 61.

19 Patrick Buchanan, presidential candidacy announcement, New Hampshire.

6

1 See Polanyi 1959.

2 Our concern here is with arguments that have fear of, and therefore animosity toward, government as their central psychic meaning. Not all arguments for the free market include this element. Some economists favor an argument for free markets that emphasizes the incompetence of government to make decisions for which appropriate information is not centrally available. While the idea of government incompetence to do what the market can do in supporting economic well being may include an element of animosity and distrust, this is not inevitable. Here, I do not consider the psychic meaning of the incompetence argument against government.

3 Friedman 1982, p. 15.

4 For Smith as for Friedman, there are ends that cannot be achieved by private means, and that thus justify minimal government.

5 Smith 1976, p. 456.

6 Weber 1992, pp. 166, 119, 163, 117.

7 Weber 1992 p. 172.

8 Keynes 1964, p. 373.

9 Interpretations of the market based on modern versions of a utilitarian ethic run into difficulty with government because of their one-sided emphasis on the aspect of self-interest that makes it particular to the individual. This emphasis makes it difficult to comprehend the more universal element in interest, and

therefore that aspect of government involved in integrating a society rather than serving different, often opposed, partial interests. I discuss the problem of integration in chapter 8.

10 Campaign speech delivered at Cedar Rapids Iowa, June 12, 1999.

11 See also Lipset, 1990.

12 Tawney 1962, p. 201.

13 Tawney 1962, pp. 227–8.

14 Tawney 1962, p. 230.

15 Weber 1964, p. 122.

16 Gingrich 1995, pp. 38–9.

17 Katz 1989, p. 231.

18 Smith 1995.

19 Koenigsberg 1977, p. 22; emphasis in original.

20 The Reverend Charles Burroughs writing in 1834, quoted in Katz (1989, p. 13).

21 Katz 1989, p. 14.

22 Katz 1989, p. 16.

23 Katz 1989, p. 236.

24 Katz 1989, p. 141.

25 Katz 1989, chapter 3.

26 Katz 19898, p. 237.

27 Katz 1989, pp. 95–101.

28 Katz 1989, p. 99.

29 It might be that those who emphasize community action have in mind a collective rather than individual will, though they may not. They may consider community action a vehicle for energizing the individual and developing in him or her a sense of personal agency.

30 Boris 1994, p. 38.

31 Riviere 1964, p. 27.

32 Riviere 1964, p. 27

33 Riviere 1964, p. 27.

7

1 The widespread support for term limits suggests how powerful is this idea about expertise in governance. George Will, in the June 24, 1993 issue of the *Washington Post*, reports that 70 percent of voters support term limits, and that this support cuts across regional, sexual, party, and racial differences.

2 Bion 1961, p. 89.

3 Alford 1994, p. 12.

4 Agazarian and Peters 1981, pp. 27–34.

5 Freud 1959.

6 See Jacques 1970.

7 Bion 1961, see also Jacques 1970.

8 Turquet 1985, pp. 74–5.

9 Alford 1994, p. 37.

10 Turquet 1985, 76; see also p. 81.

11 Turquet 1985, p. 76.

12 Turquet 1985, p. 77.

13 Turquet 1985, pp. 79, 82.

14 Turquet 1985, p. 82.

15 Turquet 1985, p. 80.

16 Hirschhorn 1985, p. 349.

17 King 1997, p. 56.

18 Dahl 1956.

19 Dahl 1985.

20 Barber 1984, p. 224.

21 Magnusson 1996, p. 31.

22 See Levine 2001, chapter 8.

23 Dworkin 1977.

24 Barber 1984, pp. 216–217.

25 Lenin quoted in Koenigsberg 1977, p. 46.

26 Koenigsberg 1977, p. 46.

27 Barber 1984, pp. 155, 232.

28 Barber 1984, p. 224.

29 Freud 1959, p. 6.

30 Lawson 1966, p. 68.

31 Quoted in Lawson 1996, p. 73.

32 I use the term myth here not to judge the reality or unreality of the claim made in American public discourse, but to emphasize its psychic meaning. On the fantasy of the promised land, see Akhtar (1995).

33 West, de Alva, Shorris 1996, p. 60.

34 West et al. 1996, p. 60.

35 West et. al 1996, p. p. 62.

36 Freud 1959, p. 52.

37 Freud 1959, p. 33.

38 Arendt 1958, pp. 50–1.

39 Arendt 1958, p. 57.

40 Alford 1994, p. 121.

41 See Glass 1995, p. 20; Kernberg 1997.

42 Kernberg 1997, p. 98.

43 Kernberg 1997.

44 Freud 1959, pp. 20, 14, 15.

45 Freud 1959, p. 49.

46 Durkheim 1958.

47 Kernberg 1997, p. 107.

48 Adams and Balfour 1998.
49 Kernberg 1997, p. 111.

8

1 Speech delivered at Carthage, Tennessee, June 16, 1999.
2 Speech delivered at Cedar Rapids, Iowa, June 12, 1999.
3 Second Inaugural Address, January 20, 1937.
4 Geertz 1963, p. 109.
5 Gellner 1983, pp. 33–4.
6 Magnusson 1996, p. 41.
7 Magnusson 1996 p. 47.
8 Friedman 1982, p. 24.
9 Kristeva 1993, pp. 2–3.
10 Kristeva 1993, pp. 16, 35.
11 It also depends on the individual's capacity to live outside the group, which is to say to find and hold a personal identity not derivative of group membership.
12 A basic assumption group is a group for which the group is an end in itself (maintaining groupness is the dominant goal).
13 Fitzgerald 1987, p. 158
14 Fitzgerald 1987, p. 54.
15 Todorov 1993, p. 173.
16 See Chasseguet-Smirgel 1985.
17 Fitzgerald 1987, p. 158.
18 See McDougal 1989, p. 41.
19 Anderson 1983, p. 143.
20 Todorov 1983, pp. 229–30, 386.
21 Broembsen 1989, p. 333.
22 See Volkan 1988.
23 Erikson 1964, pp. 161–2.
24 Anderson 1983, p. 143.
25 Anderson 1983, chapter 11, Smith 1981, pp. 52–8; Gellner 1983, chapter 5.
26 Smith 1981, p. 188.
27 Todorov 1993, pp. 172, 386–7.
28 Rustin 1991, p. 80.
29 Todorov 1993, p.173.

9

1 Goldman Family 1997, p. 75.
2 Goldman Family 1997, p. 55.
3 Goldman Family 1997, p. 78.

4 Goldman Family 1997, p. 105.

5 Goldman Family 1997, p. 97.

6 Goldman Family 1997, pp. 41, 95, 121.

7 Goldman Family 1997, p. 89–90.

8 It turns out that the family's, especially the father's preoccupation with the trial constitutes a form of abandonment of the two teenage children (of Fred Goldman's third wife, Patti) who were still living at home. The willingness of the parents to sacrifice their family to their "search for justice" lends further support to the idea that abandonment and neglect is the book's central theme.

9 Goldman Family 1997, pp. 97, 136.

10 Levine 1997, pp. 1–4.

11 Goldman Family 1997, pp. 78, 146.

12 Hegel 1977, pp. 111–19.

13 Winnicott 1971a.

14 Winnicott believes that living in the world requires a false self. I do not explore this idea here.

15 Erikson 1961.

16 The important part played by imposition of our loss on others suggests a connection between envy and the demand for justice, a suggestion emphasized by Freud (see Forrester 1997, chapter 1).

17 The words Tsvetan Todorov uses to describe the conquest of the Aztecs capture the phenomenon of gaining autonomy by acting as the agent of its loss: "The Aztecs perceive the conquest—i.e. the defeat— and at the same time mentally overcome it by inscribing it within a history conceived according to their requirements" (1984, p.74).

18 Freud 1920/1989, p. 148.

19 See Akhtar 1995.

20 This comment was made in both his 1984 and 1988 speeches before the Democratic National Convention.

21 Denver Post, May 21, 1999, p. 9A.

22 Bion 1961, pp. 151–2.

23 Freud 1917.

24 A. Freud 1936, p. 119.

25 A. Freud 1936, p. 120.

10

1 The Bible, King James Version.

2 Job 1:10.

3 Job 10:1.

4 Job 30.

5 Job 40:4.

6 Job 41:21–34.

7 Job 42:2–6.
8 Strauss 1952, p. 13.
9 Hobbes 1958, p. 86.
10 Hobbes 1958, p. 86.
11 Hobbes 1958, p. 105.
12 Wolff 1970, p. 18.
13 Fairbairn 1958, p. 382.
14 Fairbairn 1958, p. 384.
15 See Levine 1999.
16 Rousseau 1967, pp. 30–1.

Afterword

1 The second problem may be less acute in the public arena than in the private since the material used as evidence is publicly available.

2 The importance of what I refer to as subjective experience has become increasingly clear in psychoanalysis, where the impact of the patient on the analyst is now considered a primary source of information about the patient's inner world (Mitchell and Black, 1995, pp. 243–50). The nature of such information defies any suggestion that it be somehow objectively validated, or otherwise treated as purely objective data. I believe the same can be said of the sorts of information we use in attempting to explore the psychic meaning of public life.

3 Laplanche and Pontalis define psychic (or "psychical") reality, following Freud, as "everything in the psyche that takes on the force of reality for the subject." To some extent, this begs the question of the nature of psychic reality, while implicitly linking it to neurosis (though not real, psychic reality has the "force of reality," and thus might be mistaken for what is real). Then, making the unconscious conscious would tend to weaken the hold of psychic reality over the subject, and replace it with another reality. Yet, they latter define psychic reality as "the unconscious wish and the phantasy associated with it" (Laplanche and Pontalis 1973, p. 363). This gives the term a broader significance, since to lack wishes and fantasies expressive of them is not to be free of neurosis, but of desire itself, which would make us something less than human.

4 Shengold, 1989.

5 A. Freud 1936.

6 A. Freud 1936.

7 It would, however, be difficult to imagine anyone lacking subjectivity either writing a book or reading one.

8 Of course, the character does exist as a part of psychic reality both for those who made the movie and those who view it. This does not however allow us to put Mr. Smith on the couch, although we may find some of his surrogates there.

9 Bion 1984.

REFERENCES

Abramsky, S. When they get out. *Atlantic Monthly,* 283:6, pp. 30–6, June 1999.

Agazarian, Y. and R. Peters. *The Visible and Invisible Group.* London: Routledge and Kegan Paul, 1981.

Akhtar, S. A third individuation: Immigration, identity, and the psychoanalytic process, *Journal of the American Psychoanalytic Association.* 43,4:1051–1084, 1995.

Alford, C. F. *Group Psychology and Political Theory.* New Haven: Yale University Press, 1994.

Anderson, B. *Imagined Communities,* revised edition. London: Verso, 1991.

Arendt, H. Communicative Power. From *On Violence* (1969), reprinted in *Power,* edited by S. Lukes, New York: New York University Press, 1986.

————. *The Human Condition.* Chicago: University of Chicago Press, 1958.

Barber, B. *Strong Democracy.* Berkeley: University of California Press, 1984.

Bellant, R. Mania in the stadia: Origins and goals of promise keepers. *Free Inquiry,* 16:1, pp. 28–30, 1995.

Benjamin, J. Recognition and destruction: An outline of intersubjectivity, in N. Skolnick and S. Warshaw (editors) *Relational Perspectives in Psychoanalysis.* Hillsdale, N.J.: The Analytic Press, 1992.

Bion, W. *Experiences in Groups.* London: Routledge, 1961.

————. *Second Thoughts.* London: Karnak Books, 1984. Originally 1967.

Bollas, C. *Forces of Destiny.* London: Free Associations Press, 1989.

Borger, G. and L. Kulman. Does character count? *U.S. News and World Report,* 120:125, p. 35, 1996.

Boris, H. *Envy.* Northvale, N.J.: Jason Aronson, 1994.

Broembsen, F. von. Transformations of identity: Referent location, agency, and levels of integration in the progress from potential self to existential identity. *American Journal of Psychoanalysis,* 49:4, pp. 329–338, 1989.

Caporaso, J. and D. Levine. *Theories of Political Economy.* New York: Cambridge University Press, 1992.

Capra, F. *The Name Above the Title: An Autobiography.* New York: The Macmillan Co., 1971.

Cass, D. An action figure for all seasons. *Harper's Magazine,* 298: 1785, pp. 65–71.

260 — David P. Levine

February 1999.

Chasseguet-Smirgel, J. *The Ego Ideal*. New York: W.W. Norton, 1985.

Clarkson, F. Righteous Brothers. *In These Times*, 20:19, pp. 14–7, August 5, 1996.

Dahl, R. *A Preface to Democratic Theory*. Chicago: University of Chicago Press, 1956.

———. *A Preface to Economic Democracy*. Berkeley: University of California Press, 1985.

Dees, M. *Gathering Storm*. New York: HarperCollins Publisher, 1996.

Durkheim, E. *Professional Ethics and Civic Morals*. Translated by C. Brookfield. Glencoe, Il.: The Free Press, 1958.

Dworkin. R. *Taking Rights Seriously*. Cambridge, Ma.: Harvard University Press, 1977.

Erikson, E. *Insight and Responsibility*. New York: W.W. Norton and Co., 1964.

———. Reality and actuality. *Journal of the American Psychoanalytic Association*, 10, 1961.

Fairbairn, W.R.D. The repression and the return of the bad objects. *British Journal of Medical Psychology*, XIX, 1943.

———. Endopsychic structure considered in terms of object relationships. *International Journal of Psycho-Analysis*, XXV, 1944.

———. On the nature and aims of psychoanalytic treatment. *International Journal of Psychoanalysis*, XXXI , 1958, pp. 374–85.

Fields, W. *Union of Words: A History of Presidential Eloquence*. New York: Free Press, 1996.

Fitzgerald, F. *Cities on a Hill*. London: Picador, 1987.

Flanigan, W. and N. Zingale. *Political Behavior of the American Electorate*. Ninth Edition. Washington, D.C.: CQ Press, 1998.

———. *Political Behavior in Midterm Elections*. Washington, D.C.: CQ Press, 2000.

Forrester, J. *Dispatches from the Freud Wars: Psychoanalysis and Its Passions*. Cambridge, Ma.: Harvard University Press, 1997.

Freedman, N. On splitting and its resolution. *Psychoanalysis and Contemporary Thought*, 3,7: 237–66, 1980.

Friedman, M. *Capitalism and Freedom*. Chicago: University of Chicago Press, 1982.

Freud, A. *The Ego and the Mechanisms of Defense*. New York: International Universities Press, 1936.

Freud, S. *Group Psychology and the Analysis of the Ego*. New York: W.W. Norton, 1959.

———. Mourning and melancholia. *Standard Edition of the Complete Psychological Works*, Volume 14, pp. 237–58, 1917.

———. Beyond the pleasure principle. In *A General Selection from the Works of Sigmund Freud*. Edited by J. Rickman. New York: Anchor Books, 1989.

Gassner, J. and D. Nichols. *Twenty Best Film Plays*. New York: Crown Publishers,

1943.

Geertz, C. The integrative revolution. In *Old Societies and New States*. Edited by C. Geertz. New York: Free Press, 1963.

Gellner, E. *Nations and Nationalism*. Ithaca: Cornell University Press, 1983.

Gilbreath, E. The awakening. *Christianity Today*, 39:2, pp. 20–8, February 6, 1995.

Gilligan, J. *Violence*. New York: Vintage 1994.

Gingrich, N. *To Renew America*. New York: HarperCollins, 1995.

Giroux, H. Child beauty pageants and the politics of innocence. *Social Text*, 57 16:4, pp. 31–53, Winter 1998.

Glass, J. *Psychosis and Power*. Ithaca: Cornell University Press, 1995.

Glasser, M. Problems in the psychoanalysis of certain narcissistic disorders. *International Journal of Psychoanalysis*, 73,3: 493–503, 1992.

Goldman Family. *His Name Is Ron: Our Search for Justice*. New York: Avon Books, 1997.

Greenberg, J. and S. Mitchell. *Object Relations in Psychoanalytic Theory*. Cambridge, Ma.: Harvard University Press, 1983.

Grunberger, B. *Narcissism: Psychoanalytic Essays*. New York: International Universities Press, 1979.

Hegel, G.W.F. *Hegel's Philosophy of Right*. Translated by T.M. Knox. Oxford: Oxford University Press, 1951.

———. *Hegel's Phenomenology of Spirit*. Translated by A.V. Miller. Oxford: Oxford University Press, 1977.

Hirschhorn, L. The psychodynamics of taking the role. *Group Relations Reader*, 2. Edited by A. Coleman and M. Geller. Jupiter, Fl.: A.K. Rice Institute, 1985.

Hobbes, T. *Leviathan*, Parts One and Two. Indianapolis: Bobbs-Merrill, 1958.

The Holy Bible, King James Version. Philadelphia: The Judson Press, nd.

Hyatt-Williams, A. *Cruelty, Violence, and Murder*. Northvale, NJ: Jason Aronson, 1998.

Jacobson, E. *The Self and the Object World*. New York: International Universities Press, 1964.

Jacques, E. A contribution to a discussion of *Freud's Group Psychology and the Analysis of the Ego*. In *Work, Creativity, and Social Justice*. London: Heinemann Educational Books Ltd, 1970.

Keynes, J.M. *The General Theory of Employment, Interest, and Money*. New York: Harvest Books, 1964.

Katz, M. *The Undeserving Poor*. New York: Pantheon Books, 1989.

Kernberg, O. Factors in the treatment of narcissistic personalities. In *Essential Papers on Narcissism*. Edited by A. Morrison. New York: New York University Press, 1986.

———. Hatred as a core affect of aggression, In *The Birth of Hatred*. Edited by S. Akhtar et. al. Northvale, NJ, Jason Aronson, 1995.

———. Ideology and Bureaucracy as Social Defenses against Aggression.

The Inner World and the Outer World. Edited by E. Shapiro. New Haven: Yale University Press, 1997.

Kessler, R. *Inside Congress.* New York: Simon & Schuster Inc., 1997.

Kets de Vries, M. and D. Miller. *The Neurotic Organization.* San Francisco: Jossey-Bass Publishers, 1984.

King, A. 1997. Running Scared. *Atlantic Monthly.* 279,1: 41–58, January, 1997.

King, C. and C. Stivers. *Government is Us: Public Administration in an Anti-Government Era.* Thousand Oaks: Sage Publications, 1998.

Koenigsberg, R. *The Psychoanalysis of Racism, Revolution and Nationalism.* New York: The Library of Social Science, 1977.

Kohut, H. *The Restoration of the Self.* New York: International Universities Press, 1977.

Kristeva, J. *Nations without Nationalism.* Translated by L. Roudiez. New York: Columbia University Press, 1993.

Laplanche, J. and J. B. Pontalis. *The Language of Psychoanalysis.* New York: W.W. Norton & Co., 1973.

Lapham, L. Notebook. *Harper's Magazine,* 295: 1966, July, 1997.

Lawson, G. No Canada? *Harper's Magazine,* 292: 1751, pp. 67–78, April, 1996.

Lear, J. *Love and its Place in Nature.* New York: Noonday, 1990.

Levine, D. *Needs, Rights, and the Market.* Boulder: Lynne Rienner Publishers, 1988.

———. *Self-Seeking and the Pursuit of Justice.* Aldershot: Avebury, 1997.

———. *Subjectivity in Political Economy.* London: Routledge, 1998.

———. Creativity and change. *American Behavioral Scientist,* 63:2, pp. 225–244, 1999.

———. Identity, the group, and the social construction of reality. *Journal for the Psychoanalysis of Culture and Society,* 4:1, pp. 81–91, 1999a.

———. *Normative Political Economy: Subjective Freedom, the Market, and the State,* London: Routledge, 2001.

Lipset, S.M. American values and the market system. In *The Political Legitimacy of Markets and Government.* Edited by T. Dye. Greenwich, CT: JAI Press Inc, 1990.

Llhosa, M. *The Storyteller.* New York: Penguin Books, 1989.

Loewald, H. *Papers on Psychoanalysis.* New Haven: Yale University Press, 1980.

Lukes, S. *Power: A Radical View.* London: Macmillan, 1974.

Lyth, I. M. *Containing Anxiety in Institutions.* London: Free Associations Books, 1988.

Magnusson, W. *The Search for Political Space.* Toronto: University of Toronto Press, 1996.

McDougal, J. *Theaters of the Body.* New York: W.W. Norton, 1989.

Mitchell, S. and M. Black. *Freud and Beyond: A History of Modern Psychoanalytic Thought.* New York: Basic Books, 1995.

Moran, F. *Subject and Agency in Psychoanalysis.* New York: New York University

Press, 1993.

Morrison, A. Shame, ideal self, and narcissism. In *Essential Papers on Narcissism*. Edited by A, Morrison. New York: New York University Press, 1986.

Murray, C. *Losing Ground*. New York: Basic Books, 1984.

Oxford Dictionary of Quotations. Edited by A. Partington. Fourth Edition. New York: Oxford University Press.

Pew Research Center. Deconstructing distrust: how Americans view government. www.people-press.org/trustrpt.htm, 1998.

Pine, Fred. On the origin and evolution of a species of hate. In *The Birth of Hatred*. Edited by A. Akhtar et. al. Northvale, N.J.: Jason Aronson, 1995.

Pogue, L. *Another Frank Capra*. Cambridge: Cambridge University Press, 1994.

Polanyi, K. Aristotle discovers the economy, In *Trade and Market in the Early Empires*. Edited by K. Polanyi et. al. Glencoe: Free Press, 1957.

Riviere, J. Hate, greed, and aggression. In M. Klein and J. Riviere, *Love, Hate and Reparation*. New York: W.W. Norton & Co., 1964.

Rothstein, A. The theory of narcissism: An object-relations perspective. In *Essential Papers on Narcissism*. Edited by A. Morrison. New York: New York University Press, 1986.

Rousseau, J. *The Social Contract and the Discourse on Inequality*. Edited by L. Crocker New York: Washington Square Books, 1967.

Rustin, M. *The Good Society and the Inner World*. London: Verso, 1991.

Sanai, C. Community kills. *Slate*. www.slate.com, April 29, 1999.

Segal, H. Notes on symbol formation. *Journal of Psycho-Analysis*, 38, pp. 391–7, 1957.

Shengold, L. *Soul Murder: The Effects of Childhood Abuse and Deprivation*. New York: Fawcett Columbine, 1989.

Smith, A. *An Inquiry into the Nature and Causes of the Wealth of Nations*. Oxford: Oxford University Press, 1976.

Smith, A. *The Ethnic Revival*. Cambridge: Cambridge University Press, 1981.

Smith, T. Public support for public spending, 1973–1994. *The Public Perspective*, 6:3, pp. 1–3, April–May, 1995.

Strauss, L. *The Political Philosophy of Hobbes*. Chicago: The University of Chicago Press, 1952.

Tawney, R.H. *Religion and the Rise of Capitalism*. Gloucester: Peter Smith, 1962.

Todorov, T. *The Conquest of America*. Translated by R. Howard. New York: Harper and Row, 1984.

———. *On Human Diversity*. Cambridge, Ma.: Harvard University Press, 1993.

Tolchin, S. *Political Anger: How Voter Rage is Changing the Nation*. Boulder: Westview Press, 1996.

Turquet, P. Leadership, the individual, and the group. In *Group Relations Reader*, 2. Edited by A. Coleman and M. Geller Jupiter, Fl.: A.K. Rice Institute, 1985.

Volkan, V. *The Need to Have Enemies and Allies*. Northvale, N.J.: Jason Aronson, 1988.

Weber, M. *The Protestant Ethic and the Spirit of Capitalism*. Translated by T. Parsons. London: Routledge, 1992.

West, C., J. Klor de Alva, and E. Shorris. Our next race question. *Harper's Magazine*, 292: 1751, pp. 55–63, 1996.

Weyermann, D. And then there were none. *Harper's Magazine*, 296:1775, pp. 60–70, April 1998.

Winnicott, D.W. The depressive position in normal emotional development. *British Journal of Medical Psychology*, 28, pp.89–100, 1955.

———. Ego distortions in terms of true and false self. Reprinted in *The Maturational process and the Facilitating Environment*. New York: International Universities Press, 1965.

———. *Home is Where We Start From*. New York: W.W. Norton, 1986.

———. The use of an object and relating through identifications. In *Playing and Reality*. London: Routledge, 1971.

———. *Playing and Reality*. New York: Routledge, 1971a.

———. *Human Nature*. New York: Schocken, 1988.

ABOUT THE AUTHOR

David P. Levine has been professor of economics at the University of Denver's Graduate School of International Studies since 1987. Prior to joining the GSIS, he was chair of the university's Department of Economics. Between 1973 and 1981, he was assistant and associate professor of economics at Yale University. Professor Levine was educated at the University of Wisconsin (B.A., economics, 1969), Yale University (Ph.D., economics, 1973), and The Colorado Center for Psychoanalytic Studies (Certificate in Psychoanalytic Studies, 1994). He has published several dozen articles and nine books in economics and political economy, most recently *Wealth and Freedom*, *Subjectivity in Political Economy*, and *Normative Political Economy*. He has also published papers on group and organizational dynamics; the psychology of teaching and learning; ethics, tolerance, and difference; and hatred of government. He teaches courses in two fields: political economy, and group and organizational dynamics.